# CONTENTS

# Children
# Reading
# for Pleasure
# in the
# Digital Age

Sara Miller McCune founded SAGE Publishing in 1965 to support the dissemination of usable knowledge and educate a global community. SAGE publishes more than 1000 journals and over 800 new books each year, spanning a wide range of subject areas. Our growing selection of library products includes archives, data, case studies and video. SAGE remains majority owned by our founder and after her lifetime will become owned by a charitable trust that secures the company's continued independence.

Los Angeles | London | New Delhi | Singapore | Washington DC | Melbourne

# Children
# Reading
# for Pleasure
# in the
# Digital Age

## Mapping reader engagement

#Natalia Kucirkova
#Teresa Cremin

Los Angeles | London | New Delhi
Singapore | Washington DC | Melbourne

Los Angeles | London | New Delhi
Singapore | Washington DC | Melbourne

SAGE Publications Ltd
1 Oliver's Yard
55 City Road
London EC1Y 1SP

SAGE Publications Inc.
2455 Teller Road
Thousand Oaks, California 91320

SAGE Publications India Pvt Ltd
B 1/I 1 Mohan Cooperative Industrial Area
Mathura Road
New Delhi 110 044

SAGE Publications Asia-Pacific Pte Ltd
3 Church Street
#10-04 Samsung Hub
Singapore 049483

Editor: Jude Bowen
Assistant editor: Orsod Malik/Catriona McMullen
Production editor: Nicola Carrier
Copyeditor: Chris Bitten
Proofreader: Derek Markham
Indexer: Michael Allerton
Marketing manager: Dilhara Attygalle
Cover design: Wendy Scott
Typeset by: C&M Digitals (P) Ltd, Chennai, India
Printed in the UK

**Library of Congress Control Number: 2019955186**

**British Library Cataloguing in Publication data**

A catalogue record for this book is available from the British Library

ISBN 978-1-5264-3662-7
ISBN 978-1-5264-3663-4 (pbk)

At SAGE we take sustainability seriously. Most of our products are printed in the UK using responsibly sourced papers and boards. When we print overseas we ensure sustainable papers are used as measured by the PREPS grading system. We undertake an annual audit to monitor our sustainability.

# LIST OF FIGURES

# ABOUT THE AUTHORS

**Natalia Kucirkova** is Professor of Early Childhood Education and Development at the University of Stavanger, Norway. Her research concerns innovative ways of supporting children's book reading, digital literacy, and exploring the role of personalisation in the early years. She co-edits the Bloomsbury Book Series *Children's Reading and Writing on Screen* and the journal *Literacy* published by Wiley. Natalia's research takes place collaboratively across academia, commercial and third sectors. She is author of *Digital Personalization in Early Childhood* (Bloomsbury) and *How and Why to Read and Create Children's Digital Books* (UCL Press), and currently blogs for *Huffington Post* and *Psychology Today*.

©Jeanette Larsen

**Teresa Cremin** is Professor of Education (Literacy) at The Open University, UK. An ex-teacher and teacher educator, her research focuses on teachers' literate identities and practices, children's volitional reading and writing, and creative pedagogies. A Fellow of the Academy of Social Sciences, the RSA and the English Association, Teresa co-edits the journal *Thinking Skills and Creativity*. Recent edited/authored books include *Writer Identity and the Teaching and Learning of Writing; Storytelling in Early Childhood; Researching Literacy Lives;* and *Building Communities of Engaged Readers* (Routledge). Teresa leads a professional user-community website based on her research into volitional reading: https://researchrichpedagogies.org/research/reading-for-pleasure.

# ACKNOWLEDGEMENTS

The authors would like to thank all of the families who we have had the privilege to work with over the years, as well as librarians, publishers and app designers. Our thanks go to the funders of our work, including the United Kingdom Literacy Association, the Esmée Fairbairn Foundation, the British Academy, the Carnegie UK Trust and the Economic and Social Research Council. We owe special thanks to all the school teachers who have welcomed us and who have researched reading for pleasure alongside us over the years, as well as the many children from whom we have learnt.

# ACKNOWLEDGMENTS

# PRAISE FOR THE BOOK

'What an insightful book! Teachers, researchers, parents, and anyone who cares about children and reading will deepen their understanding of the crucial role that pleasure reading plays in young people's lives. The authors deftly blend scholarly analysis with practical advice for nurturing children's engagement with the written word.'

Naomi S. Baron, Author of *Words Onscreen: The Fate of Reading in a Digital World*

'This book makes a compelling case for reading as a situated, embodied experience and embraces positively the possibilities and opportunities of reading online and on screen. It will be read widely by all those committed to expanding and enriching reading for pleasure in the new media age.'

Cathy Burnett, Professor of Literacy and Education, Sheffield Hallam University

'Whether on tablet, phone, book, or wearable, reading remains a mainstay as a pleasure for many – especially children. With more routes into reading than ever, not to mention new reading repertoires involving tapping, scrolling, swiping, and curating, children must be nimble and fluid as they navigate reading worlds. In *Children Reading for Pleasure in the Digital* Age, Kucirkova and Cremin elegantly map out children's reading practices across digital and non-digital domains.'

Professor Jennifer Rowsell, University of Bristol

'Kucirkova's and Cremin's book is a timely and nuanced look at how digital technologies can play a positive role in children's joy of reading. Written in a style which is at once eloquent, engaging, in-depth, and accessible, the authors present a wealth of research on children's pleasure reading and digitisation, and provide recommendations for teachers, librarians, parents and scholars alike.'

Anne Mangen, Professor at the Norwegian Reading Centre, University of Stavanger

'This book manages to speak to both a teacher and researcher audience – no small achievement. In contrast to many publications exploring the cognitive and metacognitive aspects of reading, Cremin and Kucirkova place the child and their lives at the heart of their reasoning. They challenge us to recognise and confront our book-bound, print-related, school-centric interpretations of literacy with important considerations of the use of digital *and* print texts in developing reading for pleasure.

From a practical perspective, teachers and schools will find this book supports a journey from theory into practice – helping to situate their classroom activity within a conceptual and theoretical framework and saliently reminding us of the need to recognise and respond to the diversity of lives and lived experiences of children.'

Megan Dixon, Director of English and Director of the Aspirer Research School

'This is a book that we've been waiting for since the first Kindle was rolled out. Drawing together a range of research and case studies, Kucirkova and Cremin invite us to explore reading experiences in the 21st century through the reconceptualisation of what it means to be a reader and what we, as educators, can do to support children and families today. Anyone interested in this agenda needs to read this and become part of the long-due debate on the shifting reading spaces in this digital age.'

Mat Tobin, Oxford Brookes University, UK

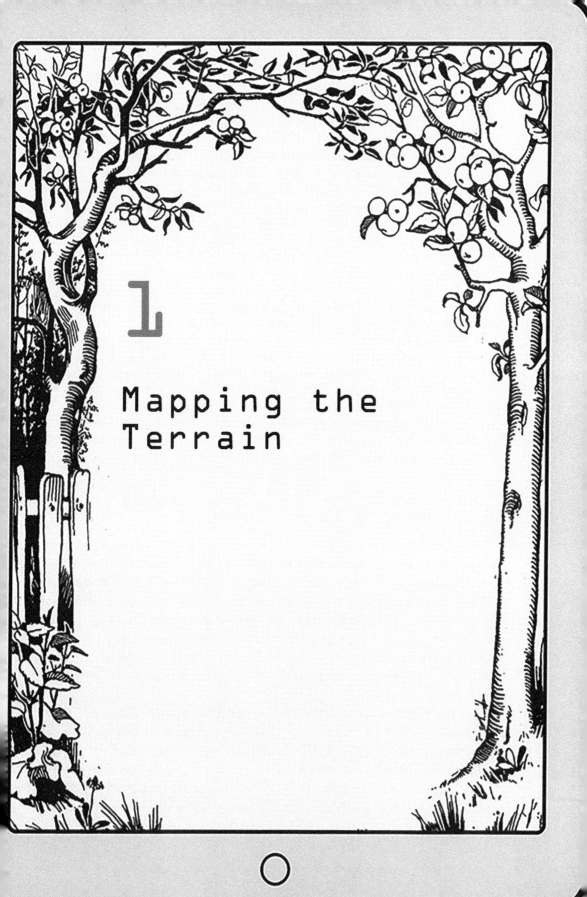

# 1

# Mapping the Terrain

R eading reflects and frames our lives, allowing us to make deep, personal connections with others and ourselves, to satisfy our curiosity and to learn more about the world. Whether children choose to read in childhood matters; it has the potential to make a difference to their learning and their life chances. Indeed, being a frequent reader can mitigate the negative influence of low socio-economic status on educational achievement (e.g. OECD, 2010). Extensive international evidence exists that demonstrates strong associations between the frequency with which young people read and their attainment, and many of these studies indicate the very significant role played in this interaction by the young reader's desire – their intrinsic motivation to read (e.g. Schiefele et al., 2012; Sullivan and Brown, 2015; Taboada et al., 2009).

Reading for pleasure (RfP), that is volitional reading in which we choose to engage, can involve any kind of text, in any shape or form. In this new media age, such reading almost always includes digital texts, since digital technologies influence nearly every important aspect of human life: education, relationships, health, communication and work. Technologies combine and integrate key elements including portability, availability, connectivity, multimedia and personalisation, and as a consequence, they are powerful game-changers for the book industry. In this book we seek to draw attention to the positive influence digital technologies have had on children's RfP and the ways in which the Internet has diversified the quality and augmented the quantity of texts available to children. Digital technologies have contributed to the process of children's texts becoming increasingly multimodal, individualised and connected to others. Such texts, as parents and educators know, quickly draw in and engage young readers and they deserve our attention alongside more traditional printed texts. What texts children read matters. But do all texts incite their desire to read equally?

## Narrative Texts

Children choose to read multiple forms of texts. In particular they engage with those that are of high interest and are meaningful to them, including for instance: advertising, comics, magazines, newspapers, fiction and non-fiction, all of which may be read on and/or offline. Drawing on our own research and that of others, we are particularly interested in children's reading of fiction and we focus mainly on children's literature, in print and digital book form. Whilst there is no officially agreed nomenclature for digital books, they typically relate to fictional narratives that are presented on digital devices, including dedicated reader devices (such as Kindle or Kobo) and multifunctional devices (such as iPads and smartphones).

In profiling fiction, we draw on the widely recognised power of narrative for constructing reality. Humans use narratives of various sorts as linguistic and cognitive tools to represent and reflect on the past, to structure and evaluate the present and to shape and inform their futures. Educationalists and literary scholars (e.g. Bruner, 1986; Hardy, 1977) as well as novelists (e.g. Gottschall, 2012) have highlighted the importance of narrative and reading narratives for human development and higher order thinking.

Nature designed us to enjoy stories so we could benefit from practice. Fiction is an ancient virtual reality technology that specialises in simulating human problems. (Gottschall, 2012: 59)

In addition, researchers have found that narrative texts, in part perhaps due to their inherent personal and emotional allure, involve and challenge young readers, enhancing their desire to spend more time reading (e.g. McKeown et al., 2015; Mol and Bus, 2011). More recent research demonstrates the existence of a substantial 'fiction effect' (Jerrim and Moss, 2018). Drawing on large scale data of 15 year olds from 35 OECD countries, this study reveals that those young people who read fiction frequently, have significantly stronger reading skills than their peers who do not. Importantly, this effect does not hold for the four other text types: magazines, non-fiction, newspapers and comics (Jerrim and Moss, 2018). Whilst we recognise that RfP contributes to far more than children's academic attainment, and deserves to be valued in its own right as an aesthetically engaging experience and a way of making sense of experience, we find the argument for a 'fiction effect' compelling and foreground it accordingly.

We consider that reading literature in narrative form distinctively excites and enhances the imagination, helping children consider myriad possibilities and connections. Connecting to Craft's framework of possibility thinking (e.g. Craft, 2001; Cremin et al., 2006) we conceptualised children's pleasurable engagement with print and digital texts, and identified six facets linked to narrative. These comprise: sustained, shared, interactive, affective, creative and personalised engagement (Kucirkova et al., 2017) and we use these to underpin our arguments in this book. Children's engagement in narrative encourages them to persist, to read on, to read more frequently and to interact with others about what they are reading, but how does this operate with print and digital books and what difference does the social context make? These are some of the issues we address, whilst always cognisant that what young people read, *and* the social context of reading are crucial to them finding pleasure and satisfaction in the process. The context always matters; it shapes their engagement in the reading experience.

## Reading as Social Practice

Reading, Knoester (2010) argues, has historically been misconstrued as a solitary not a social practice. In education in the English-speaking Western world, it is also frequently framed as a set of neutral cognitive skills that can be taught and tested. This framing and assessment of reading is underpinned by what Street (1984, 2008) describes as an autonomous model of literacy. This views literacy/reading as a set of skills which are independent of context (where and how we use them), and can thus be taught through an authoritarian form of pedagogy in school. The model assumes a hierarchy of skill levels with literacy acquisition as a ladder that children have to climb. It categorises learners according to the level of skill that they do not yet possess and as such is a deficit model, as no attention is paid to what learners can do on their own terms. It also implies these skills are transferrable from the classroom context to the outside world. Yet as Luke and Freebody (1997) remind us, teaching and learning are made possible through social inter-action and discourse exchange, not through knowledge transmission or the acquisition of specific skills at a particular point in time.

In this book we view literacy and reading as a social practice, located in interaction between people; we recognise it is socially and historically constructed and framed by the context of its use. We adhere to Street's (1984, 2008) ideological model of literacy which takes account of difference – of different texts and different contexts – and we recognise the uniqueness of each learner. We do not envision a perfect twenty-first century reader, rather we recognise, as Barthes (1975) highlighted, that we continue to give ourselves reading lessons throughout our lives as we encounter texts which make new and interesting demands on us, demands that we choose to respond to for our own reasons. In addition, we recognise that reading varies in response to different cultural norms and discourses (e.g. relating to gender, identity) and that it is always embedded in relations of power. For children at home with their siblings and caregivers, or at school with peers and teachers, the reading experience and the sharing of these experi-ences with others is influenced by what counts as reading in these contexts, by their relationships (including power relations), and by the agency afforded them, as well as by the texts and identity positions they adopt or that are made available to them. These and other contextual factors contribute significantly to the pleasure involved. Working from a socio-cultural perspective, we seek, in alignment with Dyson (1995), to under-stand RfP both through the unofficial lens that frames children's everyday reading lives and practices at home, and through the official lens that frames their experience of reading in school.

## Positioning RfP

Although we are placing RfP under the spotlight, we are acutely aware that in many countries where high-stakes testing holds sway, this non-assessed aspect of reading is mar-ginalised. There is an inherent suspicion that RfP is not actually 'work', but is merely an additional extra, (albeit a desirable one), that will take time away from the serious and important business of learning to read (predominantly through phonics) and learning to comprehend. Since schools are assessed on these aspects, children's volitional reading too often remains backstage. It is rarely rigorously planned for, and merely afforded a real role to play in celebratory events such as World Book Day or Night.

In addition, since narrow conceptualisations of reading underpin the curricula of many countries, teachers can come to unquestioningly accept these, and view reading as merely proficiency – a universal set of technical skills that are defined for them by the nation or the state. Such skills are perceived to be independent of text and context, yet as adult readers we know that what we are reading and where we are and with whom during particular reading events influences our interest and engagement as readers. Intriguingly a disjuncture often appears to exist between teachers' personal engagement in RfP as a choice-led affectively engaging, cognitive and social process, and their pedagogic practice as professionals within the system.

Nonetheless, there are schools that place RfP at the centre of school life, and build children's delight and desire, even with limited budgets. Such schools eschew RfP as a series of activities or slots in the timetable and instead they plan and integrate RfP pedagogy that is responsive to their children's interests and home reading practices – print and digital, on and offline. Such practice is also reliant upon teachers' subject knowledge of children's literature and other texts and is enriched by staff adopting a Reading Teacher stance, as a teacher who reads and a reader who teaches. This positions the teacher as a fellow reader, helps to build reader relationships and over time, combined with the chance to read, hear and talk about texts in a highly social reading environment, contributes to the creation of reciprocal reading communities (Cremin et al. 2014).

## Mapping the Journey

Drawing on work in developmental psychology and education, we seek to consider the value, challenges and opportunities of children's engagement in contemporary RfP. Through this book we explore the personal and social nature of RfP; an approach that invites theory–practice dialogue from which to discover and elaborate new meanings. In the process we work towards three goals: to theorise the experience and practice of RfP, to deploy an interdisciplinary approach and to engage in an examination of the inter-relationships between personal and collective RfP in school.

In relation to theorising RfP, whilst the empirical base regarding print texts is reasonably well-established, empirical evidence concerning children's volitional reading of digital books is slim due to the recent appearance of digital reading devices. We orient our analysis of the field around the reader's engagement with texts which is inherently personal, and aim to bring the children's reader identities to the fore. So that our readers can trace our claims back to rigorous empirical analyses, most of our arguments are drawn from peer-reviewed journal articles and books based on research projects. We have both worked with teachers, early years practitioners and professionals, literacy charities, publishers and children's app designers in consultancy or voluntary positions and draw on these experiences to substantiate our practical recommendations. As such, we present our readers with insights that have been set out in scholarly literature, but also tried and tested in educational practice. We interweave reflections and observations from practice with empirical and theoretical work in all chapters in order to foster non-hierarchical relationships between practice and research.

We adopt an interdisciplinary approach to examine the fabric of reading with and on screens and the enchantment that is possible through narrative. The need for increased interdisciplinarity in designing and interpreting children's reading in the digital age has been recognised by the European Union, which has several funding streams dedicated to the study of children's reading on screen. We discuss and conceptualise children's RfP from the perspective of multiple disciplines and combine insights from our empirical work that has followed different disciplinary origins, including psychology, education and literary studies. Interdisciplinarity is essential for fostering multi-stakeholder conversations and is therefore a key goal for us as reading researchers. Employing a socio-cultural lens, we are particularly interested in the roles of personal agency and the nature of social mediation in RfP; the ways the individual reader and communities of readers are positioned, enabled and enriched through their engagement with texts, print and digital.

Our focus on the interrelationship between a personal and collective response to reading offers a rich conceptual space from which to explore the experience of RfP in the twenty-first century. We argue that the nature of RfP has been affected by the emergence of multimedia, customisable and highly versatile texts, and that these socio-technological changes influence children's responses to reading fiction. In this book, we propose a new theoretical construct – reciprocal RfP – which unites the psychological and socio-cultural research on children's reading at home and school, and honours the interrelationship between personal and collective responses to narratives. We study these personal–social interrelationships at the meso and micro levels. The meso level relates to the influence of adults who mediate children's experiences and the micro to the characteristics of the reading medium itself.

In examining contemporary children's engagement in reading print and digital books and profiling the personal as well as social aspects of RfP, we aim to offer both teachers and researchers additional tools to think with as they document, develop and nurture children's volitional reading.

# 2

# Reading for Pleasure in the Digital Era

Our shared interest in children's volitional engagement in reading is motivated not only by scholarly concerns, but also by policy and practice questions. International evidence reveals that the frequency with which young people, and particularly boys, engage in volitional reading markedly decreases as they move through the years of schooling (Mullis et al., 2012; OECD, 2010). Furthermore, reading for pleasure (RfP) is not always foregrounded in schools in ways that nurture young readers and enable reciprocal reading communities to be built. We believe that more attention needs to be paid to the experience of reading, the inner satisfactions and pleasures, as well as those experienced through shared engagement and discussion. Our research, and that of other colleagues, reveals that it is more than possible to entice and engage children as readers in this digitally saturated era. Much depends however on our knowledge, understanding and practice, and the print and digital texts made available to them.

In order to examine contemporary children's RfP explore the reading experience and consider how to build affect and reciprocity in action in classrooms, we frame our discussions in this chapter and throughout the book around a set of encompassing dimensions of reading engagement (Kucirkova et al., 2015). These include: affective, creative, interactive, shared, sustained and personalised reading engagement and can be applied to reading any text, including for example interactive story apps or classic narrative poetry printed on hand-made paper. We examine these facets towards the end of this chapter, having explored the nature of RfP and the benefits that accrue to those who develop a love of reading in childhood. In addition, we voice our concerns about children's attitudes to and engagement in reading, reflect on print and digital books, and critically examine the quality of many e-books, our primary digital text focus. We try to avoid a digital–print books divide; rather we seek to consider the rich experiences, challenges and opportunities of children's contemporary engagement in reading.

# R f P

Reading for pleasure, a term more frequently used in England than elsewhere, is fundamentally volitional, choice-led reading of any kind of text. Often described as 'free voluntary' or 'independent reading' in the US (Krashen, 2004) and as 'recreational reading' in Canada (Ross et al., 2006), it is closely associated with intrinsic motivation and feeds our desire for more such engagement. It is the reading that we do of our own free will, anticipating the satisfaction that we will get from the experience. It also encompasses reading which, whilst it might have begun at someone else's request, is sustained by the reader in response to their personal interest (Clark and Rumbold, 2006). RfP thus refers to a positive attitude towards the act of reading and involves sustained engagement with books and texts. For many educators, RfP is associated with two easily observable features: children's motivation and desire to read, and their engagement. Such a perception is well aligned with the OECD's (2016) recently widened conception of reading which they use in the influential Programme for International Student Assessment (PISA) tests.

> Changes in our concept of reading since 2000 have led to an expanded definition of reading literacy, which recognises motivational and behavioural characteristics of reading alongside cognitive characteristics. (OECD, 2016: 7)

This re-conceptualisation serves as a reminder that as educators and researchers we need to avoid accepting the narrow notions of reading that dominate tests and policies internationally, and tend to view reading as simply decoding and comprehension. Instead we need to re-consider reading and RfP, learning from our own experiences as readers as well as those of the young, and seeking to understand more fully the available theoretical arguments and emerging empirical evidence. Such considerations will help us as we work to nurture young people's identities as readers, enrich their affective affiliation with books, texts and narratives and enhance their desire and capacity to read, reflect and discuss their chosen texts. A representation of the OECD's (2016) expanded definition initially developed by colleagues at the UK's National Literacy Trust, usefully summarises some of the affective processes and reading behaviours of readers who not only can, but *do* choose to read (see Figure 2.1).

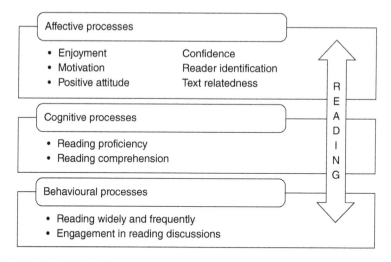

**Figure 2.1**  Top-level tripartite conceptualisation of what we mean by 'reading'

Source: Figure adapted from Clark and Teravainen, 2017a: 2

These scholars, drawing on work by a coalition of literacy organisations, argue that a skilled reader is someone who has strong cognitive skills, demonstrates particular reading behaviours and engages affectively (Clark and Teravainen, 2017a). Skilled readers are motivated to read, they relate to texts and confidently identify as readers.

They read widely from a range of texts and they engage in reading-related discussions, online and off. In terms of the cognitive processes that they engage in, skilled readers are proficient in using various reading strategies to understand and deeply engage with texts. RfP is frequently associated with the concept of 'reader engagement', since engaged readers tend to display positive dispositions towards reading, choose to read and self-identify as readers. As Figure 2.1 illustrates, however, reader engagement encompasses several interacting components and these components bear upon the quality of a reading experience.

Readers can be deeply and meaningfully engaged with print or digital books. We deliberately focus on RfP and the cognitive and emotional impact it has on the reader to avoid dichotomous interpretations of the power of different reading media. Indeed, a focus on the reading medium would, in our view, undermine what literature is about. Just as a poor framing can influence our appreciation of a painting's aesthetic qualities, so too can a good novel get lost in a poorly printed paperback or a cluttered e-book. With increasing text-digitisation, some book formats, such as silk books might soon disappear, but the act of reading, the exchange of words between the author's and reader's minds, always remains (Price, 2019). In other words, RfP has and will continue to influence our thoughts and actions, and we focus on the types of engagement that characterise this in digital and print books. Despite the rapidly changing publishing landscape and some alarm bells to which we need to pay attention to, children's reading is on the rise.

## The Benefits of Becoming an Engaged Reader

Children's engagement in reading is examined in two major international surveys: the Programme for International Student Assessment (PISA) which assesses 15 year olds' performance in reading, mathematics, science and problem solving every three years and its sister survey, the Progress in International Reading Literacy Study (PIRLS), which assesses reading in 10 year olds and is repeated every five years. These highly influential surveys are used by governments worldwide to compare their students' reading performance and their country's success on a worldwide scale. The survey results significantly shape both policy and practice. In PISA, reader engagement is deployed as a hybrid term to determine more than reading attainment – in this context it encompasses numerous elements, such as: frequency of leisure reading, attitudes, interest, diversity and 'depth' (measured by the comprehension strategies that the students report using) (Marks, 2000).

International results from the PISA and PIRLS studies show a strong relationship between children's independent, choice-led reading and reading attainment. This is supported by empirical research, which, since the 1980s has documented a strong correlation between the amount of reading children do outside of school and their reading achieve-ment in school (e.g. Anderson et al., 1988). For example, in England in the last PIRLS, children who reported liking reading the most, scored, on average, 45 points more than those who reported that they did not like it (McGrane et al., 2017). Additionally, the work of Sullivan and Brown (2015) has shown that those children who read in childhood make substantial cognitive progress between the ages of 10 and 16. This analysis of data from the 1970 British Cohort study further reveals that such progress is not simply evidenced in higher literacy scores, but is also associated with progress in mathematics and a marked increase in vocabulary.

Other studies also show RfP and reading engagement are strong predictors of reading attainment, including one in the USA with over 165,000 children aged 9–10 years old (Schugar and Dreher, 2017). These researchers documented positive associations between children's out-of-school reading engagement and their information text comprehension, and argue that motivated readers are more likely to be able to handle the cognitive demands involved (Schugar and Dreher, 2017). Drawing on longitudinal data from a national study of over 4000 students, German research confirms that intrinsic reading motivation and reading competence are positively correlated and that this is mediated by reading amount (Miyamoto et al., 2018). In other words, the more children are motivated to read, the better readers they are and this influences the number of books or texts they read. The mediating influence of reading volume on reading achievement was also noted in another German study, which pinpointed the positive influence of challenging text materials (Schaffner et al., 2016). As the researchers note however, it is often only the able or the 'academic track' readers who have access to such layered texts, thus disadvantaging less assured readers. In a not dissimilar manner, research in the UK highlights the posi-tive impact of teachers reading challenging, complex novels aloud (and at a fast pace) on the skills and attitudes of less experienced 'poorer' readers (Westbrook et al., 2018). These readers were offered the opportunity for sustained engagement with such material, which in turn influenced their readerly dispositions, their motivation and engagement, and contributed to their enhanced attainment. They made 16 months progress over a 12-week period which is remarkable for 12–13-year-old 'less able' readers.

Examining the influence of different text types, another recent study is of particular note. Drawing on large international survey data from 35 OECD countries who partici-pated in PISA 2009, involving more than 250,000 students, Jerrim and Moss (2018) reveal that there is a strong association between reading fiction and young people's academic attainment compared to reading other types of text (such as non-fiction, newspapers or magazines). There are several possible reasons for this 'fiction effect'. As the authors acknowledge, reading fiction requires sustained time and commitment, the capacity to concentrate for long periods and the use of one's meta-cognitive capacity to ensure understanding. In addition, extended narratives of a complex nature make high cogni-tive demands upon readers, and are likely to contain new vocabulary and syntactic structures that not only demand, but potentially enhance, the reader's capacity to handle this experience (Oakhill et al., 2015). Wolf's (2018a) argument is that 'deep reading' of fiction books is at risk in the digital era. We build on international evidence that shows that it is not the format of reading, but rather the interplay between content (fiction), the format characteristics (short novel on an iPad or a thick printed volume), the context of reading and reader characteristics that jointly determine the 'depth' of reader engagement. We argue that fiction reading in print and digital books can involve considerable concentration and deep engagement with meaning – a point we discuss later in this chapter and more fully in Chapter 3.

RfP has also been described as a form of ludic play (Nell, 1988), and in the case of fiction it offers a temporary escape from everyday life and the possibility of learning through sustained imaginative engagement, so the marked potency of fiction noted in Jerrim and Moss's (2018) PISA re-analysis, is not that surprising. In addition, fiction's significance is underscored by the human propensity to 'narratise' experience and to think through stories and narratives of life (Bruner, 1991).

Young readers who enjoy reading fiction and choose to make time for it in their lives beyond school predictably develop their skills as readers. This in turn nurtures their desire to read more, to read more often and to read more challenging texts. As the studies already noted indicate, the will influences the skill and vice versa; there is a strong bi-directional relationship between reading enjoyment and reading attainment. In another analysis of the large-scale PISA survey data (an increasing trend in education contexts internationally that prioritise children's numerical scores and national percentages), it is argued that enjoyment of reading can predict as much as 18% of variation in achievement at the country level (Chema, 2018). However, this varies between countries. For example, enjoyment of reading on its own explained 17.6% of the variation in reading achievement in Australia, although in Tunisia it explained only 0.1% of such variation. Looking across different countries' results, the authors observe that reading enjoyment is positively associated with reading achievement mainly in high and mean academic performance countries. They posit that cultural differences may be influential in shaping some of the differences noted, and comment that in some cultural contexts, parents may discourage children from reading (and engaging in other forms of 'entertainment') in order to ensure that there is no reduction in the time set aside for schoolwork (Chema, 2018). This highlights the need for parental information and guidance about the value of RfP, both academically and more widely.

Other benefits associated with reader engagement and RfP include a wider general knowledge (e.g. Clark and Rumbold, 2006), enhanced imagination, empathy and mindfulness of others (e.g. Kidd and Costano, 2013; Kucirkova, 2019a; Nikolajeva, 2014), and enriched narrative writing (Sénéchal et al., 2018). In addition, research studies indicate that RfP supports personal, emotional and cultural development (Arizpe et al.,

2014; Cliff-Hodges, 2010a), offers young people opportunities to explore their personal and social identities (Appleyard, 1990; Rothbauer, 2004), and develop new reader-to-reader relationships in classrooms (both teacher–child and child–child), which in turn help to build socially supportive communities of readers (Cremin et al., 2014). Readers, depending on text and context, often become affectively engaged in their reading, and are motivated by a legacy of past pleasurable engagements, both in the text and in the interaction often triggered by it. Thus, multiple cognitive, social and emotional benefits, as well as cognitive ones, accrue for those young people who choose to read in childhood and beyond.

## Young People's Attitudes to and Engagement in Reading

Considering these wide-ranging and undisputable benefits, it is disheartening to note that national and international surveys report declining levels of interest in reading and reductions in enjoyment and frequency of RfP in the young. This represents serious cause for concern for policy-makers, teachers and parents. In the UK, the National Literacy Trust found that four in ten children and young people say they don't enjoy reading and that RfP declines significantly as children grow older, with 78% of 8–11 years olds reporting enjoying reading compared to 44% of 14–16 year olds (Clark and Teravainen, 2017b). In the USA, Common Sense Media found that 27% of 17 year olds report that they never or hardly ever read (Common Sense Media, 2019). Boys are a key factor in this internationally, with girls continuing to outperform them in reading achievement (e.g. OECD, 2010; Rutherford et al., 2018). In England, children's attitudes to reading are comparatively low compared to their skills; in the most recent PIRLS survey, far more children than the international average reported disliking reading (McGrane et al., 2017). Furthermore, England had the lowest ranking for enjoyment in English speaking countries and the lowest for pupil engagement in reading except Australia (McGrane et al., 2017).

Large scale international studies have their limitations, however. They 'frame reading more as a measurable result than a lived experience and a process' (Cremin et al., 2014: 7), and many of the factors which interact to develop young people who self-identify as readers remain undocumented. Furthermore, and significantly, the complex social, affective and relational nature of reading and being a reader is ignored in such work. Studies such as PIRLS and PISA can only report on measurable reading scores and self-reports from young people in response to the survey's set options. Nonetheless, they can and do record shifts over time. Class or school reading assessments and surveys have not dissimilar limitations, although children's self-reports of their own reading habits are subject to the same socio-desirability biases as any survey data and in school will be influenced by their perceptions of reading. It could be for instance that children enjoy reading at home, but find limited satisfaction in reading texts from the school's mandatory reading list or the box of colour-banded books graded according to 'reading ability'. It could be that they enjoy reading the detailed instructions for playing the latest version of Minecraft at home, or love reading comics, but do not think this counts as 'reading'. Many will assume 'reading' is book bound and school-related if multiple choice options, open discussions or strategies such as 24 hour reads are not encompassed – an issue we discuss in more detail in Chapter 7. But, combined with observation and other evidence, surveys can be useful, and we do need to reflect upon the evidence they offer, whilst recognising that they offer a limited and partial view.

Motivation is key in developing volitional readers. Readers who are intrinsically moti-vated are more likely to be reading for their own pleasure and satisfaction and to have a positive self-concept as a reader (McGeown et al., 2012a). The presence of, and access to texts that interest, involve and challenge the young are aspects of intrinsic motiva-tion that have been found to predict comprehension (Wang and Guthrie, 2004). Another intrinsically motivating factor is the actual experience of reading itself which Ross et al. (2006) argue markedly motivates readers. Such intrinsic motivation is particularly triggered by the experience of reading narrative texts. In a meta-analysis of 108 studies, Lindsay (2010) found that access to print material improves children's performance, and encourages them to read more and for longer. In a longitudinal study across 27 countries, Evans et al. (2010) also found that having books in the home was as influential on attain-ment as the education level of their parents. Of those pupils in the England PIRLS survey who reported having 10 or fewer books in their homes, 42% reported that they do not like reading, compared to just 12% of those pupils who reported having more than 200 books at home (McGrane et al., 2017). Children are also motivated by digital texts, which as Bearne argues 'have changed the ways in which young people expect to read, the ways they think and the ways they construct meaning' (2003: 98); they value and enjoy the capacity to personalise such texts and the interactivity involved. This is why we dedicate significant space to digital texts in this book.

Studies of extrinsic motivation reveal it can have a limiting effect on readers. The greater the emphasis placed on performance and grades, on competitions and material rewards, the less keen children are to read (Orkin et al., 2018; Schaffner et al., 2013). Compared to the development of reading activities that support children's need for autonomy, belonging, competence and meaning, extrinsic motivational strategies (such as gold stars, popcorn, points and prizes) appear to be far less effective (Orkin et al., 2018). This is not a simple dichotomy however; young people may be motivated by both intrin-sic and extrinsic aspects. They may read for their own pleasure and be obliged to (and later derive some satisfaction from) reading for others' purposes. Nonetheless, excessive extrinsic motivation and pressure to perform within the school system as a reader can negatively influence young people's interest and pleasure in reading. We need to ensure that the young find pleasure in reading for themselves; they should not be reading to please their teachers or parents, or to conform to expectations within the school system.

In England, RfP has been part of the mandatory national curriculum since 2014 (DfE, 2014). This is a welcome recognition of its importance in children's education and their lives. However, without wider curriculum reform and significant professional support, the formalisation of RfP into a statutory requirement carries risks. Schools, overburdened by detailed knowledge-focused curricula and assessment regimes, may embroil themselves in 'performing' RfP to showcase their commitment to this agenda to parents, governors and inspectors. We have observed this tendency and see it reflected in schools investing in expensive book buses, book sheds, reading tents and endless cushions for reading corners, at the expense of staff developing knowledge of children's reading preferences and practices and widening their own knowledge of texts, both print and digital, that would motivate young readers. In such contexts RfP becomes little more than an 'act of window dressing' (Cremin, 2016). Additionally, in many schools, few opportunities are afforded children to use the school's reading spaces in ways that would nurture their journeys as readers. RfP pedagogy is not always given the curriculum time it deserves, and planning and reviewing the efficacy of this pedagogy is rarely prioritised. Furthermore, the backwash of assessment frames RfP pedagogy, restricting its efficacy, particularly for those who struggle (Hempel-Jorgensen et al., 2018). In Chapter 5, we discuss in more detail how schools differ in their approaches to RfP and based on some exemplary practice, we suggest ways forward. For schools that offer only a facsimile of RfP, time is often seen as a limiting factor. Senior management, often pressed to ensure standards are raised, tend to prioritise activities that promise to deliver short-term gains and in effect sideline RfP, despite unequivocal evidence of the long-term benefits of reading in childhood. Balancing the will and the skill remains an ongoing professional challenge.

## Print and Digital Texts

Within the RfP agenda, digital books have received relatively little attention and they are often portrayed negatively in the media (e.g. Crum, 2015; Ensor, 2013), with observers constructing narratives of anxiety and concern among many parents and practitioners. This book seeks to redress that balance in offering a detailed understanding of the potential of children's digital books alongside print texts. We do not privilege one medium over the other, but rather foreground different types of reading engagement with diverse reading media recognising that children learn with and from all types of texts, as well as para-texts and meta-texts. The latter type are texts that are hyperlinked and available exclusively online (via the Internet). Our main focus in this book is on digital books that are not hyperlinked but that can be accessible offline and online, and are narrative in nature. When we discuss children's reading of digital books and digital texts, this reading is reading on a screen, but it could have been preceded by reading on paper and may be followed up by reading on paper. Indeed, research suggests this is frequently the case with children using both formats and flexibly switching media according to their purposes and preferences (O'Donnell and Hallam, 2014). This is why we refer to children's contemporary reading experiences as happening on and with screens, resisting the seductive tendency to perceive one reading medium in isolation from the other.

Nonetheless, the question of reading digitally or on paper continues to divide researchers, albeit studies increasingly indicate that comparing print and digital reading creates a false dichotomy. Some studies have found greater learning benefits for print books (Munzer et al., 2019) and some for digital books (Strouse and Ganea, 2017b), depending on which type of book was tested, with which group of children and in which context (Courage, 2019). Pitching one format against the other is like comparing apples and oranges. Both digital and print books can be of good and poor quality, contain interesting or inappropriate content and have design features that may or may not encourage a meaningful experience for the reader. The quality of a text shapes our desire to read it, as poorly written and constructed texts are far harder to read than engaging well-written ones. The pleasure and meaning involved will also depend upon the context and the reader. For example, if you were sitting at home on the sofa one winter weekend, with a mug of hot coffee beside you and the children tucked up in bed, then sensory and embodied factors will influence your experience of reading, as well as your personal response to the message and meanings in the text, regardless of whether your chosen novel or newspaper is in print or digital form.

Adults' preferences regarding print and digital reading vary; many feel a strong preference for print books and would not trade a good hardback for a Kindle, while still others report their choice depends upon the situation and their particular purpose for reading at that moment. For instance, a recent European study highlighted that when reading for the purpose of study in a library, or when reading for leisure at home, young adults mostly preferred print texts (Kuzmičová et al., 2018). In public spaces however, more reported a preference for reading on their smartphones (this included newspapers, magazines, books and poetry) as these offered privacy; there was no need for them to worry about what others might think about their reading material. In the company of friends in such public places, digital texts were also seen as more acceptable than print texts, since such reading tends to be transient and does not prevent interaction in the way that print texts may (Kuzmičová et al., 2018). With regard to young children's reading, those paediatric researchers and experimental psychologists who have conducted experiments comparing one format with the other, strongly recommend reading print books only, especially for children under 5 years old (Klass, 2019). The reasons for this recommendation are multiple, including adopting the precautionary stance (in the absence of insufficient evidence, harm is avoided by prohibiting new resources), as well as the concern, that e-books increase children's solitary use of screens. These are valid concerns but portraying digital books in exclusively negative colours is counter-productive. Digital books and reading on screens will not go away; we cannot put the genie back in the bottle, so to speak.

In our work and throughout this book, we recognise the importance of personal attitudes and preferences, and the influence of place, space and purpose when it comes to RfP, but we also acknowledge that children's choices are typically mediated by their caregivers or educators. This has implications for children's experience of RfP and it is therefore important to consider parents' and teachers' attitudes towards young children's texts. National survey data in England shows that parents strongly prefer reading print books with their children, especially for bedtime reading. Many parents voice an active dislike of reading digital books with their children (Kucirkova and Littleton, 2016), although, perhaps unsurprisingly, their children seemed to show the opposite preference (Strouse and Ganea, 2017b). In a US study, children again expressed a personal preference for 'recreational digital' reading (seen here as the use of websites, messaging and social media) before 'recreational print' reading with 'academic print', 'academic digital' following (Lupo et al., 2017). Research suggests adolescents tend to perceive school-based reading as an academic event, one tethered to the proficiency agenda and reading at home or beyond school as more personally positioned, based on their own interests and preferences (e.g. Manresa, 2018). In early years and primary school settings, practitioners mediate children's access to different texts for particular educational purposes. Frequently though, this establishes hierarchical relations between texts and may inadvertently create the beginning of a separation between the 'unofficial' texts available to be read (and often desired) at home, and those officially endorsed and made available in school (Hopper, 2005). In the case of school texts, these are more likely to be in print format.

Whatever the format, fostering readers' engagement remains of critical importance and cannot be guaranteed. As educators we need to develop our understanding of the experience of reading, both of print and digital texts, and consider what counts as reading and RfP in our lives, in those of the children we teach, and in our schools and classrooms. In widening our conceptions and comprehension of reading in the twenty-first century, and eschewing populist assumptions, we will be in a better position to support children who are at the beginning of their journeys to become life-long readers.

## The Shifting Nature of Texts

The rise of the Internet undoubtedly paved the way for almost universal access to digital texts. Online texts with hyperlinks, images and videos have become the primary way to access information globally, 24/7. Questions remain concerning the many new ways in which readers engage with such digital texts and what constitutes a successful or less successful digital reading practice. The growing unease of many educators with digital texts is not surprising if we consider how quickly the reading landscape is changing and how slow the education system has been to accommodate it. Teachers, who closely observe these new habits in their classrooms, face questions that preoccupy many literary scholars too:

> Does the concept of literacy change along with the change of reading substrate, for example, from knowing how to navigate paper-based texts to knowing how to navigate the multiplicity of ever-changing hardware and software configurations involved in screen-based reading? How does the growing digital infrastructure change the social position of books and other texts and that of reading in general? (Mangen and van der Weel, 2016: 117)

Considering the historic emergence of e-books, we can see that the appearance of reading devices, such as the Amazon Kindle reader in 2007 and the Nook reader in 2009 drove the availability of adults' e-books. For children the increased use of touchscreen tablets and smartphones was significant. When children's e-books first appeared, there were concerns in some quarters that they would eliminate print books. The opposite happened: the appearance of e-books has reinvigorated interest in print books and the e-book continues to thrive as a book format in its own right (Baron, forthcoming). The variety of e-books is greater for children than for adults given the possibility of using images, moving characters, drawing and colouring features which are rarely used in adults' e-books. Enhanced digital books are sometimes referred to as story apps (Yokota and Teale, 2014) and are characteristically presented on iPads and other tablets. They typically contain some or all of the following features: audio (which can be activated through the 'Read to Me' option), audio with text highlighting, embedded audio and/or video, inbuilt camera and microphone, text magnification, background music, interactive elements or shared passages online. So story apps offer numerous possible entry points and forms of potentially pleasurable story engagement in ways that are different from traditional paper-based books.

Digital books are transforming the ways in which children read, write, engage with and produce their own stories (Burnett, 2010). These books have several benefits. The most salient identified in relation to adult e-reading include: intimacy of the reading experience, convenience, cost, environmental benefits and democratisation of access (Baron, 2015). Digital books also have some limitations: they can be easily copied and their content misappropriated and they do not offer tactile or olfactory feedback in the way that print books do (Benedetto et al., 2013). We focus on these almost exclusively, conceptualising them as a specific type of digital text that is particularly salient for children's RfP. Given the distinct benefits and limitations, it is more appropriate to judge digital books on their own terms. Ryan (2006: 180) captured this approach with uncommon precision when she wrote:

> (...) digital texts should not be expected to be enhanced versions of the novel, or drama, or of the cinema. Their achievements reside in other areas: freely explorable narrative archives, dynamic interplay between words and images, and active participation in fantasy worlds. Digital narrative is only a failure if we judge it by the criteria of the literary canon, this is to say, by the criteria of another medium.

We follow Ryan's perspective in our work and approach digital books as a new and unique medium expanding children's reading experiences that become visible in different ways and impact differently on children's learning trajectories. We use the umbrella term 'digital books' to encompass the various kinds of digital texts developed and designed for children's reading of stories on screen, including what Benedetto et al. (2013) and others refer to as 'e-books' and also ibooks, storyapps, bookapps or LeapReader books. When we use the term digital books, we do not mean simple e-books that are merely printed text presented on the screen in the form of PDF files. We mean texts that are enhanced with the digital medium and that present the content in several modes (audio, text and illustrations) with some kind of interactivity, such as, for example, the possibility to customise the text or tap on hotspots in the story. Many children's digital books contain a game or encompass a playful activity, such as the option of colouring in a picture or moving the story character to perform a certain activity.

For instance, in the app *Little Red Riding Hood* developed by the publisher Nosy Crow, the reader is encouraged to be the Little Red and knock on the door to grandma's house or tickle the big bad wolf with feathers. With such digital books 'the boundary between book and animation becomes blurred' (Al-Yaqout and Nikolajeva, 2015: 3). The blurring of different genres represents, in our view, a particularly important point of innovation for RfP in the digital age. The effects of reading digital books with added multimedia and interactive features on children's story comprehension and vocabulary levels have been documented with contrasting results (Takacs et al., 2014, 2015). We discuss the nature of interactivity in digital books in Chapters 4 and 6.

Many print books also prompt interaction and trigger playful engagement. For example, some offer opportunities to lift flaps to discover new characters and objects (e.g. *Spot the Dog* books by Eric Hill), turn flaps to make new creatures (e.g. *Flip Flap Safari* by Axel Scheffler), or unfold the concertina text to look underground (e.g. *The Street Beneath My Feet* by Charlotte Guillian). Others offer opportunities to open tiny cards and letters from envelopes in the text (e.g. *The Jolly Postman* by Alan Ahlberg) or engage with different textures and sensory additions for instance. Such books can blur the boundaries between books and play, as they frame and support reading as a playful social activity. Printed picture books often serve to support shared engagement between readers due to their size, and their visual, multimodal and polysemic nature. The non-linear nature of reading pictures can reveal new insights through interaction with others and research using wordless picture-fiction books has demonstrated their value as rich sources for discussion and identity exploration (Arizpe et al., 2014). Some books exist in both digital and print formats and may be accompanied by merchandise which again seeks to trigger interaction and play; soft toys, props and miniature characters can enable young readers to bring the story to life physically, with and without screens, alone and with others.

## Digital Books and Quality Concerns

For all the potential of digital books, the current international landscape of children's e-books and story apps is rather depressing. For instance, in assessing the quality of the best-selling apps on the Google Play and iTunes App Store in four European countries (Hungary, Turkey, Greece and the Netherlands), a research team found that many were not even available in local languages and all were very poor in terms of teaching children literacy skills (Sari et al., 2017). Similar conclusions were drawn from an analysis of the quality of apps developed for Greek pre-schoolers and available on the Google Play store (Papadakis and Kalogiannakis, 2017; Papadakis et al., 2017). These researchers reported that the majority of the apps that they scrutinised were inadequate, developmentally inappropriate and simply not teaching children anything worthwhile, let alone affording them engaging opportunities as readers. Many of these so-called educational literacy apps did not promote the readerly dispositions that are conducive to developing RfP. Instead, they contained simple games designed for rote learning, cause-and-effect tapping on the screen and offer limited scope for creative engagement. In their analysis of a selection of US English apps, Rowsell and Wohlwend (2016) also raise the issue of inadequate designs. They focused on the potential of children's digital books to support children's participatory literacies, which Rowsell and Wohlwend define as literacies that enable children to engage in multiplayer, productive, multimodal, multilinear, pleasurable and connected literacies. Such literacies connect children to the text, the author, other readers and themselves as readers. In contrast, the current designs of children's apps rely on the simple notion of cause–effect teaching and feed information to their young users in a behaviourist fashion (Guernsey and Levine, 2015). Such digital books cannot fulfil their potential to support new literacy skills or build new readers.

We are prompted to ask why is it that children's digital books are not designed in ways that facilitate children's reading journeys? Why are they so poor? The answer is complicated. Books with interactive and multimedia effects are very expensive to produce but very cheap to buy, thus only a few publishers can afford such a low return on investment. High-quality content does not always have to be expensive, but it is the case that illustrations, interactive features and multimedia (original music, sounds, voiceovers) do not come for free. This means that digital books that are developed at a lower budget, are almost inevitably of lower quality, particularly those that are offered for free and are typically put together by experimental developers or publishers. Given that the places that sell digital books – the Apple App Store or Google Play store – have no content-related acceptance criteria, there is an abundance of mostly low-quality digital books and story apps. In addition to finance, the production of higher-quality digital books requires input from award-winning authors and publishers as well as literary scholars and literacy researchers. Children's authors who write print books know that bestsellers for the young engage both children and adults alike, so their content needs to work on multiple levels. However, this awareness is not reflected in the children's digital book market as most such books seem to be designed for individual rather than shared use, and often lack sophisticated narratives, rich vocabulary and strong grammatical structures. Another reason why digital books are generally of poor quality relates to adults' attitudes. Teachers and parents mediate children's access to books and their conceptions of reading and the value they assign to print and digital books will influence the variety of reading resources and experiences children receive.

One could easily jump to the conclusion that given this poor quality, the paediatricians' recommendation to not use digital books with young children is the best solution. We disagree. The quality of digital books will not be increased if parents are discouraged from using them. A more productive approach, in our view, is to encourage greater involvement of all stakeholders involved in the production and use of children's digital books. Strategic collaboration between designers and researchers interested in digital books is currently pursued in the International Collective of Research and Design of Children's Digital Books (www. Childrensdigitalbooks.com). Such initiatives hold promise as they can address the currently low quality of children's digital books (Sari et al., 2017) by bringing researchers, designers and teachers into dialogue. Collaboratively designed digital books can be developed to connect parents and children around a shared reading experience and thus address the prevailing concern that they distract the child or disrupt parent–child reading experiences. In addition, parents, teachers and children can be actively involved in the creation of digital books to increase the books' quality; there are several platforms that offer the tools and space for adults and children to develop their own multimedia books, with the illustrations, voiceovers and storylines they desire (e.g. Storyweaver, Unite for Literacy).

In one of our projects, teachers were supported to develop researcher dispositions and undertake Learner Visits to children's homes in order to find out about their everyday literacy practices and later build on these in school (Cremin et al., 2015). We found that initially teachers were somewhat 'digitally blind' in that they had to be helped to notice the presence of digital media in children's homes and not to perceive this as 'mere entertainment' or a distraction, but as an embedded part of their literacy lives. It appeared that in some cases the teachers' own conceptions of literacy were book-bound, print-related and school-centric. For example, when a 5 year old was texting on her mother's phone, or an older child was searching online for computer game 'cheats', their focused engagement and the skills they were using in these contexts were not recognised as being 'valid' or relevant to literacy in school. Over the year of the project, however, as they shared the data gathered in children's homes, and reflected on their own literacy practices which encompassed digital texts, the teachers' conceptions of twenty-first century literacy widened, and they slowly began to value the marked digital competencies of the young. As we discuss further in Chapter 7 the teachers came to recognise the power in children's personal, affective and creative engagement in digital (and print) texts. As a consequence, they sought to widen the textual diversity available in school. Nonetheless many of the teachers found it hard to 'turn around' (Comber and Kamler, 2005) their pedagogies to connect to and build on the children's digital practices, as other studies have also shown (see Abrams and Merchant, 2013).

With regard to parents' attitudes to digital texts, as noted earlier many prefer print-based texts (Kucirkova and Littleton, 2016), whilst their children prefer digital texts; indeed young people from lower income families are reported to spend longer amounts of time with digital media (Kabali et al., 2015) and to prefer to read on screen rather than off screen (Picton and Clark, 2015). They are also, the research suggests, more likely (than children from wealthier families) to use them on their own, without adult support or guidance (Kinzer et al., 2016). If these children are also using poorly designed apps, they will become trapped in the 'second app gap' (Guernsey and Levine, 2015). EU Kids Online revealed that many low-income families have infrequent or no Internet access at home, creating the first gap (Livingstone et al., 2011). The second gap relates to the quality of content accessed by low-income children. Wealthier parents have the option of paying for subscription services which push apps that have been verified through some quality control, or at least have no advertising or inappropriate content. Such parents download digital books for their children in a manner not that different from buying print books (Guernsey and Levine, 2015). But for children who do not benefit from such adult mediation, the Wild West of children's digital books may become their daily, hours-long experience of story. This is a matter of social justice. The issue of adult mediation of books and children's access to high quality material is not isolated to digital books; it can be a challenge with print books too. Once children can read, reading too often becomes 'an orphaned responsibility' (Merga, 2016: 159) with teachers and parents stepping back from offering ongoing social and relational support that could enable children to develop and sustain a love of reading.

# Facets of Children's Reading Engagement

In considering the changing nature of childhood in the digital age and the seamless ways in which technology is integrated into children's daily lives, Craft (2011: xvii), a scholar of creativity, identified two dominant discourses in approaches to childhood and youth. The first, she argues, views children and young people as vulnerable and at risk, needing adults to protect them in this vast and rapidly changing technological world. The second, by contrast, sees them as capable and agentic, such that the role of adults is to enable and empower them. These contrasting discourses typify societal approaches to the digital revolution and are evident in adults' different, yet often overlapping, views about reading and technology. Theorising possible education futures, Craft identified four salient dimensions of digital childhoods: Pluralities, Possibilities, Playfulness and Participation. These can be understood as 'plurality of identities (people, places, activities, literacies), possibility awareness (of what might be invented, of access options, of learning by doing and of active engagement), playfulness of engagement (the exploratory drive) and participation (all welcome through democratic, dialogic voice)' (Craft, 2011: 33). We have built on these 4Ps of childhood in the digital age to consider how the key socio-cultural transformations of the twenty-first century position children as readers, recipients and (co-)constructors of digital texts. In order to conceptualise key facets of children's pleasurable engagement with print and digital texts, we also adopted Craft's framework of possibility thinking (e.g. Craft, 2001; Cremin et al., 2006) which focuses on the transformation of 'what is' to 'what might be'. We identified six facets linked to narrative: sustained, shared, interactive, affective, creative and personalised engagement (Kucirkova et al., 2017). Figure 2.2 offers a visual representation of these six facets of reading engagement mapped onto Craft's (2011) 4Ps.

We draw on this conceptualisation and in particular the six facets of engagement to guide and underpin our arguments in this book, seeking not to isolate them but to connect them to our own and others' work in the field. For affective engagement we consider how this relates to feelings and behavioural engagement with print texts, literacy apps and digital books. For shared engagement we discuss the collaborative possibilities and shared experience during the reading experience. For interactivity we pay attention to the connection between the main narrative and the interactive features of books. For sustained engagement we reflect on children's long-term and repeated engagement

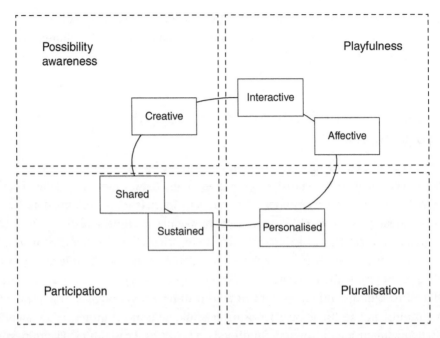

**Figure 2.2** Six facets of engagement and their position in relation to Craft's 4Ps of digital childhoods

Source: Kucirkova et al., 2015

with a narrative. For personalised engagement we examine the possibilities for choice, customisation and relating the material to self or others. For creative engagement we focus on imagination and hypothesising. The six facets interact and overlap and these interactions and overlaps manifest in different ways for digital and print books. For example, some digital books encourage children to envision story alternatives which can be embedded in the book in different modes (sounds, pictures, written text). This carries considerable potential for developing the children's creative as well as interactive engagement, which couldn't be achieved with print books. At the same time, some digital books save the reading progress and can be revisited later, while many print-based books can be marked up with highlighted texts or curved book corners. These markers of repetitive engagement often result in affective engagement, which manifest in different ways with digital and print books.

For teachers keen to support RfP in their classrooms, these facets of reader engagement provide both a framework for evaluating contemporary digital books and a new conceptualisation of reading engagement. A simplified version of the facets, together with some guiding questions and related criteria are used by the teacher judges of the annual UKLA Children's Digital Book Award. The criteria have also been incorporated into the National

Literacy Trust's guide to children's literacy apps and have the potential to inspire future international design, practice and scholarship in digital books to enrich and even transform children's RfP.

## Conclusion

We often associate RfP with print texts, but our understanding of RfP and its connection to readers' lives must continue to evolve in order to reflect contemporary childhoods. In framing this book, we have drawn on our work which focuses on facets of reading engagement that can be applied to reading both print and digital books, in any format or genre. From this perspective, we understand volitional reading as responding to the affordances of different reading media and the richness of literature. While national and international surveys indicate declining levels of children's interest in RfP, more nuanced research studies note an increase in volitional reading of diverse types of texts, online and offline. Readers who are motivated to read become skilled readers, and such readers typically also become lifelong readers. So, an essential question to ask in relation to life-long and long-term RfP, is how can we harness the connection between reading motivation and reading attainment, in current and future forms of narrative texts?

   In considering readers' motivation and engagement, we are challenged as both educators and researchers, to reflect on the multiple ways in which digital books are reshaping the landscape of reading. Children's reading of digital texts is a rapidly developing area of research in RfP; and considers both the quality of children's e-books, as well as their impact on children's motivation to read. Drawing on Craft's (2011) 4Ps of digital childhoods, we introduced our six facets of reading engagement that understand children as readers, co-readers and co-authors of texts. It is this more expansive stance towards the future that takes Craft's work well beyond a narrow focus on the medium of reading to the key socio-cultural transformations of the twenty-first century. The task for those who teach and carry out research in the area of RfP is to consider this wider understanding of reading and remain cognisant of the many ways in which 'words can change worlds' (Allyn, 2009: vii).

# 3

# The Personal and the Affective

T he potency of the personal in reading needs to be re-asserted and re-examined. It is one of the six facets of reader engagement underpinning this book and the specific focus of our attention in this chapter alongside the affective. In education, personalisation has at times become a buzzword; it seeks to capture difference and diversity and acknowledges that education needs to be responsive to individual children. In relation to personalised engagement in literary texts, we foreground the making of life to text and text to life analogies, relating the story to ourselves and others, and readers' affective engagement with and empathy for characters. The personal and the affective are significant forces in reading for pleasure (RfP) – not only in motivating readers to persevere and to read on (or to exercise their rights and step away), but in deepening engagement and potentially transforming their understanding of the text and of their own and others' lives.

Initially, we revisit the power of literature and the role of narrative and connect this to reader response theory in order to highlight the active role of the reader as a meaning maker. In exploring a conceptual model that connects affect and personalisation to contemporary reading practices and texts, we then introduce affect and personal resonance theories arguing that these can help to mobilise readers' deep engagement and understanding. Affect and personal resonance intersect with playfulness and pluralisation – two of Craft's (2011) 4Ps framework we introduced in Chapter 2. We consider these are essential for the reciprocal reading for pleasure (reciprocal RfP) we aspire to in our work. We also reflect on reading as a spatial and physical experience linking this to the intersection of personalisation with affect.

## Literature

Literature serves multiple purposes, but when it comes to children's literature, it is often perceived in binary terms, as either a didactic or creative tool (Nikolajeva, 2005). Our understanding of literature builds on the view of writers, critics and scholars who perceive it as a distinct genre of literature, characterised by unique aesthetic and educational qualities. It is not a watered-down version of adult literature, and represents far more than an educational–utilitarian resource; it has the potential to create aesthetic and pleasurable experiences and to enhance our understanding of the human condition. This potential links to the role of narrative as a fundamental human practice and a tool for thinking, for interaction and for development. In documenting how humans use narrative, Bruner (1990a) shows that we use it to make sense of experience and to represent and reflect on our broader social world. This perspective is widely recognised by scholars from many disciplines, for example Turner asserts that:

Narrative imagining – story – is the fundamental instrument of thought. Rational capacities depend upon it. It is our chief means of looking into the future, or predicting, of planning, and of explaining. (Turner, 1996: 4–5)

In addition, the linguist Langer (1953) describes narrative as a major 'organising device' and Barthes (1977), a literary theorist, claims it is 'international, transhistorical and transcultural'. Anthropologists have documented rich cultural diversity in storytelling traditions, both oral and literary (e.g. Heath, 1983; Hymes, 2003) and development psychologists such as Priddis and Howieson (2010) emphasise that in narrative thinking, emotions, memory and imagination are combined. Indeed, Hardy famously asserted that narrative is 'not to be regarded as an aesthetic invention used by artists to control, manipulate, and order experience, but as a primary act of the mind, transferred to art from life' (1977: 12–13).

Children's literature contributes to young people's identity constructions (Sumara, 1998) and plays a highly significant role in their desire to read and the frequency of their volitional reading, which as we argued in the previous chapter, has considerable cognitive, social and emotional benefits. Later in this current chapter we refer to texts that reflect our own reader identities, both from childhood and adulthood, but are acutely aware that children need access to diverse texts that reflect all readers in our multicultural world. A wide definition of diversity is needed however, as Courtney (2019) reminds us, one which encompasses representations of race, class, sexuality, disability, gender and religion alongside other areas. Texts which represent diverse realities have the potential to connect to children's lives and reflect their experiences, although as the children's author Katherine Rundell observes:

> This isn't to say children need to see exact replicas of themselves in every story they read – fiction, in giving you a front-row seat to another person's heart, allows you to be male, female, an armoured bear – but every child does urgently need to be able to find themselves *somewhere*. (2019: 58)

This metaphor of the mirror of fiction is useful since it suggests that through reading fiction and positioning ourselves within the text, we can come to understand ourselves more fully, such that the texts begin to 'reveal what we think we have successfully concealed even from ourselves' (Meek, 1988: 35). Narrative texts enable young people to explore new possibilities for selfhood and may lead to a deeper understanding of one's own culture and practices (Gopalakrishnan, 2011). The metaphor of children's literature as a window which opens onto the life worlds, practices and understandings of others, also helps us recognise its potential to enable readers to acknowledge difference, develop empathy and explore others' values and viewpoints. The metaphor of mirrors and windows is developed further by Botelho and Rudman (2009) who suggest that narrative can also operate as a doorway, a liminal space in which children can explore boundaries safely and develop both new self-knowledge, and new knowledge and understanding of others, this may contribute to the development of critical cultural awareness. However, as Arizpe et al. (2014) point out, if children don't choose to read and are not supported by a pedagogy that enables critical engagement and analysis of texts, such awareness will not develop.

Whilst recognising that notions of 'good' children's literature are highly context and culture dependent and intensely debated, we foreground fictional narratives in this book. Children's literature occupies a significant space and plays a unique role in motivating and engaging young readers, indeed Meek's (1988) seminal assertion that texts 'teach' what readers learn has underpinned much of the use of children's literature in the classroom. However, its potential is not always capitalised upon in relation to children's RfP, due to multiple issues including the financial resourcing of schools, teacher subject knowledge and the use of literature as a means to teach key literacy skills (for a research review see Arizpe et al., 2013). In exploring readers' engagement with literature in narrative form, we draw in particular on Rosenblatt's (1978/1994) reader response theory. Her conceptualisation, which is now widely recognised, views reading as an active meaning-making process between reader(s) and text(s), acknowledging that texts are not fixed, but develop their potentiality through the reader's engagement with them. An educationalist and literary scholar, Rosenblatt drew attention to the role of the reader and the memories, experiences, prior knowledge and understanding that they bring to bear on whatever text they are reading. As she observed:

> The special meaning ... the submerged associations that these words and images have for the individual reader will largely determine what the work communicates to him. The reader brings to the work personality traits, memories of past events, present needs and preoccupations, a particular mood of the moment and a particular physical condition ... in a never to be duplicated combination. (Rosenblatt, 1978/1994: 30–31)

It is the transaction between readers and texts and these notions of the reader's life, past and present, and the 'physical condition' and 'particular mood of the moment' that in large part shape and influence their affective engagement in reading, fostering their RfP.

## Affective Reading Engagement

Affect can be understood as a non-conscious/pre-conscious bodily intensity that cannot be named and can only be felt and sensed. It is arguably a space of potential (Massumi, 2002) that enables meaning to be given to an event/situation. In the psychological literature, affect is defined as the agglomeration of feelings, attitudes and perceptions towards an object or activity (Crone and Dahl, 2012). In studying affect, educational researchers tend to be interested in children's affective response to school, their feelings of belonging at home and their interest in and motivation for learning (e.g. Archambault and Crippen, 2009). An ongoing debate in psychological studies in this area focuses on the role of choice in affective engagement; some studies show that increased choice increases the feelings of positive affect (e.g. Cordova and Lepper, 1996), whilst other studies point to a possible threshold beyond which choice becomes undesirable (too many choices can be confusing, the so-called paradox of choice – Schwartz, 2004).

Affect is widely recognised as an underlying dimension in reading. Scholars comment that whilst reading, affect is experienced in both the mind and the body (Waller, 2019) and that there are socio-emotional lessons to be learnt, particularly with regard to empathy when reading literature (e.g. Kidd and Castano, 2013; Nikolajeva, 2013). In adults, empirical research indicates that after reading fiction, at least in the short term, their theory of mind scores increase (Kidd and Castano, 2013) and they demonstrate pro-social behaviour, such as increased generosity to a charity related to the fictional text (Koopman, 2015). Individuals who frequently read fiction seem to be better able to understand other people, empathise with them and see the world from their perspective, which researchers have documented in frequent readers in relation to reduced out-group prejudice (Johnson, 2013).

Texts which engage us emotionally can prompt us to pause and reflect upon the moral and ethical issues that they raise, the characters' actions and the consequences of these for others. In one of our studies, the *Teachers as Readers* project, when the 45 project teachers shared their favourite childhood books, strong 'affective traces' (Waller, 2019: 90) were in evidence. In studying the re-reading of such salient books from yesteryear, Waller suggests that these traces or points of connection, 'act like threads that resonate as they are first spun or as they are touched again in remembering or re-reading' (2019: 89–90). The teachers remembered these early texts and reflected a sustained emotional investment in them. As C.S. Lewis (1966) infamously observed 'no book is really worth reading at the age of ten which is not equally (and often far more) worth reading at the age of fifty' (1966/1982: 14). When the teachers discussed self-chosen current adult books, they again repeatedly and without prompting foregrounded affect and meaning. In their small group conversations, personal views and intense emotional responses were voiced, and social, cultural or moral issues were spontaneously discussed, often in considerable depth (Cremin et al., 2014). Drawing on their personal remindings the teachers shared myriad connections to their own lives and in the process got to know more about one another – their values, families and life histories, for example.

In complete contrast, when these same teachers discussed self-chosen children's books from their classrooms, their talk was dominated by a professional focus: they concentrated on what literacy objectives the book was good for (e.g. teaching character, plot, setting and specific language and literary devices), and often noted how long the book would sustain a literacy focus and the amount of work it could generate. This talk was largely at the expense of mentioning the content or meaning of the narrative, or of how individual books affected them personally or might affect children. The absence of the affective dimension and the marked disconnect between the talk which surrounded children's texts and their own adult reading material, was significant. The teachers were largely unaware of these different personal and professional discourses and the consequences for children's experience of reading. Gradually however, with support and reflection, and through reading and being encouraged to respond to children's literature as individuals and not as pedagogues, they came to talk about it as worth reading for its own sake – to be experienced and discussed. Recognising that affect and engagement were crucial in motivating their own reading, the practitioners began to share their own responses to texts in class and gave increased attention to children's personal and emotional responses. They also set considerably more time aside for reading aloud as we discuss further in Chapter 5, and observed the way in which children's emotional investment in particular characters drove their desire to read on or to hear more.

In reflecting on RfP in our digital age, Burnett and Merchant (2018a) adopt a somewhat broader conceptualisation of affect in relation to RfP. They view it as more than an individual's emotional response to a text, although they acknowledge this might well ensue. In exploring Bennett's (2001) work on enchantment and her concept of 'thing power', they argue for 'seeing RfP as an affect generated in the relations between readers, texts and things' (Burnett and Merchant, 2018a: 63). They draw attention to diversity in literacy practices and the pleasures that are often generated as we read, respond and engage, often ephemerally, with digital media. In stressing the social-relationality of reading digital texts and the materiality or 'thingness' of digital devices (e.g. their shape, size, weight and interactivity), these scholars argue that children's and adults' everyday engagement with digital media has the potential to create a mood of playful enchantment, and that it is this that propels interaction and further engagement. In this work, affect becomes a generative force, an 'affective encounter' with people and materials, which can 'allow something new to come to the fore' (Burnett and Merchant, 2018a: 64). It is this focus on affect, as a force that can produce or originate new experiences, that we connect to personal resonance theory.

## Personal Resonance

Personal resonance in reading is encapsulated by a group of theories concerned with the relevance/relevancy of a piece of text to an individual. In the context of adult literary reading, Larsen and László (1990) coined the term 'personal remindings', which they describe as conscious associations between the text and the reader's memory. Personal resonance is experienced as readers engage with fictional narratives (and other texts) and relate their personal history to these. Research indicates that keen adult readers gain considerable pleasure from activating their life-experiences when reading literature, for example through conjuring up mental images, personal memories or identifying self-relevant character traits and pondering on their future selves (for a review see Kuzmičová and Bálint, 2019). Research also shows that such remindings or 'life-resonant reading experiences' as Kuzmičová (2019) describes them, can enhance adult engagement with complex stories and offer them support as readers. The act of self-referencing through reading literature involves readers in comparing story content and character features to their own self-schema and through this process the narrative is connected to the readers' past experiences which are surfaced as remindings (Seilman and Larsen, 1989). Personal connections to texts are different from text-to-text (intertextual) connections, that we mention in Chapter 5, in that they are not in any way characterised by reading proficiency or reading experience; they offer a context for connecting readers' own knowledge, cultural background and personal histories to texts.

Although not formally investigated, it might be the case that remindings enhance adult pleasure in reading, and support one's understanding of others' mental states and capacity to empathise with them, since the mechanism of connecting to a fictional story character simulates the social connections in everyday life (e.g. Oatley, 2009).

Whilst little empirical research has applied the concept of personal resonance and remindings to children, historically, early years practitioners have sought to enable the young to make personal and affective connections to texts in order to make sense of them. This work has drawn, often unconsciously, on Rosenblatt's (1995) reader response theory, and on the potential power of literature and narrative in particular for personal, social and emotional development. In addition, the relationship between personal response and narrative has been examined by many scholars, but perhaps most intensively by Bruner, who as we noted earlier pioneered research on narrative. Bruner argued that 'stories make "reality" a mitigated reality' (1990a: 97), that is they act like a buffer between what we viscerally experience and what we tell others we have experienced; thus narratives act as a guide for locating our self in relation to others (and ourselves). This notion is evidenced in the psychological literature concerned with children's identity and oral narratives (e.g. Congleton and Rajaram, 2014; Engel, 2005; Nelson and Fivush, 2004; Wang and Fivush, 2005). In these studies, it is clear that narrative provides a framework for interpreting life events and understanding how children think about themselves and their experiences. In studying the relationship between children's autobiographical memory and self-definition, this body of work shows that autobiographical memories provide children with self-regulation mechanisms and a sense of continuity and coherence. It follows that if children recount stories of personal resonance or if they read stories with many personal remindings, it will have a beneficial effect on their identity formation. We propose that it may also contribute to children's greater affective engagement with texts. Indeed, we contend that personal resonance and affect are at the heart of transformative literary experiences.

## Transformative Literary Experiences

In this text we seek to offer an expanded theory of RfP, which perceives reading as a balancing act between personal and shared approaches to meaning-making, with reading experiences anchored in authentic, individual and complex responses to texts. In this regard we find Rosenblatt's (1986) transaction theory invaluable in conceptualising the process of meaning-making between the reader and the text. She acknowledged that 'the reader's attention to the text activates certain elements in his past experience – external reference, internal response – that have become linked with the verbal systems' (1986: 11). From this perspective, texts are sites full of potential which can limit or expand the reader's mind; all interpretations of texts are grounded in the transaction between the reader and the text, and are influenced by the wider social context of the reading. So, while Rosenblatt recognised the particularity of context and temporal dimensions in reading, she positioned the reader, or perhaps the dynamic interfusion of reader and text, at the centre of the 'lived experience' of reading (2005: 96).

One can think of this dynamic interfusion as a space of growth, where readers stretch their minds, scaffolded by the text. Vygotsky (1986) conceived of space for learning more broadly, supported both by other learners and objects of learning. His concept of the zone of proximal development applied to reading does not refer to a simple transfer of knowledge from the more knowledgeable other (the author) to the novice reader. Rather he recognises that learning happens on both cognitive and emotional levels (Chaiklin, 2003), that motivation and affect are highly significant and that choice counts. Vygotsky (1978) stressed the close entanglement of learning with the novice's personal desires, emotions and specific interests, as he noted:

 Thought is not begotten by thought; it is engendered by motivation, i.e., by our desires and needs, our interests and emotions. Behind every thought there is affective-volitional tendency, which holds the answer to the last 'why' in the analysis of thinking. (Vygotsky, 1978: 252)

The connections between personal resonance, socio-cultural theory and meaning-transactions are myriad, but in the context of reading they underscore the role of affect as a driving force in RfP. Transaction theory provides a concentrated focus on readers as active makers of texts, who in their roles as readers, story-makers and storytellers transact with text meanings. The notion of personal resonance endows this transaction with the reader's unique personal connections, such that each time they give voice to or perform a text, silently or with others, an affective encounter is generated. This can 'allow something new to come to the fore' (Burnett and Merchant, 2018a: 64) and fresh understandings or insights to be grasped (see Figure 3.1). The extent to which experiences are transformative will vary depending on the reader, the text and the context, but the potential is evident, powered by the affective dynamic interfusion between reader and text.

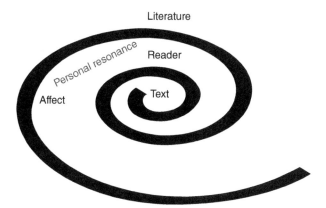

**Figure 3.1**   A simplified model of the relationship between affect and personal resonance

## Personal Resonance and Affect in Action

In applying these theoretical arguments to young children's reading, we draw on two examples of novice readers – the former involves a 5 year old telling a story and the personal resonances identified, whilst the latter recounts a 7 year old's personal and affective encounter with Jacqueline Wilson's *Sleepovers*. Both examples emerge from our research projects and have been selected to demonstrate theoretical patterns and provide practical illustrations of our argument.

One of our projects sought to understand the story-based approach developed by Vivian Gussin Paley (1990) and its contribution to children's learning (Cremin et al., 2018a). In Paley's approach, children dictate their stories to the teacher who writes them down verbatim, and then later the same day, the children act their stories out with their peers on the classroom 'stage' (as their story is being read aloud). We listened to many children's invented narratives and analysed these by examining the written versions captured by the teachers as well as stories that the children told us as researchers. The latter were captured with a multimedia app, *Our Story*, which records the voiceover and children's drawings or pictures accompanying their stories. We share two stories, both from 5-year-old Maddie (a pseudonym), one from her using the app and one from her teacher's notebook.

> the cat went to the shop without his mummy and the mummy was cross because he went there because he's only little. the cat, then the mummy came and put some food in, then next page, then the cat spitted it out and then the cat into a ehm to go to a shop and she got her favourite one and that's the end.
>
> Recorded by Maddie with the *Our Story* app

> Once upon a time there was a butterfly and then Mrs Leeke came and Mrs Leeke thought I'm going to get a horse and she ride on it very fast, then the mum came. The mum feeded the horsey.
>
> As told by Maddie to the teacher

In Paley's (1990) storytelling/story-acting approach, there are no constraints, no guidelines, so in our project, children were free to tell any story they wished, and teachers transcribed their narratives verbatim. It is interesting to note that in both Maddie's tales, the character of the mother was not initially present, but her arrival represented a turning point in the tales (the stories took new directions as soon as the mother appeared). In both stories the mother character interrupts the child's activity and feeds the animals (cats, horses). Maddie's tales appear to fictionalise her internal mental state – the cat and butterfly characters want to go to the shop on their own and to ride a horse very fast, reflecting perhaps a growing desire for increased independence. The tales reflect fairly advanced cognitive skills of perception, comprehension and projection. More importantly for our discussion, Maddie's stories, whilst fictional, were rich with personal resonance, and drew on her experience and knowledge of the world (she was learning to ride a pony). Our observations of the storytelling sessions across 12 weeks showed that she enjoyed telling her stories to others and was often strongly and affectively engaged. There was however no evidence of a sequence to her re-tellings in relation to personal resonance and affect. The two were entangled in the experience. As Vygotsky (1987: 50) observed, affect and cognition are inherently bound together: 'every idea contains some remnant of the individual's affective relationship to that aspect of reality which it represents'. The opportunity to tell her own stories created the conditions for Maddie to experience personal resonance and this experience became visible in her affective engagement with each of her stories.

On discussing other children's stories with their teachers, we found that many of these alluded to or fictionalised their real-life experiences (e.g. moving to a new house, dad leaving, a puppy getting lost). We recognise these as personal resonances which were often highly affectively charged. Whilst telling a story is of course different from reading a story and critics might argue that story-reading involves different affective and personal resonance processes, we posit, in line with Engel (2005), that children's oral stories enable them to slip between play simulating everyday life ('what-is' narratives) and a pretend world of fantastic possibilities ('what-if' narratives). Children's narratives in our research often remixed and recontextualised elements from these worlds, and many also drew on characters from popular culture such as Harry Potter, Power Rangers and Little Kitty (see Cremin et al., 2017 for a fuller discussion). In addition, it has been argued that children's ability to playfully inhabit imaginary situations is 'a basic aspect of narrative experience that endures through the lifespan' (Gerrig, 1993: 195), and that later this is realised in adults' engaged and absorbed mental states or flow whilst reading (Harris, 2000). In other words, the imaginary story worlds children compose do not disappear – they are carried over to other literary experiences and real-life accounts.

Our second example is of Holly, a popular 7 year old who loved being read to, would sit attentively listening to stories at home and school, but when it came to reading independently, Holly shied away. While she was able to decode text and was assigned to the yellow box (mixed scheme books) for 'able' readers, she appeared to read these to her mother as a job to be done. She rarely continued reading alone and although her mother tried to tempt her with other texts, this was to no avail. Until one day Holly brought home a copy of Jacqueline Wilson's *Sleepovers* and told her mother excitedly that Jade, one of her close friends, had recommended it. From the outset Holly's attitude to this book was different, she declined a bedtime story and announced she was going to read it herself. She was found with a torch still reading it late that night. It didn't go back to school but was placed under the pillow where it remained for weeks, as she read it again and again, possibly six or seven times. The book represented a significant life-resonant reading experience for Holly who had, her mother explained, always been somewhat hesitant about her friends coming for a birthday sleepover. The previous year she had procrastinated about what to do for her birthday, and whilst all her friends had sleepovers which she adored, she had avoided this, suggesting there wouldn't be room and that her older brother Darren would be difficult or get in the way. In a not dissimilar manner, Daisy, the book's main protagonist, is uncomfortable about the expectation of holding a birthday sleepover at her house, as she has an older sister with special needs. Daisy and Holly also shared the dilemma of a challenging school 'friend' (one fictional, one real) whom neither were sure they could trust. At the time Holly did not discuss the story with her parents, and she chose to keep her personal meaning transaction private, so the analogies here remain interpretations. But there is no question that *Sleepovers* became an important – affectively charged – text for Holly. It arguably launched her as a reader, creating both desire and powering a new interest in reading. Following this experience, Holly read voraciously, first many of Jacqueline Wilson's other books and then a wider range. That Christmas, she requested a copy of the book and began to plan for a birthday sleepover. The dynamic interfusion between this reader and this text, between affect and personal resonance appeared to shape her new engagement with reading.

## Personal resonance and print books

Personal connections to narratives or books are not necessarily visible, although well attuned teachers or close family may be aware of resonating features. As an adult perhaps you too have a book that you cherish more than any other, that you keep in a special place in your library at home or even carry with you when you travel. One of us for instance has a cherished childhood copy of *The Family from One End Street* by Eve Garnett, dogged and faded on a particular shelf in her study; the other has *Gathering Moss: The Natural and Cultural History of Mosses* by Robin Wall Kimmerer.

The content and form of these texts contribute to their value, but it is the personal resonance they retain that set them apart from others. Shaped by our early and later life experiences, we have strong memories attached to these physical objects which serve to create a personal aura around them, setting them apart from other copies of the same texts. In the former, the pages are brown with age, the binding frayed, the line drawings of the Ruggles family and the local shops were coloured in decades ago. Holding it conjures a sense of warmth and comfort, of family and play, and the picture of the Ruggles' train trip even now brings to mind reading the book on an overnight sleeper to Inverness and intermittently watching the 'fairy lights' of towns rush past. The latter book brings back memories from particular hiking trips to Norwegian mountains, covered in moss, a seemingly small and unimportant plant, yet so powerful in surviving the harshest conditions. Kimmerer's poetic descriptions of how moss can stay green year-long and adhere to driftwood or stones, sends a powerful reminder of the importance of collaboration (not competition or survival of the fittest) in ensuring continued growth. The book carries a transformative message for humanity and for individual readers. Should these books get lost, we could buy new copies, but they would not contain the emotional residue attached to these particular texts. Personalisation is at the core of affective engagement in texts; it touches on both their format and the content.

While commercially produced personalised books, such as those created by *I See Me Ltd.* for example, aim to recreate some of this, they cannot replicate the deeply personal resonances individual readers have for particular texts. The range of publishers providing services for custom-made photobooks, diaries and children's books has grown exponentially in the past decade; people are craving personalised products and services. Parents can send their child's name, pictures, even their child's friend's names to such book publishers and receive a 'unique' personalised book in return. Personalised book publishers have templates into which customers can insert personal memories, in any format. Customers can get multiple copies printed, update their books with latest photos and share them with others. Whilst such books are personalised, they can only contain a limited number of personal resonances.

Imagine a different personalised book, one which contains pictures of you as a child, some poems written to you by your first lover, an old concert ticket or some perfume on its pages, all held together with stitched Coptic binding. A personal aura breathes from each page. Losing this book would be losing a part of you. Such is the nature of genuine personal resonances: they are deeply affective and carry bodily, material and mental associations that outweigh any attempts at replication.

## Personal resonance and digital books

In what follows, we highlight digital stories as an example of personalisable reading resources (not as deeply personal as the preceding example but with features that can be appropriated by a single reader). In one of our studies, we compared the key design features of paper-based books, simple electronic books (available for desktop computers without animation/interactivity) and highly interactive digital books (which combine multimedia and interactive features) (Kucirkova, 2018a). We found that personalisation is a key defining feature in more recent interactive digital books – the more advanced or evolved a book format is, the more personalised and personalisable it is. Paper-based books contain very simple features of personalisation, such as name-based personalisation (a child's name written inside a book indicating ownership), or face-visualisation (a mirror at the end of toddler books shows them their face). Digital interactive books, however, allow for the immediate and seamless insertion of a child's selfie into a book and the enhancement of a story with an authentic audio-recording. Moreover, children can share their multimedia story with others, receive feedback and personalise it further.

Such personal resonances in digital books can be interpreted in two ways. On one hand, they could be perceived as 'forced' personal remindings. There is no distance between the reader and the story character as the reader *is* the story character. There is no need for the text to prompt a personal resonance as the readers can see themselves in the book. Reflecting on such digital personalisable books, we propose a Distancing Hypothesis, according to which the distance between the reader and the story character determines the depth of engagement in reading. The closer the story character to the actual reader's persona, the less cognitive work is necessary for identification and thus the less deep the reader's engagement with the story. Conversely, if the story character is very distant from the reader, the story needs to be of high literary quality and engage the reader through subtle personal remindings. Not all authors achieve this.

The short distance between the reader and the story character might lie at the heart of concerns about children's 'shallow' engagement with digital books. In many quarters, digital books are seen as less emotionally involving because all the senses are not recruited for engagement. The haptic and olfactory cues which print books afford have been identified by literary scholars as key to our autobiographical attachment to book titles (Mackey, 2016) and even the ability to deeply process long literary texts (Wolf, 2018a). The more senses that are engaged in a reading experience, the deeper the engagement. Haptic and olfactory cues are currently missing in digital books, but we could imagine them being developed in the next decade. Nevertheless, we contend that sensorial engagement is not a permanent feature that could explain the depth of readers' affective engagement. The distance between readers and story characters points more precisely at the possible mechanism here. The distance between the reader and text does not need to involve story characters alone, personal resonance can also be felt towards other content features or specific format characteristics.

In particular, some young readers may feel greater individual affinity with digital formats as these are closer to their personal experience of texts. It follows too that readers' feeling of personal relevance with specific texts is linked with greater enjoyment of reading those texts. Distancing and personal resonances might thus be at the heart of young people's increased motivation to read digital books rather than print books. Research undertaken by the UK's National Literacy Trust (Picton and Clark, 2015) indicates that using the e-book platform RM Books in schools can positively influence children's attitudes towards RfP. The findings need to be interpreted with caution however given that the research was correlational and commissioned and published in a report rather than a peer-reviewed journal. Nonetheless, the report describes some interesting patterns: boys' reading levels increased after participating in a 4-month-long trial with the RM books and their confidence in reading as well as perception of reading being a 'cool activity' increased (15.9% to 28% increase and 34.4% to 66.5% respectively). It could be that these reluctant readers identified with the digital medium more readily than with print books given the personal connection they have to digital devices. This point should not be interpreted in terms of dominance of one format over the other. Print books are here to stay and young readers need diverse choices in both print/digital formats. The question is how to skilfully combine texts with important topics that children need to learn about while preserving their affective and volitional engagement in reading.

## Personal resonance and reading aloud

Reading aloud to children is a technique that has been used from time immemorial to evoke personal resonances and affective response to narrative by children. We discuss this as a key strand of effective reader-led RfP pedagogy in Chapter 5, but want to stress here that such reading, whether at home or at school, not only offers rich opportunities for making personal connections and engaging affectively, but also serves to motivate children as readers. Through listening to texts read with passion and pleasure, children are invited to imagine, predict and participate. They can be involved in looking closely at the visual or constructing their own mental images, can be prompted to share what the text reminds them of (e.g. people, places, predicaments, other texts) and can explore how different characters' actions and values make them feel. The book as a whole may even lead to the consideration of world issues, such as war, refugees, children's rights, the environment and so forth, and from awareness to social action at a local level. Though much will depend on the quality of the text, who chose it, and the adult's capacity to bring it vividly to life, reading aloud represents an affinity space in which all readers, including the adults, can connect personally and affectively.

Significantly, the shared experience of being read to draws parents and children, and teachers and children together, as remindings are shared and emotions voiced – a sense of belonging, intimacy even, tends to develop. Over time, these 'books in common' (Cremin, 2018) become a communal resource, a shared frame of reference for families and classes of children. Such books in common build connections and bonds between readers which are highly supportive of RfP and can impel readers forward with the desire not just to find out what happens, but to read more by this author or in this genre. Relating this practice to Rouxel's (2005) notions of *interpreting* text, which involves specific skills taught within comprehension for example and *using* the text, which suggests personal appropriation of the key messages and emotional engagement, we can see that reading aloud predominantly involves the latter, although such notions are not absolutes as there is always interplay. Nonetheless in relaxed informal spaces, reading aloud, potentially a richly resonant and affective encounter, can help develop young people's awareness of themselves, of others and the wider world.

# Reading as a Physical and Affective Experience

As we have argued reading is not confined to the brain as a cognitive activity, nor is it just a cognitive-affective experience – it involves the whole body. In each act of reading, embodiment and phenomenological processes intersect with cognitive processing, shaping the reader's understanding of the words and their relationship with the writer. For example, the experience of reading a summer novel in print or on a digital device might encompass a strong sense of place, a beach in the sunshine perhaps, one's friends or family nearby, the book itself and the physical experience of thumbing through the pages or scrolling onwards, as well as immersing oneself into story and living through the characters' experiences. The affect at play in this context will also influence the physical experience of reading.

The embodied and situated nature of reading has been investigated by a team of EU researchers who explored the role of the environment in influencing the reader's purpose, text type and device (e.g. print book, laptop, e-reader, smartphone) (Kuzmičová et al., 2018). Unexpectedly the team found that the young adult readers regardless of where they were reading and for what purpose, (leisure or study), were very aware of the presence and activity of others. In homes, in dedicated reading spaces (e.g. university libraries) and in non-dedicated more public spaces, they documented the 'affective impact of the unobtrusive physical presence of others' (Kuzmičová et al., 2018: 73). Home reading experiences for instance, were spontaneously reported to be enriched by the presence of others who, whilst they may have disturbed the reader's silent focus, created a sense of belonging. Reading for study was also shaped by social and affective factors, including the presence of others, irrespective of whether this reading was on paper or with screens. This work is resonant of Burnett and Merchant's (2018a) conception of RfP as an affective encounter with people and materials.

If we turn to the literal physicality of books, the immediate features that come to mind with print texts are weight, spine, cover, feel and the order of the pages. These predominantly visual and tactile features contribute to our reading experience, they can entice us to select a particular book, prompt us to avoid one, affect our mood, and serve to trigger engagement, to mention but a few of the consequences of this materiality. There is also an inner physicality that has to do with the feel of individual pages, perhaps prompting us to pause as we read, and fill gaps as we turn them. Proust (2013) is credited with the first reference to the connection between olfactory memory and the physicality of print books. A print book can evoke autobiographical memories as we noted earlier and act as a reminder of a particular moment in time. Such a personal memory connection is as much a result of the book's content as of its physical characteristics.

Whilst digital books do not – as yet – contain olfactory cues, their materiality can, we have argued, be divided into two categories: external material properties, which are peripheral, easily noticeable and common to all, and internal material properties, which are embedded and different in each book (Kucirkova, 2017b). Since the appearance of the first Kindle on the market, concerns were raised around the physicality of the new medium and its impact on the experience of reading. Digital books do not hold the history of giving and receiving as traditional books do, and have no 'aura' around them (Wu, 2010). More specifically, accessing long narrative texts with hyperlinks might interrupt and fragment a reading experience. Anecdotal evidence suggests that if readers are given easy access to hyperlinks that diverge their focus (to other texts or words), the original personal–social rapport between the reader and the text will suffer. Readers might become more interested in shorter snippets rather than engaged in longer literary texts, their reading is also likely to be faster when reading such digital texts and possibly somewhat superficial, maybe even reducing the affective experience. This concern is not only expressed by some teachers and parents, it is also the focus of research that focuses on the materiality of texts. With digital texts accessed online, researchers have documented that readers use different reading strategies, recruiting different memory and intellectual skills. Given that the Internet carries an unprecedented amount of information that we don't need to remember (it is enough to type the right search word to retrieve information), it reduces the need to recall information and for in-depth processing (Sparrow et al., 2011). From this perspective, while text digitisation represents a significant practical advantage, it also poses risks for basic memory functions, such as the depth and accuracy of information processing. This line of research emphasises the materiality, the physical properties of texts, rather than the reader's individual response to texts. It is thus different from our perspective, but not necessarily different from public perception concerning the value of e-books and digital texts.

The physical properties of texts, Wolf (2018a) argues, influence not only our affective and subjective feeling of reading, but also our cognitive processing, shaping adults' and children's capacity to understand texts, to learn from them and influencing their ability to empathise with story characters. Through studying the acquisition of reading skills from a neurobiological perspective, Wolf (2018a) seeks to explain the complex 'design principles' of the human brain implicated in the reading process. Our brains have a unique capacity to connect old and new information and to generalise patterns from specific examples/ instances. This process is intimately linked to our senses in the embodied experience of reading. Wolf (2019) is concerned that the short, fast-paced, two-dimensional engagement with digital texts diminishes our capacity for deep engagement, and that this has negative effects on cognitive and emotional processing. She focuses in particular on the 'deep reading' processes that, in her definition, consist of internalised knowledge, analogical reasoning and inference; perspective-taking and empathy; critical analysis and the generation of insight. Wolf's (2019) main argument is that these processes are threatened by the digital medium of reading. She hypothesises that the spatial arrangement of printed (analogue) texts encourages more 'looking back', which, when complemented with the sense of touch, help with readers' orientation to the chronological nature of texts. The quick accessibility of hyperlinked texts via screens is believed to encourage specific reading habits that are not conducive to deep reading. In particular, Wolf (2019) is concerned that digital reading promotes skimming, and that with the currently high levels of digital engagement, this may also influence our reading of print books.

This is a significant concern, but there is also the potential for the opposite correlation: just as the digital medium carries the potential for possible fragmentation of meaning, it also carries the potential for the integration of meaning. For example, it could be argued that as the reading size (the reading screen) becomes smaller and more portable, the reading experience may become more personal, immersive and intimate. Young adults appear to value the privacy it affords as we noted in Chapter 2 (Kuzmičová et al., 2018). Scholars also hypothesise that the opportunity that some children's digital books afford to interact directly with story characters (by moving them around the page and performing certain actions for instance), is likely to encourage greater identification with the characters' feelings (Zhao and Unsworth, 2016). Also, when processing texts, digital or non-digital, readers make diverse and often circular connections between memories, associations and judgments related to specific words (Calinescu, 1993). Over time, they develop textual and intertextual connections between the texts they have read in the past and the texts they anticipate reading in the future. Digital texts will surely broaden the landscape of textual interconnections, enriching the experience of reading. So, whilst the digital format may be limiting in one respect, it may well be enriching in another.

Returning to our focus on the physical and material attributes related to the experience of reading on and off screen, we know that reading books in print engage all our senses with different levels of intensity according to the text and the context. Nonetheless we focus on the visual representation offered, engage with the sound of turning pages, draw on the book's aroma to remind us of places where it was or where we read it before, and use haptics to hold it and estimate our reading position within it. In contrast, as Mangen notes:

> When reading on screen, we may see (for example, using page numbers), but not kinaesthetically sense, our page-by-page progress through the text. On an iPad or a Kindle, the display of each page in a text rests on a different logic of sensorimotor contingencies. A print book informs the brain about the length and volume by concurrent tactile, haptic, and kinaesthetic information as we gradually move through a lengthy text. When reading on a Kindle, there is no such sensory feedback – only visual information about progress. (Mangen, 2016: 465–466)

Perhaps in the light of the importance of readers' physical experience of texts, some of these limitations will be overcome with book design developments in the twenty-first century. There are several prototypes underway that focus not only on overcoming the lack of physical engagement in the digital format, but augment it to levels that would be impossible with physical books. For example, the prototype digital book developed by Kindoma Ltd. offers parents and children who are not co-located in the same geographical location, the possibility of connecting around the same digital book with a video conference call. The parent can see on their screen where the child is pointing on the digital page and guide the child's finger by moving it across the screen and literally across the distance. Thus, in seeking to understand the potential of digital books for children's RfP we argue that this needs to involve bodily engagement, since 'those who read for pleasure know that the desire to read almost seems to have a physical sensation with which it is associated' (Grainger et al., 2005: 66). From this perspective, a Kindoma digital book that brings together parents and children who cannot read together in person (for example in the case of displaced families for work, war conflict or health reasons) represents an exciting step towards future directions.

## Reading as a Personal and Spatial Experience

We also want to recognise the influence of space and place in RfP. Reading as a spatial experience and the relations between reading, place and identity are increasingly being studied (e.g. Cliff-Hodges, 2016a; Mackey, 2010, 2016; Spring, 2018) and are frequently highlighted in reading memoirs (e.g. Mangan, 2018; Spufford, 2002). Mackey's (2016) extensive autobibliographical work is seminal in this area. She analyses her childhood reading history growing up in St. John's Newfoundland and in so doing reflects upon and reveals the importance of place in the development of readers. Drawing from this particular place, she does not seek to generalise, but there are lessons to be learned for all readers. Mackey emphasises the physical and social situation of herself as a 'placed child' (2016: 13) – a situated reader – and explores how the immediate locality, its history and the point in time at which she grew up there all influenced her literate experiences, shaping her personal perspectives. Her detailed account foregrounds the embedded and situated nature of her own RfP which she recognises was/is never free from emotional involvement. As Mackey acknowledges:

> Whether reading for the first time, or repeating an encounter with a text, we necessarily embed the textual experiences inside the events and understandings of our local life at the time. It is not an optional extra; it is woven into the experience itself. ... We read our own worlds into the words of our books, and these worlds will not be subtracted from the understanding we develop from the texts. (Mackey, 2016: 263)

In Mangan's (2018) early encounters with texts, she too recognises that the context counts. The church hall 'nursery' and her mother's NHS clinic were places, where, left to her own devices, she become engrossed in books. Later, the local library and the study of a family friend played their part, alongside many other specific places and spaces. For us as readers too, place has played and continues to play a role in our experience of reading, influencing our personal responses and affective engagement in particular texts. As children we individually recall reading Eleanor Brent Dyer's books alone in the sand dunes at the back of Achnahaird beach in Wester Ross, and Milan Rúfus's *Modlitbičky* (Little Prayers) at the grandparents' cottage in the northern Slovakia mountains. As adults, one of us remembers devouring Joanne Harris' *Chocolat* in bed in a cottage in the Dordogne and seeking out local chocolateries to buy the richly described shining mendicants, later eating these while reading the text. The knowledge and experience of reading this novel whilst in a small French village one Easter enabled different interpretations and connections with the text. As the author Tim Wynne-Jones observes, reading involves consideration of fictional and real places 'the one that we live in and the one the writer takes us to' (Wynne Jones, 2011, quoted in Spring, 2018: 108). The other one of us remembers reading Elizabeth Gilbert's *The City of Girls* on a plane to Boston, USA and thinking about how different New York must have been in the 1940s, where the story is set. The story was about a 19-year-old Vivian Morris who moved to New York with two personal belongings: a suitcase and a sewing machine. Reading the book in the air on a digital reader led to an interesting experience: the book was a page-turner (even though there were no physical pages to turn) and made the reader literally forget about how much 'time flies' when we are absorbed in a story. The connection between the place of the fictional story and the actual destination gave the reader an even greater thrill of anticipating the destination.

In sum, reading places us. We are always situated readers, in a particular space and time and this serves to shape our meaning-making, contributing to the personal connections possible, to the surfacing of resonances and to our affective engagement. This has consequences for pedagogy as we discuss later in this book. In the transactional process of reading we draw upon our prior knowledge and experience of place, and deploy it in order to personalise our response, perhaps connecting or transforming the fictional place to another place, a real place we know. In the process we use 'the representations of place provided by the author to scaffold a reflection of our own place identity, outside of the text' (Spring, 2018: 109). Reading and making meaning-transactions with texts necessarily involves exploring place; it is never static, rather it shapes and is shaped by our experience of the 'what if' and 'what is' worlds we inhabit.

## Conclusion

Literature plays a key role in readers' engagement, it has a unique potency and power, enabling young readers to transact meanings 'from the stuff of memory, thought and feeling' (Rosenblatt (1978/1994: 12)) in a never to be repeated event. The digital and print books and the reading practices that readers encounter, create the conditions for them to experience personal resonance which becomes visible in affect. This is evidenced in their deep engagement, their enhanced intrinsic motivation to read and potentially in their comprehension. Significantly, as remindings are shared and emotions felt and voiced in shared reading contexts, whether at home or school, a sense of connection and belonging is created. This serves as a motivating factor and supports children's RfP.

Readers of all ages are highly active meaning-makers, not passive receivers of others' words. In drawing on their present lives and past memories, their vicarious experience and their emotions, readers make sense of the words and images on print or screen, personalising the meanings as they engage in this cognitive–affective experience. Each act of reading is also a physical and spatial experience, an embodied and situated one that shapes reader engagement. The personal and affective dimensions of reading drive readers forward in diverse and individual ways and are enriched by the social and relational dimensions of RfP, which we turn to in the following chapters.

# 4

# The Personal Entangled

onnecting to readers' personal responses and the impact of personal relevance on children's reading engagement which we discussed in the last chapter, here we again draw on Rosenblatt's (1978/1994) emphasis on the reader's active quest for meaning, and her assertion that a text either expands meanings or 'limits or controls' these (1978/1994: 129). Inspired by this, we conceive that reading for pleasure (RfP) involves a potentiality possessed jointly by the reader and the author, and consider how the personalised features of texts limit or facilitate readers' contributions and transactions. Digital texts which use personal data and algorithms offer more acutely perceived personalised engagements than print books. However, the extent to which this personalised engagement is agentic (led by the readers) or passive (led by the designer/publishers) is key.

In order to appraise the extent to which books mediate the boundaries between the personal and the social, or the 'self' and the 'other', initially we unpack the notion of subjectivity. We start from the premise that no 'self' exists in isolation from others and therefore personalised engagement is deeply entangled with social engagement. As in the other chapters, we focus more fully on one of the RfP facets of engagement, but remind readers these overlap. The personalised–social engagement overlap is particularly salient here. Authorship requires audience; a personalised text created by a child deserves to be shared with others. While the advent of digital texts revolutionised text-sharing through immediate and global channels, it has also altered the intimacy of one-to-one author–reader dialogues. To understand the conceptual shift brought about by text digitisation, we synthesise the most influential schools of thought on subjective meaning-making with texts and draw on Vygotsky's (1978) and Bakhtin's (1981) insights – they inject a structural component into our discussion. We illuminate these with examples from our studies and new analyses, arguing that books which contain personalisable features offer a unique context for experiencing, expressing and maintaining subjectivity that bridge the personal and social worlds of stories.

## Subjectivity

In conceptualising personalised reading engagement, and the reader's experience of 'self' within a shared social world, we opted for the word 'subjectivity' in this chapter. Subjectivity shares some attributes with agency, a key concept in RfP. Agency, subjectivity and independence all relate to the 'self' and the ways the 'self' relates to others. For this reason, we tend to avoid the term independent readers, which, while popular among the education profession, implicitly foregrounds an understanding of the 'self' as apparently autonomous. In seeking a balance between personalised and shared reading engagement, we consider the boundaries between readers, authors and the text features that facilitate or constrain such boundaries. Dialogic and dialectical socio-cultural theories are particularly helpful here for clarifying the dynamic exchanges at play. They locate subjectivity at the intersection between the personal and the shared.

Unlike the term 'independent readers', subjectivity has the qualities of action and process rather than a static status. This is important for understanding reading as an active mental exchange between meanings encountered in books, and meanings held in the readers' minds. Also, subjectivity encompasses intra- and inter-personal dimensions. The experience of 'me, myself and I' is not a personal quality or trait that is fixed in time, but rather an ongoing process of meaning-making with others, as family psychologists such as Skowron and Schmitt (2003) would say, or the collective and individual identity, as social psychologists, following the tradition of George Mead (1934), would describe them.

## Dialogic Approaches to Subjectivity

Lev Vygotsky barely needs an introduction to educationalists. Although little known and virtually unpublished during his lifetime, the influence of his work (1964, 1980, 1986) on early childhood education is undeniable – all contemporary textbooks on children's development include references to Vygotsky's socio-cultural theory. His thinking is often contrasted with Jean Piaget's constructivist development theory, although the two theories share more similarities than dissimilarities (Cole and Wertsch, 1996). We focus on Vygotsky's unique contribution for two reasons: first, unlike Piaget, Vygotsky emphasised the role of external influences on child development, notably the influence of more knowledgeable others, such as children's teachers, parents or guardians, who actively shape children's thinking and development. Whilst socio-cultural influences in children's development were not central to Piaget's work, he too acknowledged that children's learning happens through others' mediation. Secondly, we draw on Vygotsky's (1978) work as he stresses the role of cultural artefacts, such as books and adults' mediation of them with children. As Cole and Wertsch (1996) explain, tools and cultural artefacts were central to Vygotsky's description of mediated learning. His work supports our discussion of children's engagement with and use of digital and print texts as specific cultural artefacts, and the mediation of these by parents and teachers.

### Dialogic mediation of meaning with books as cultural artefacts

Vygotsky (1978) proposed that the internalisation of subjectivity with cultural artefacts occurs in a sequence. He argued that any higher mental function appears first between people and then becomes internalised, placing the social influence above individual subjectivity (Rey, 2009). In other words, the 'self' is not free from external influences but is shaped by others' words, perspectives and actions and these influences happen before the self can establish his or her agency. This suggests that when individual readers engage with particular books, their engagement and interpretations are influenced by their life experience, including their experience of reading other texts or discussing stories with teacher/parents/peers.

The importance of previous experience in shaping readers' engagement is inherent in Schank and Abelson's (1977) argument about scripts and schemas and how people make sense of stories. Rosenblatt (1978/1994) refers to scripts in terms of well-known texts by other authors, but for Schank and Abelson scripts are 'specific knowledge to interpret and participate in events we have been through many times' (1977: 37). They stress these 'are an important part of story understanding' as they fill in the 'obvious information that has been left out of a story' (1977: 43).

In Chapter 1, we outlined the power of narrative for constructing reality (e.g. Bruner, 1986, 1991; Hardy, 1977) and we focus on fictional narratives throughout this book. The reason why narratives have become the main discourse genre is that they are based on social scripts and closely aligned to everyday experience. Humans draw on narratives to explain their experiences, past, present and future and this facilitates their personal and social understandings. One could say that the history of mankind is in the form of narratives that have been passed from generation to generation in oral, written and multimedia forms (e.g. Connelly and Clandinin, 1990; Graesser et al., 2002). Given that stories are so deeply embedded in our culture and 'DNA', it is not surprising that social science has experienced a 'narrative turn', with blossoming theories of narrative comprehension and increasing use of narrative methodology as a research tool (Czarniawska, 2004). Narrative-based studies are concerned with cultural scripts, that is the kind of stories that get shared in specific cultural groups and that can reveal cultural differences. Story-driven investigations are useful in studying children's learning and reading too: 'Through the use of narrative we are able to recognise the power of subjectivity in allowing open dialogue and co-construction of meaning' (Garvis et al., 2015: 10).

In our focus on RfP, we are also interested in the text-to-text reminders which literary scholars refer to as intertextuality. Whilst Rosenblatt (1978/1994) did not use this term she did, as we discussed in the previous chapter, discuss the ways in which readers draw on their past experiences with texts. Intertextuality, as the name suggests, is about inter-connecting and linking texts or as Worton and Still (1991: 1) describe it 'cross fertilisation'; the process of the reader creating meaning by making intertextual connections (to their own life narratives and experience of other texts), thus creating an intertextual synergistic relationship. Hartman (1995) reminds us of the origin of the word 'texts' and the characteristic nature of textual connections.

> Even the Latin derivation of the word text (n. textus, which means 'woven,' as in a fabric) suggests that the composition of a text is interwoven with previous resources that give it a particular texture, pile, and grain. As an ideogram, a text is a kind of 'textile,' with the threads of the warp trailing off in one direction and those of the woof in another. (Hartman, 1995: 523)

Intertextuality is a desirable feature of experiencing subjectivity in RfP. Studies, including those by Hartman (1995), show that while all readers connect their current reading to previous readings, proficient readers do so to a greater extent. While intertextuality is about linking texts, Vygotsky's (1978) theory is about connecting the 'self' and 'other' around a shared learning activity. The most familiar example of this connection is his notion of the 'zone of proximal development' (ZPD) which is the space between what a learner knows (actual level of development), and what the learner can learn with the help of more knowledgeable others (potential development). In the description provided by Vygotsky (1978), the connection happens on a mental (cognitive) and verbal (oral) level, and relates to new information and knowledge transfer. The adult or more experienced peer provides knowledge that is new to the child but within a ZPD, and offers scaffolds and examples that help the child integrate new knowledge with their existing understanding. The adult's scaffolding needs to be attuned to the child's individual needs and unique background knowledge. This understanding of scaffolding as mediated by adults and resources was introduced by Wood et al. (1976), who conceived of scaffolding as a prime instructional tool. Scaffolding has been shown to be supportive of children's language development, for example Landry and colleagues (2002) established that when mothers engage in reciprocal conversations with their 3 year olds, they are directly increasing their children's verbal ability (which the researchers measured a year later). Scaffolding within ZPD is not only beneficial for children's direct adoption of adult words and ways of talking, it is also beneficial for children to guide their own behaviour and internalise this approach of gradually growing their competence. Books and other resources can support and enrich this learning process, especially if they are written to appeal both to adult and child readers.

## Books as scaffolds for learning

Good children's books bridge several gaps, for example the gap between:

* what the child knows and what the child could know (as in Vygotsky's ZPD)
* the adult writer and the child reader
* the adult and child as co-readers
* words and illustrations
* fiction and reality
* the individual's inner (personal) world and the wider social world.

Given the tangible learning benefits for children of adult scaffolding, book publishers, authors and illustrators make efforts to bridge these gaps with various techniques. Some adults craft stories that are positioned at the intersection of self/other, and others craft narratives that creatively leverage the power of the personal/shared tension.

Texts that foster readers' agency, that is texts that involve the reader directly and actively in the story, offer a particularly enjoyable and satisfactory RfP experience. In Barthes's (1975) terms these are likely to be 'writerly' texts whose meaning is not immediately evident and which demand effort on the part of the reader. This literary critic suggested such writerly texts contrast with 'readerly' texts which are by nature more straightforward. Although Barthes was referring to adult texts, children's authors also create 'writerly' texts and use various techniques to engage the reader personally, for example, addressing readers directly as in *The Monster at the End of This Book* by Jon Stone. In this tale, the main story character, Furry Old Grover, is positioned as an agent to scaffold the child's reading experience. Throughout the book, Grover begs the reader not to turn the page because there is a monster at the end of the book. The tension between the child's curiosity and the book's direct scaffolding enriches the book's appeal and drives the reader onwards. The reason the child disobeys Grover's instructions is that the child draws on the social script of what is and what is not allowed (in most cultures it is seen as inappropriate to disobey others' instructions). In another picture fiction text, *The Stinky Cheeseman and other Fairly Stupid Fairy Tales* the co-creators Jon Sciezka and Lane Smith play with the tales, the text design, and their position as authors. They offer a narrator role to Jack, who pops up throughout the book, alongside his accompanying talkative co-narrator the Little Red Hen. Between them they make connections (often bizarre ones) between the retold tales and again they address the reader directly. For instance on the playful upside-down dedication page when read the right way up, Jack talks to the reader saying:

> I know. I know.
> The page is upside down.
> I meant to do that.
> Whoever looks at that
> dedication stuff anyhow?
> If you really want to read
> it – you can always stand
> on your head.

Once reversed, the page offers the following dedication in very large font:

> This book is dedicated to our close, personal,
> special friend:
> (your name here)
> J.S. and L.S.

Textual features and creative typography are playful throughout in this post-modern text and even on the back cover the Little Red Hen chats on asking, 'What is this doing here?

Who is this ISBN guy? Who will buy this book anyway? Over fifty pages of nonsense and I'm only in three of them. Blah, blah, blah, blah blah, blah'.

Other picture fiction texts and novels make use of first-person narrative to draw the reader in, enabling them to experience the tale through the eyes and voice of the narrator and engage affectively. Those in which the illustrations serve to underscore this scaffolding device include for example *Me and My Fear* by Francesca Sanna, *My Name is not Refugee* by Kate Milner and *I go Quiet* by David Oimet. These texts personalise the story as it unfolds and is voiced through the protagonist's perspective, such that the visual depictions, which tend to be emotive in nature, are perhaps more acutely felt than when distanced by a third-person narrative.

With digital books, the author–reader meaning exchange can be enriched by more than the text and illustrations through interactive features. For example, in Nosy Crow's digital version of *Little Red Riding Hood*, the reader is encouraged at the crossroads to choose a path for the Little Red – will she take the path to the flowers or the path to the feathers? Depending on which direction the reader's finger pushes the character on the screen towards one of two possible paths, the story finishes with either Little Red defeating the bad wolf by tickling him with feathers or with dandelions. The book runs a simple algorithm in the background that selects one of several possible story endings depending on the reader's choice. The child's personal choice is sustained through the publisher's pre-designed possibilities, extending the reading experience into a shared space where the personal and shared entwine. This entanglement is possible through the combination of reader agency (in selecting a story path), the publisher's selection of a story with a familiar cultural script (a version of Little Red Riding Hood appears in most European folktales) and inclusion of scaffolding features (such as an uncluttered e-book design that is easy to navigate).

Despite such supportive scaffolding, children's books are most beneficial to RfP when they are conceived as shared objects for adults and children to read together. A solid body of literature exists on the educational benefits of shared book reading for children (see Ezell and Justice, 2005 for an overview). In particular these stress that shared book reading by parents to children is beneficial for parent–child bonding (van Kleeck et al., 2003) and that parental verbal scaffolding around books read to their child can significantly advance children's language and literacy skills (Wasik and Bond, 2001). Recent studies reveal the benefits of e-books that are specifically designed to support adult–child dialogue (Troseth et al., 2019). Some scholars even argue that digital texts can replace adults in the traditional shared book encounter. Exploring this, a meta-analysis of 29 studies (involving 1272 children) examined whether digital books are more beneficial than print books when experienced by children without an adult (Takacs et al., 2014). The authors found that when an adult was not present, digital books offered more benefits with regard to comprehension and word learning than print books. When an adult was present, there was no difference between the stories appearing digitally with embedded multimedia, or on paper. The authors conclude that: This suggests that multimedia features like animated illustrations, background music and sound effects provide similar scaffolding of story comprehension and word learning as an adult (Takacs et al., 2014).

The authors acknowledge however, that the multimedia stories used in their meta-analysis were not the usual low quality of commercially available digital books – they were specifically designed for this study. There is a significant difference between laboratory studies, such as the ones included in the meta-analysis which strategically scaffold children's comprehension through carefully designed digital stories, and the kind of reading that happens in homes and schools with commercially available e-books. Researchers have established that the educational quality of most popular children's e-books published in the last 10 years has been very low (Korat and Falk, 2019), and little progress has been made in embedding the learning benefits noticed in research studies into actual designs. This underscores the importance of adult presence during shared reading of e-books.

For Vygotsky (1978), the forms in which we access cultural scripts (in our case the digital or print text forms that children access) matter to the meaning we can make or the higher mental functioning we can engage in. Vygotsky and other Russian philosophers focused on cultural artefacts because of their 'assumption that the special mental quality of human beings is their need and ability to mediate their actions through artefacts and to arrange for the rediscovery and appropriation of these forms of mediation by subsequent generations' (Cole and Wertsch, 1996: 252). In other words, children's daily engagement with texts, mediates their understanding of culture and higher mental functions, such as learning of new words, understanding how other cultures work and how characters in different situations behave, feel and talk. Higher mental functions also refer to interpreting what an author's narrative means for an individual's personal life and how this story might relate – intertextually – to other tales, read and viewed. This unique human capacity connected to texts gives rise to collective memory, culture and history.

Vygotsky asserts that cultural artefacts, such as books, clocks or technologies, not only reflect and represent socio-cultural values and practices, but also shape and propagate them. Subjective and collective memory is not just located in individual bodies, but also in the artefacts the body interacts with; the personal extends to the social and the social feeds back to the personal. This notion that knowledge is distributed through artefacts (and humans who interact with them) has later become central to several neo-Vygotskian theories of distributed intelligence (Pea, 1993), distributed knowledge (e.g. Hewitt and Scardamalia, 1998), distributed self (e.g. Wetherell and Maybin, 1996), and distributed mind (e.g. Cole and Engestrom, 1993).

If knowledge is distributed, how does it become internalised by individuals, or, more specifically for us, how do children learn about the self and others from and through books? As we noted earlier, Vygotsky argued learning occurs through a dialogue between more knowledgeable others and the learner. Another Russian philosopher, Mikhail Bakhtin, agreed that higher mental functions are generated within situated dialogue and emphasised the phenomenon of 'heteroglossia', that is the multiplicity of different view-points and voices in this dialogue. In particular Bakhtin (1981) was interested in the negotiation of meanings and perspectives among several voices. He did not focus on children reaching a learning goal or stretching their understanding to a higher level, but explored the social possibilities available to individuals in meaning-making. All per-sonal voices are in relation to each other, Bakhtin argued, and it is this interrelationship between past and present voices that gives cultural artefacts their reality (ibid.). What is crucial for Vygotsky's approach is the emphasis on the relationship between the reader and co-readers, such as children and parents reading together. For Bakhtin, however, the emphasis is on the reader's meaning-making with a text, which in Bakhtin's view, is a passive object. This is different from Rosenblatt's view, she distinguished between types of texts that are passive and texts that are dynamic companions to readers' meaning-making, and foregrounded the reader's own perspectives as influencing the value derived from a text. Bakhtin, on the other hand, emphasised the perspective of the text's author and the author's active voice:

> The text as such never appears a dead thing; beginning with any text – and sometimes passing through a lengthy series of mediating links – we always arrive, in the final analysis, at the human voice, which is to say we come up against the human being. But the text is always imprisoned in dead material of some sort ... . (Bakhtin, 1981: 88)

The ways in which text is imprisoned in children's digital books has changed significantly since Bakhtin's lifetime. Indeed, digital books, with their interactive features, the capacity to collect personal data and use it to adjust the reading experience in the moment of the child reading are far more active than Bakhtin envisioned. Technology is not 'dead'; it lives with algorithms which have interaction agendas embedded in their codes that can connect the reader to other readers, authors and story-makers.

Bakhtin's quote brings us to the issue of materiality in RfP and the old question of how much a book is a passive or living object that captures or disrupts 'the prolonged (or intense) exposure of one mind to another' (Brodkey, 1985 cited in Mackey, 2005). It is clear that the materiality of texts matter, but it is not clear which aspects of material-ity matter for RfP. Researchers have attempted to answer this question empirically since the appearance of children's digital books in the early 2000s, but the evidence has been inconclusive. Some comparison studies show that digital books are superior for children's learning (e.g. Korat, 2010), while others show higher learning gains with print books (e.g. Krcmar and Cingel, 2014). However, a third strand of studies show that print and digital books produce similar educational outcomes (e.g. Lauricella et al., 2014). Several explanations for these findings have been offered, including the fact that the studies use diverse methods, outcome measures and types of digital books, and that young children's maturity levels (notably their executive functioning) may have been influential (Courage, 2019).

With their focus on the haptic exploration of the page, easy manipulation and access to the story through hyperlinks, digital books are new cultural artefacts that offer multiple ways into a story (Flewitt et al., 2015). For emerging and early readers, these additional meaning-making modes are appealing, and some researchers argue they can foster more intense learning. For example, Strouse and Ganea (2017a) conducted an experiment with over 100 toddlers (17–26 months old) and two books with the same content, although one was digital, one print format. They found that the children paid more attention and learnt more new words from the digital book than the print book, possibly through their increased attention to the content on the screen. This could have been due to the novelty effect, since many children have restricted access to digital books at home and could relate to the digital book's high visual and audio stimulation. However, as more children access digital books and more print books adopt the trend of highly stimulating visual designs, this is likely to alter in the next few years.

To interpret the mixed findings from print–digital book comparison studies, we need to look deeper and beyond the books' formats. Both are cultural artefacts that can mediate children's mental functioning, depending on content and the context of use. Both formats are likely to provide different benefits for different children. We therefore sought to identify shared features that play a role in children's reading engagement (Kucirkova et al., 2017) and one such format feature is personalisation – to which we now turn.

## Children's Digital Books With Personalisation Features

In this next section, we focus on the ways in which children's digital books are personalised in their construction, and personalisable, that is unique for an individual child. As we have highlighted previously, digital books offer additional levels of personalisation, for instance children can add their own audio-recordings, drawings or pictures to the story. Such personalised features thus connect to the child's culture, background and previous experiences, and from a Vygotskian perspective, are examples of cultural artefacts that might be implicated in higher mental functions. We offer two examples of parent–child interactions with digital books drawn from one of our studies – the Personalised Stories Project (Kucirkova, 2019b).

In the first vignette, Darren (aged 3 years 11 months), an only child, read the book with his mother, who observed she was moderately confident in using digital media, whilst she thought her son was highly competent. In the second vignette, the video data shows Hasim reading with his mother, who rated both her own and her son's confidence as moderately good. Hasim (aged 3 years and 2 months) attended a local nursery and had an older sister. Both Darren and Hasim frequently engaged in playing with the family's iPad and in reading print books, but they had not read digital books on a tablet device before.

## Darren and his mum reading

The first example focuses on how Darren and his mother used the *Fairytale Play Theatre* app (Nosy Crow) in relation to the name feature – a personal textual marker. Interestingly, not all the children in the project added their name to the title page of their digital narratives.

## Vignette 4.1 *Fairytale Play Theatre* App

| Time | Textual description of the videoed interaction |
|---|---|
| 01:45 | The mother holds the iPad, Darren tries to interact with the story characters (little dwarfs) on the screen. His mother taps the app icon which returns the page to the opening scene, with a theatre curtain and a rectangle on top of it. |
| 02:27 | His mother reads the text in the rectangle: *'OK, brand new story. Tap here to change.'* |

*'I can change.'* Darren says. His mother taps the white space which pulls up the iPad's embedded keyboard.

She asks: *'Right, who is it by?'*

*'Me!'* Darren exclaims.

*'Me?'* his mother smiles, *'Okay, where is M?'*

Darren hovers his index finger above the letter W on the keyboard.

*'Oh, very close. That's Woo. Where is M?'*

Darren hovers his finger above the letter D.

*'Well, that would be the first letter of your name, wouldn't it. You want to do that one then, go on, you want to put* Darren?

Darren presses D. His mother sounds out the second letter of his name. He repeats the sound and asks: *'Where is...?'*

*'I give you a clue, it's in the bottom line'* his mother says and points to the bottom line of letters on the keyboard.

Darren spots the letter and taps it.

*'There you go and what's next?'* his mother asks.

*'I don't know'*, Darren replies and his mother sounds out the third letter from his name. The interaction continues with the mother sounding out the individual letters and Darren finding them on the keyboard.

We can see that for Darren and his mother, the book app, the *Fairytale Play Theatre*, became an object of joint attention and a socially constructed context around which they had a dialogue. His mother used gestures and eye gaze to get Darren's attention, but the book's personalisation features heightened the child's focus on 'self' rather than the 'other'.

Significantly, Darren attributed the story ownership to 'me'. From a developmental psychology perspective, his correct use of the personal pronoun shows his linguistic capacity, as well as his ability to position himself in relation to others. The use of this pronoun is a developmental milestone because children's first references to self typically involve the use of their own names/nicknames, that is the names that others use to refer to them (see Levinson and Bowerman, 2001).

## Hasim and his mum reading

Our second example and analysis of the digital text's contributing features connects to the use of a mirror – a visual marker of self in children's books. In Nosy Crow's *Cinderella* book app, there is however no sentence directly related to the mirror feature, or any marker directing the reader's attention to it. The mirror appears on several 'pages' of the digital book, and is part of the mirror illustrations in the narrative. For example, in the scene where Cinderella is helping her step-sisters get ready for the ball, the mirror is placed in the left corner of the illustration. The mirror is not a reflecting surface but the front facing camera of the iPad, which becomes activated as soon as the reader swipes to a page in which it is present. In what follows, we share selected extracts of the video transcript that illustrate some instances of Hasim's response to this mirror feature (the time indicates each of these).

## Vignette 4.2 Hasim's Response to the Mirror Feature

Time    Textual description of the videoed interaction

01:03   Hasim is on the second screen of the *Cinderella* story. He is tapping small circular blue dots on the illustration of Cinderella and her mean sisters, which triggers audio-recorded dialogues between the story characters. He is distracted with what is happening in his home: his sister is playing Twister with her school friends. He is about to leave the iPad when his mother arrives. She points to the screen: '*What's inside, I wonder what happens when you tap it again?*' She helps him progress to the next page.

02:36    The app plays short dialogues between the story characters, highlighting individual words in red as they are being spoken. Hasim and his mother watch the story unfold on the screen. Hasim tilts the iPad slightly towards himself and his mother spots his face in one of the magical mirrors in the scene.

'*Who's that?*' she asks loudly and points to Hasim's face in the mirror. They both laugh. Hasim smiles into the mirror.

03:09    Hasim swipes left and returns to the page where the stepmother receives a letter invitation to the ball. The page contains a big letter, which, when tapped, releases many stars and sparklers. He taps the letter to see the sparklers. His mum helps him find blue dots to make the story characters move.

'*What about these?*', she points to hotspots but Hasim swipes right and moves again to the page with the mirror. When he looks into the mirror and sees his face, she laughs with pleasure.

04:11    '*I can see your teeth!*' his mother teases as Hasim makes grimaces.

'*What can we do on this page or shall we just look into the mirror?*' she asks and taps on other parts of the screen to explore other interactive elements on the page. Hasim is fixed on the mirror feature, he gives it his full attention and keeps making grimaces.

'*What happens if you press that?*' his mother asks and moves the story to the next page.

Initially, it was Hasim's mother who first spotted the mirror feature and drew his attention to it. She provided the necessary scaffolding to elicit a response from him by asking: '*Look who is there?*' Neither of them expected the mirror feature and both laughed when his face appeared in it. Even though the spoken and written narrative was about Cinderella, the mirror made Hasim visually part of the story. It distracted him from the storyline and directed his attention to his face, to Hasim himself. In this way, the app acted as a cultural artefact that triggered self-expression, within the confines of a cultural narrative.

Returning to our conceptual argument around subjectivity, cultural artefacts and meaning-making to interpret the vignette findings, we reflect on the ways in which the subjective 'self' is represented in children's digital books and in their printed equivalents. In a deliberate attempt to complement the existing empirical focus on print–digital comparisons, we consider Nosy Crow's print books with similar person-alisation features and contemplate the possible influence on the patterns we observed with digital personalised books.

# Children's Print Books With Personalisation Features

Print books often offer a space for personalising the text by writing the owner's name, and digital publishers too have taken advantage of the flexibility of the medium and launched titles that can be personalised in this way. On the first page of many children's books, children or their parents, can add their name. Once a name is written down, it is difficult to change or remove it from the glossy page making the book unique, a personal object that belongs to one named child.

This is different from a digital book that can be multiplied on an iPad, with several copies of the same book marked as belonging to different children and stored on a virtual bookshelf in the iPad's library. Names can be easily deleted or edited but are however typed in, so they do not carry the unique signature characteristic of hand-written letters. Given that young children will not be able to write their names yet, help from parents/caregivers will be needed to type this using the iPad's keyboard or write using a pen/pencil. In both cases, writing the child's name can enhance their awareness of written language, letter recognition and the direction that writing unfolds in English. With print books, this might also include learning to hold the pen/pencil the right way and perhaps tracing letters.

The use of a mirror in books is another feature that foregrounds subjectivity. Several print books for young children contain a mirror embedded in the pages. For instance, Nosy Crow's print title *Where is the Lion?* contains both felt flaps and a shiny mirror, which is a central feature of the story. It culminates on the last page with the question 'Where are you?' and a bright yellow flap hiding a mirror. The book is about several jungle animals hiding behind the flaps, but only one flap, the final one with the mirror, drives the child's attention to the self. With digital books, the mirror features are cameras, which might raise concerns about privacy. In print books, the mirror feels 'safer' than a camera given the fleeting nature of images reflected by mirrors and the potential sharing options of digital texts.

Reflecting on these personalisation features of print and digital books, it is worth highlighting the age groups targeted by the publisher. The digital book *Cinderella* is labelled as suitable for children aged 3–6 years, whereas Nosy Crow's print titles are targeted at younger children – *Where is the Lion?* is a hide-and-seek book for babies and *Toddler Time* speaks for itself. The placement of the personalised features in the print books is either at the very beginning or end of the story, while in the digital books, they are interspersed in the story. This indicates the importance the publishers assign to personalisation – in the two print books, personalisation appears to be used to frame the story experience, while in the digital book it was one of the e-books' many interactive features.

In Chapter 6, we highlight the text features that draw the child's attention to others' perspectives and the social arena of meaning-making as a reader. The examples we provide here do the opposite – they draw the child's attention to the personal sphere of interpreting the world. The importance of personalised features, not only for a balanced understanding of subjectivity, but also for assessing the place of personalised books in children's literature, is difficult to overestimate. Our main interest in this chapter was to highlight the nature of personalised features, therefore to close, we connect this more clearly to children's personalised engagement in RfP. We offer a practical consideration of the importance of diversity in children's books and a theoretical consideration focused on Vygotsky's (1978) notion of 'perezhivanie' and empathy.

## Personalised Engagement and Reflecting Realities

The diversity of children's literature is a hot topic not only among literary critics or researchers, but also among the general public. A social media campaign #WeNeedDiverseBooks grew into a global movement demanding greater representation of ethnic minorities in both adult and children's literature. Despite the increasingly urban, ethnically mixed and diverse lives that today's children experience, the literary canon of children's books is insufficiently diverse (Graves, 2019). Indeed a 2018 survey investigating the representation of Black, Asian and minority ethnic (BAME) characters in children's books found that of the 9115 books published and submitted for analysis in 2017, only 4% featured a BAME character and in only 1% was there a BAME main character (CLPE, 2018). This is in marked contrast to the 34% of children in state primary schools in the UK who are not White British (DfE, 2018). Yet as we argued in Chapter 1 all children deserve to see themselves reflected in literature – to have their lives recognised, this fosters RfP.

One way of beginning to address this issue is to draw on the concept of agency and involve children in the text-production process and text evaluation. If we widen the authorship possibilities, we invite more voices into text production and through crowd-sourcing of content for instance, we can increase the possibility for diverse content. On a theoretical level, story authorship options offer an avenue for stretching the individual side of subjectivity to the shared end of the personal–shared continuum (Kucirkova, 2016). Some initiatives have been undertaken in this direction, for example, some book awards include children as book judges and involve them in national and international book selection initiatives (e.g. Children's Book Awards run by www.lovereading4kids. co.uk/genre/pw/Book-Awards.html). In addition, some research-led projects include children in selecting literature (The International Children's Digital Library – http://www. icdlbooks.org), and the UK national newspaper *The Guardian* has run a children's books site with children's reviews, pieces of their creative writing, and authors and experts sharing their own reading choices and writing advice. Similarly, the annual BookTrust Best Book Awards, which celebrates excellent books for babies, children and teenagers, are judged by young people. In several community programmes too, children are involved in the planning of books used in their public library or classrooms (see Dresang and Koh, 2009).

These approaches seek to address aspects of the problem of low diversity in children's books by nurturing young people's evaluation skills and critical awareness of quality literature, and they also offer opportunities for deeper insights into book authoring (Haug and Jamissen, 2015). Early authoring from a socio-cultural perspective focuses on how children's texts are shapedh by the cultural practices of writing in their homes, schools and communities and how these practices shape what it means to be an author in these contexts (Rowe and Nietzel, 2010). If early authoring and book evaluation processes are combined, the book cycle, or Authoring Cycle as Condon and Harrison (2007) call it, becomes complete. Currently, children are rarely invited to be part of the voting systems or reviews of digital books and very few children's digital book review sites include the child's voice. Yet, there are multiple sites for parents and teachers to offer their views on such texts (e.g. Common Sense Media; Children's Technology Review). Personalisation theory serves here as a theoretical base for the Book Cycle, a reminder that reading is an active process during which readers personalise the text. The more story-evaluators and story-authors there are, the higher the likelihood that the resultant content will be diverse, reflecting a wider range of realities and experiences. It is also the case that teachers and librarians need to work as 'agents of change' (Horning, 2014) to influence this agenda.

## Personalised Engagement and Vygotsky's Perezhivanie

Although Vygotsky's (1978) theory is typically associated with children's cognitive development, he has made significant contributions to the theorisation of emotional development too, particularly in his writings about perezhivanie. This Russian term is difficult to translate and is easier to describe than capture with a direct translation. It relates to 'an emotional experience' that unifies the personal and communal or the individual and the contextual. As Smagorinsky explains: In an emotional experience [perezhivanie] we are always dealing with an indivisible unity of personal characteristics and situational characteristics, which are represented in the emotional experience [perezhivanie] (Smagorinsky, 2011: 342).

It describes the subjectivity of experience or the authenticity and uniqueness of a personal experience. Two children in the same context (e.g. a classroom) who read the same book will relate differently to it, that is they will experience the text and visuals differently. This is because as we argued earlier when discussing Rosenblatt's (1978/1994) work, readers bring their own life experiences and memories to the text.

In addition, as we noted in Chapter 3, there are always two sides to reality: the cognitive, rational and objective side and the emotional, irrational and subjective side. At the time of Vygotsky's writings, in the 1910s, paying attention to the emotions was revolutionary in psychology – European psychologists were preoccupied with Freudian psychoanalysis and American psychologists were steeped in the behaviourist tradition of John B. Watson. One could argue that not much has changed. Most contemporary reading curricula are preoccupied with fostering the skills of reading (children's story comprehension, concepts and language learning), at the relative expense of the will to read, the affective processes and reading behaviours of those who choose to read for pleasure.

Fiction in digital and print formats has considerable potential for engaging children aesthetically and affectively as we highlighted in Chapter 3. In the example earlier of Darren adding his name to the digital book we saw how this created a playful parent–child exchange with cognitive (letter recognition) as well as emotional markers (laughter). The personal textual marker of inserting his name added to the authentic character of this shared reading experience. In one of our earlier studies, we argued that when parents and children co-create digital stories, both serve as teachers and apprentices (Kucirkova et al., 2015). Such interactions may give rise to perezhivanie experienced as a 'unit of consciousness' (Veresov and Fleer, 2016: 56).

According to Veresov and Fleer (2016) and Fleer (2017), young children experience perezhivanie as a unit of consciousness when they engage in role play. Role play offers them the opportunity to experience 'double subjectivity': the experience of self as players inside and outside the play. We suggest that fictional texts with personalisation features offer opportunities for double subjectivity too, as children can be positioned both inside and outside the story. In the *Cinderella* app, children are positioned inside the story (through the mirror), while in the *Fairytale* app (a story-making app by Nosy Crow), children are positioned as owners of the story. The boundary is not clear-cut, however. With the former, the mirror does not need to feature the child; if the camera is tilted towards a parent reading alongside them, it will be the parent who enters the narrative. Conversely, in the latter, the *Fairytale* app, children can audio-record their own retelling of the story, thus adding their voices inside it.

Focusing on perezhivanie as a unit of consciousness, we can conceptualise a child's interaction with a print or digital book as an interaction that affects not only their understanding of self but also others, 'as a developing whole where changes of a child's concrete perezhivaniya bring dynamic changes to the whole organization of consciousness' (Veresov and Fleer, 2016: 65). The self does not begin or end; subjectivity is on a continuum depending on context. Digital books with personalisation features that are read together by parents and children may offer a unique context for experiencing this continuum. Significantly these insights point to the processes of deep reading and in particular, empathy.

Empathy brings us to the complex territory of narratives fostering different types of emotional responses, depending on both their content and medium of representation. While cognitive effects, such as children's understanding of the story or acquisition of new words featured in the story, can be measured before and after a reading episode, emotional responses are not easily or immediately measurable. We can only speculate whether a child's increased focus on self might influence his ability to identify with Cinderella's experience. In Hasim's example the book provided an opportunity for parent–child dialogue about self and elicited a positive emotional response from both him and his mother. Hasim returned to the mirror feature and repeated the grimaces, presumably to make her laugh again, thus the feature enabled him to attract his mother's attention. It could be argued that the mirror distracted him however, centring his attention on self and subjective feelings rather than those of Cinderella, who in this scene was helping her step-sisters get ready for the ball.

At the time of writing, no study has formally evaluated children's empathic abilities in relation to RfP. For adult readers, however, there is an emerging empirical basis for the relationship between literary fiction and empathy, with several psychological studies showing that adults who read literary texts perform higher on tests of empathy (e.g. Djikic et al., 2013; Kidd and Castano, 2013; Koopman, 2016). In this body of literature, there is a theoretical assumption that empathy is fostered through the simulation of social experience (Oatley, 1999) and the presence of a narrative that evokes the personal experience of emotion. For example, a narrative in which the protagonist dies may evoke sadness through activating adult's memories (see Hogan, 2003). In the digital format, however, there are several features that interrupt the narrative flow. Although Fleming (2013) claims that the use of the digital novel *Inanimate Alice*, which follows the storyline of a young girl across the world, contributed to children's development of empathy in the classroom, scant evidence is presented. Indeed, over 30 years ago, Abelson (1987) hypothesised that the digital format might disrupt literary appreciation. More recently, Mangen and Kuiken (2014) found that literary fiction accessed through iPads or Kindle may break the flow of a literary reading experience with hyperlinks, reducing the opportunity of a strong emotional or empathetic response.

In the absence of empirical evidence however, it would be amiss to extrapolate from adult studies to young children or to assign the digital format a causal role in changing children's emotional or empathetic responses to narrative. It is, however, worth noting the features that might be implicated in the deep engagement process nurturing empathy. To empathise with a story character, children need to engage in a dual process of character identification and story immersion (Kucirkova, 2019b). Personalised features in digital texts might be particularly important for character identification, especially if the main character carries the child's name or represents the child. If used strategically, personalised books could draw children's attention to story characters they don't know, offering new positions, perhaps as the villain or a minor character, and new emotions through double subjectivity. As such, personalised features in digital narratives provide a unique context for experiencing perezhivanie as a unity of knowledge and emotion, and shared reading of digital books can become an emotionally positive experience for parent and child, operating at the intersection of their subjectivities. However, personalised features can, as we have seen, disrupt story immersion and draw the child's attention to the self rather than the story and its characters. Regardless of the books' design, teachers can encourage children to contemplate different characters' perspectives and emotions through discussion and dialogue, role play and drama for instance, and this may, if supported, lead to pro-social action locally or more widely. The work of Empathy Lab in the UK (www.empathylab.uk/) offers professional support for ways forward in this regard.

## Conclusion

In considering specific personalisation features in texts we concur with Rosenblatt's (1978/1994) assertion that texts can expand or constrain meaning-making, and that this depends on the extent to which the text supports the child's agency and the possibility of interaction with other co-readers. In recognising the value of the dialogue that mediates children's meaning-making with texts, we connected to the work of Vygotsky (1978) and Bakhtin (1981) and highlighted books as scaffolds supporting children's RfP. Examining parent–child interaction with digital books which contained personalisable features, we tracked their potentiality for experiencing, expressing and maintaining subjectivity. We conclude that subjectivity is embedded in texts, providing for the meeting of minds and bodies between authors and readers, and the socio-cultural context in which they respond.

# 5

# Reading for Pleasure Pedagogy

I n the English-speaking Western world, reading curricula and related pedagogies are subject to high levels of scrutiny and accountability. Whilst reading for pleasure (RfP), volitional child-led reading is mandated in England (Department for Education, 2014), it is challenging to foster this in the current culture in which individual assessment and public accountability holds sway. Children are obliged to undergo a phonics screening check in England at the end of Year 1 (when they are aged five or six), and a standardised assessment test at the end of Year 2 (when they are aged six or seven) and again at the end of Year 6 (when they are aged 10 or 11). The backwash of such frequent assessment, which exists in many countries, serves to constrain professional practice, prompting a pedagogy of conformity and compliance, not of principled practice that draws on and contributes to the evidence base around RfP. Furthermore, it frames and often limits children's experience of reading within and beyond school. In such contexts, what counts as reading as we discussed in Chapter 2 is underpinned by an autonomous model of literacy (Street, 1984, 2008) which views literacy/reading as a set of discrete skills, independent of the context of their use. Yet as we have argued from the outset, children's reading, like ours, is embedded in different social and cultural practices and is thus socially (and historically) situated, shaped by text and context.

In this chapter we consider the evidence base about practice that develops motivated, engaged and socially interactive young readers. Connecting in particular to the shared and sustained facets of reader engagement, we foreground the participatory nature of effective RfP pedagogy and highlight the value of creating social reading environments in which children can exert enhanced ownership of their reading. In particular we explore the interrelated strands of RfP practice identified in our two-phase study *Teachers as Readers* (TaRs): reading aloud, social reading environments, child-led reading time and informal text talk and recommendations (Cremin et al., 2014). Such practice is premised upon teachers' knowledge of texts (discussed here) and their knowledge of the children as readers themselves (discussed in Chapter 7). We highlight the need for teachers to value and validate both digital and print-based texts and argue that knowledge of texts and of individual readers are prerequisites, enabling practitioners to sensitively shape the four strands of RfP pedagogy and support volitional reading. We also offer insights from our study of boys' dis/engagement in reading which revealed the very significant challenges that beset teachers working in low socio-economic schools, and the need to avoid 'pedagogy of poverty' in relation to RfP in order to ensure struggling readers are not held back (Hempel-Jorgensen et al., 2018).

## Teachers' Knowledge of Children's Literature and Other Texts

Teachers' knowledge of texts is the cornerstone on which interactive and reciprocal communities of readers are built, but such subject knowledge cannot be taken for granted. Research reveals that teachers have very limited knowledge both of children's print literature (Clark and Teravainen, 2015; Cremin et al., 2009; Laurenson et al., 2015) and digital texts (Roskos et al., 2012). Digital texts can be accessed on stationary (e.g. interactive whiteboards, desktop computers) or mobile devices (e.g. tablets and iPads) and come with various levels of interactivity and multimedia possibilities. While the impact of print texts on children's concurrent and future reading lives is well-studied, much remains unknown about digital books. For many teachers, the use of digital texts, and of digital media more broadly, are an unknown territory. Roskos et al. (2011) have documented the ways in which teachers can introduce digital books to the classroom, with suggestions for creating a digital reading corner or gradual enrichment of the classroom reading routines.

In the TaRs study, we undertook a survey of 1200 teachers from 11 education authorities across England and found considerable cause for concern (Cremin et al., 2008a, 2008b, 2009). Namely, while teachers were readers themselves in their own lives (73% had read for pleasure within the last month), they had remarkably restricted repertoires of children's fiction. Their knowledge was strongest with regard to children's authors; nonetheless less than half of the teachers could cite six 'good' authors. 'Good' was explained as referring to writers whose work teachers found valuable to use with primary-aged learners. 'Celebrity' authors and long-standing authors from the teachers' own childhoods held sway. These tended to be those who had been children's laureates for instance, or whose work was high profile in the media, in bookshop chains and had been made into films. Roald Dahl gained the highest number of mentions (744), followed, after a large gap, by Michael Morpurgo (343), Jacqueline Wilson (323) and J.K. Rowling (300). It is of note that whilst these teachers were not leading literacy in their schools, all were responsible for nurturing readers year on year. When asked to name six good poets 22% named none and only 10% named six poets. The most frequently named were: Michael Rosen (452), Allan Ahlberg (207), Roger McGough (197) and Roald Dahl (165). The teachers' knowledge of picture fiction creators was the weakest: 24% named none and again only 10% named six. Quentin Blake (423) was the most frequently named (illustrating as he did many of Dahl's texts as well as his own), followed by Anthony Browne (175), Alan Ahlberg (146), Shirley Hughes (123) and Mick Inkpen (121). Very few women poets were named, and scant knowledge of writers of multicultural literature was demonstrated.

More recent studies have affirmed that this impoverished subject knowledge remains a very significant professional problem (Clark and Teravainen, 2015; Laurenson et al., 2015). In the predominantly secondary phase UK teacher survey with 2300 teachers, Dahl was again in a league of his own (Clark and Teravainen, 2015). The profession has, we have argued, become somewhat 'Dahl dependent' and whilst newer popular authors such as David Walliams may figure more highly today, the reliance on celebrity authors or those from teachers' own childhoods deserves concerted attention. A US study of the different genres of children's literature that teachers know, also documented very limited professional repertoires (Akins et al., 2018). 'Realistic fiction' and 'fantasy' genres were the most well-known, few teachers recognised the texts presented that were picture fiction, historical novels or multicultural genres, and again, Dahl and Rowling were amongst the most well-known, alongside classic US writers such as Mildred D. Taylor and Judy Blume. Such limited professional repertoires have serious pedagogic consequences.

International studies have persistently shown that in order to effectively support children in becoming independent, fluent readers, teachers require secure knowledge of children's literature and of reading development (Cremin et al., 2008a; Dreher, 2002; Flynn, 2007; Medwell et al., 1998). For those teachers supporting readers in the early and primary years, this encompasses knowledge of a range of contemporary and classic children's authors, books, poets and picture book creators, as well as knowledge of comics and magazines for the young, graphic and verse novels and online hypertexts. Inadequate repertoires constrain professional practice and limit teachers' capacity to make tailored recommendations to individual children in order to motivate them as readers. A lack of subject knowledge will also prevent practitioners in engaging in casual reader-to-reader conversations about particular texts as well as in-depth discussions, both of which have been documented as key in fostering children's pleasure in reading and helping them make their own discerning choices (Cremin et al., 2014; Maine, 2015).

Children deserve to be introduced to literature and non-fiction which inspires them, that connects to their personal interests, enables them to develop text and authorial preferences and fosters their sense of self as a reader. Whilst the classic work of the popular writers of yesterday may well be 'old but gold', their writing may have less relevance for motivating the young readers of today. Contemporary writers often connect to current issues and concerns for children and society, and write in different styles and experiment with new genres which can engage and entice young readers. Their work also needs to be known and shared. However, it is genuinely challenging for teachers to keep up to date with children's texts. This is where digital libraries and reading recommendation systems can offer significant support: these platforms provide reading commendations that can supplement teachers' knowledge of children's authors (see Chapter 6). Digital library systems can suggest titles that correspond to children's preferences, reading history and abilities and are potentially important assets for teachers seeking to expand children's RfP. However, in their current designs, they are not an effective substitute for teachers' personal knowledge of texts because they tend to position teachers as monitors and curators of children's reading, not as fellow readers. While digital libraries and their recommender systems offer valuable supplementary tools that can support the profession, teachers' personal knowledge, when deployed strategically and socially, affords significant support for children's RfP.

## Conceptualising RfP Pedagogy

In the second phase of TaRs, which was a research and development project, 45 teachers from five education authorities were enabled to widen their literary repertoires and share their enriched knowledge with each other, their pupils and colleagues in school

(Cremin et al., 2014). They talked about texts (in their local groups and on national project days) and began to take risks, reading outside their comfort zones and responding aesthetically rather than instrumentally to children's texts. At the start of the project, the practitioners viewed such texts primarily as tools to teach the skills of literacy and did not fully appreciate their potential for nurturing young volitional readers. Significantly, they came to recognise their professional responsibility to expand and sustain their repertoires of children's literature and other texts, and in addition they sought to find out about the children themselves, as individuals and as readers. Finding out about the children's everyday reading experiences and honouring and celebrating these, was recognised as important, prompting teachers to offer and validate a wider range of digital and print-based texts in school. The research, which tracked the teachers' journeys revealed the pedagogical consequences of this wider subject knowledge and knowledge of the children as readers.

A quartet of practices were identified, which, when carefully and responsively combined, were seen to be an effective evidence-based RfP pedagogy. These included: creating a social reading environment, setting time aside for independent choice-led reading and reading aloud, as well as considerable informal book talk, inside-text talk and recommendations (teacher to children, children to children and children to teachers). In effect the teachers were offering sustained opportunities for the children to be read *to*, to read *with* others and to read *by* themselves, an underlying tenet of reading recovery programmes, in that context albeit within one-to-one reading sessions (Clay, 1977). In TaRs the teachers read to the whole class, creating 'books in common' and also made individual recommendations. They also read alongside the young as fellow readers and afforded opportunities for the children to read and share their reading with one another. Over time a subtle shift in the locus of control around reading was observed; children had a stronger degree of agency as readers. Reciprocal and interactive reader relationships developed within new communities of readers (Cremin et al., 2014). Such reader collectives and shared cultures of reading are examined further in Chapter 6.

There was strong evidence that the teachers' enhanced subject knowledge and enriched pedagogic practice impacted on the children's desire to read, their perceptions of their abilities as readers and their self-confidence (Cremin, 2010a; Cremin et al., 2014). They became drawn into reading and began to read more regularly and more independently, participating as members of the emerging classroom reading communities. The specific RfP pedagogy strands that contributed to this impact are discussed in the remaining sections. However, it is important to acknowledge it is not merely a case of teachers introducing these practices as stand-alone activities, since 'pedagogic situations are always unique' and need to be subtly orchestrated and responsive to the learners' needs (van Manen, 1990: 155). If the four strands become routinised, timetabled and offered without teacher knowledge of texts, of the children and a deep understanding of the nature of reading and being a reader, then they are unlikely to be successful in developing readers who find pleasure in reading. All practices position children in particular ways and not all equally (for example less experienced readers are often offered less intellectually and affectively engaging texts), and all practices have consequences for how reading is perceived by the young. For example, expecting children to sit at tables to read (which is far from conducive to relaxed engagement), or enforcing silence during such reading time with no book swapping and requiring written reviews when books are completed, is likely to result in children who feel 'obliged' to read. Some may even 'pretend' to do so, remaining disconnected from the literature and each other, yet reading time will have been offered.

In the name of RfP, many schools undertake 'fun' reading activities week in week out across the year, as well as participating in World Book Day and other transient celebrations. This tends to foster an activity orientation to children's RfP, one without a secure pedagogical underpinning based upon research. In addition, few schools currently track the development of such activities, assuming perhaps, that by simply offering more relaxed or 'fun' reading opportunities this will foster readers. In other areas of the curriculum, teachers commonly track children's progress, and evaluate the efficacy of their pedagogic interventions, but when it comes to RfP, this does not appear to be the case. Children's reading skills are regularly assessed, but their sense of self as a reader, their confidence, interest and attitudes to reading are rarely tracked or recorded. This is a lacuna that needs filling in order to support the development of positive reading identities and ensure readers are supported and sustained over time. We cannot measure their pleasure, but we can and should evaluate RfP pedagogy and understand, track and document children's journeys as readers. This issue is discussed more fully in Chapter 8.

In planning and assessing the efficacy of RfP pedagogy, four principles are key: all practice and activities need to be Learner-led, Informal, Social and with Texts that Tempt (see Figure 5.1). This RfP pedagogy teacher check LIST helps to ensure the activity is focused on developing children's intrinsic desire to read, fostering agency, authentic engagement and interaction with texts that tempt the children (not just or even the teacher). Being conscious of the pedagogic orientation of any reading activity, whether it is to enrich the children's skills as readers, or to foster the will to read is important. This research-informed RfP pedagogy check LIST helps to avoid pleasure-oriented activities being inadvertently misappropriated or reframed by teachers working within the pressured 'reading as proficiency' agenda, which, research suggests, is all too common (English et al., 2002; Hall, 2012; Hempel-Jorgensen et al., 2018; Kwek et al., 2007). We offer examples of this misappropriation in discussing the four strands of RfP pedagogy next.

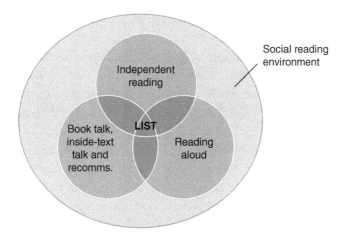

**Figure 5.1**   RfP pedagogy and the RfP check LIST

## Reading Time

Assigning dedicated time for children to read in school is essential if we are to develop engaged and committed readers. No young footballer will improve their skills without practice, without taking the space and time to kick a ball around with friends. Many will spend hours informally practising on the playground, after school and in the community. Some may also attend a club where training is offered, and most will follow their favourite football club on the media and by attending matches. Intrinsically engaged, keen young footballers seize every opportunity to participate in their beloved sport and enjoy it, honing their skills as they travel. RfP has some similarities: intrinsically motivated young readers make the space and time to read alone and with others. Whether at home or school, at a friend's house or on holiday, their desire to know what happens next in a story, to find out more about a particular pop group or computer game drives their actions and they read more frequently, enrich their stamina and enlarge their reading volume. Keen readers find the experience deeply satisfying and this in turn re-fuels their desire. Some readers, however, have not yet found 'what reading is good for' (Meek, 1998) and need more support; they need to be offered a range of texts that might tempt them and be given time to develop the reading habit in a socially supportive community of engaged readers.

However, if such time is only sporadically offered, is very short, or is highly routinised, its potential to support readers is markedly reduced. In an Open University project focused on boys' disengagement in reading, the time set aside for children's 'own reading' differed very considerably across the four case study schools (Hempel-Jorgensen et al., 2018). In the four classes of 9–10 year olds, it ranged from 45 minutes a week in School C (five sessions of 5–11 minutes each), to 3 hours and 36 minutes in School B. The latter involved almost twice daily reading sessions and represented 16% of the school's timetable. Whilst this clearly denoted that independent reading was important, the time set aside was beset with interruptions, so it was difficult for children to develop their reading stamina and no interaction was allowed. It may have been that the staff were responding to concerns about low reading standards and negative attitudes, and were trying to compensate for a perceived lack of reading undertaken at home, but it did not appear to be effective. In all the schools, the children were seen to be inattentive and disengaged during reading time. Thus, assigning time to 'just reading' as one teacher voiced it, is not a panacea; much depends on the context and the mediating support offered by adults and peers. Conversely, well-shaped and owned by the children, assigning time to 'just reading' can be a rich opportunity for learning and a space for them to progress their interests and preferences as readers, develop and consolidate their reading habits and enhance their stamina. This can lead to increased reading volume (Manresa, 2018). Research reveals that high reading volume is associated with high reading attainment (Allington, 2014) and thus offering time to read, which is learner-led, informal and social, with texts that tempt is supportive of reader development. In the TaRs study reading time in many classrooms was a partly social affair, with book conversations being held alongside focused reading, and much depended on the readers and their choices (Cremin et al., 2014).

Reading time is also deployed in other countries. For instance, in Japan, the good morning reading movement has four principles: everyone reads, read every day, read what you want, and just read. Its value and success has been well documented and suggests that the relaxed atmosphere of morning reading times support students in voluntarily stepping up to more complex readings over time (Han, 2012; Lim, 2018). Similarly, in Scandinavia (Lerkkanen et al., 2012) and the USA (Moses and Kelly, 2018), researchers found that when emphasis was placed on child-centred reading practices and time for reading was set aside (often with informal conversations and RfP oriented activities which were LIST), this led to increased engagement and interest in reading.

Allowing children to choose their texts for independent reading time is essential. Considerable research evidence indicates that choice and reader interest significantly enhance readers' motivation, self-determination and engagement (e.g. Moss and Macdonald, 2004; Pihl, 2012). Whilst within the literacy curriculum children's choices are likely to be compromised by appropriate teacher selection of texts to study, in reading time child choice should be retained. During reading time in the boys' reading research, children in all the schools were allowed to choose their own texts (Hempel-Jorgensen et al., 2018). Predominantly they selected books from their classroom collections, although a few were brought from home, which was accepted but not explicitly encouraged. However, the book numbers in the four classes ranged from 147 in one classroom to 802 in another, thus affording some readers very considerable choice and others much more limited options. The quality and diversity of texts also varied: no poetry was available in one classroom, and no magazines or newspapers were available in two. Additionally, no texts were read on screens during this free reading time, despite the classrooms having computers and in some cases iPads (Hempel-Jorgensen et al., 2018).

Clearly children's choices are always constrained: by the texts available, by institutional and personal knowledge of authors and illustrators, by the degree of support offered by teachers, parents, peers and the environment and by their own sense of identity as readers perhaps restraining their risk taking with an unknown genre for example. In addition, the use of colour-coded boxes for readers of different 'reading abilities' can constrain their choices. Even when teachers value and validate children's interests in digital texts during this time, access issues will constrain their choices. Nonetheless it is only by recognising these limitations that we can work towards reducing them. Opportunities to read online can also be offered and to supplement classroom collections, boxes of quality non-fiction, poetry and comics can circulate around classes. Many teachers seek to document children's choices in some way. Not to monitor them in the sense of surveillance (as in systems such as Accelerated Reader), but to better understand children's preferences, enabling more tailored and personal text recommendations. Such recommendations need to ensure children have some agency and choice, so more than one text needs to be suggested (Cremin et al., 2014). Indeed, there is a big difference between agentic personalization, generated and led by the child, and automatic personalization, driven by algorithms (Kucirkova, 2019b). As an example, consider 'personalized' recommendations provided by Amazon or Goodreads, based on a reader's personal data. This data might include previously viewed book titles or purchased books without any direct input from the reader, versus recommendations provided verbally by a librarian or teacher, based on multiple conversations with the reader about reading, their preferences and being a reader. In addition, if we want to foster volitional reading, allowing children the choice of where to sit during reading time can be supportive. As Kuzmičová et al. (2018) found, readers are sensitive to the physical presence of others during silent reading, and embodied and social factors endow the reading environment with a supportive sense of belonging.

Whether talk is encouraged, allowed or banned during reading time is likely to be influenced by the teachers' conception of reading, and the extent to which they view reading as a solitary activity or a social and relational one. The titles afforded such time in schools often denote an emphasis on silence and a sense of focus, for example, SQUIRT – Silent, Quiet, Uninterrupted Reading Time, USSR – Uninterrupted Sustained Silent Reading and DEAR – Drop Everything And Read. For some young readers, depending on the text and context, such silence may be alluring, affording time to concentrate and re-connect with the unfolding text. On other occasions the opportunity to talk quietly, to share a book with a friend or to read aloud to a small group may be desired and more supportive of them as readers. If children's autonomy is prized and the sessions are to be learner-led, then teachers will want to offer children choices around the use of this time, whilst ensuring interruptions are kept to a minimum and regular practice reviews of the efficacy of the approach are built in.

In the boys' reading study, we found that the nature of the interaction differed; two schools required silence and actively monitored this (B and C), one allowed quiet exchanges (D) and in the last (A), interaction was allowed, but not encouraged (Hempel-Jorgensen et al., 2018). In schools A, B and C we observed that the 'struggling' boy readers changed their chosen material daily, often several times during the allocated time. Jack for instance frequently flicked through different *Horrible Histories* magazines looking at the visuals and occasionally remaining on a page for a minute or two before becoming distracted. Once he chose to tackle a longer text (Roald Dahl's *Granny*), but after a couple of minutes he gave up and in a desultory manner picked up a spare *Horrible Science* magazine lying on the table. Tracking Jack across the week, his lack of concentration and disinterested attitude towards reading was evident. He had no drawer in which to keep his reading material, so his practice of seizing a different magazine to peruse during the 5–11 minutes assigned each day was sensible and strategic. He may have seen it as a time-filling, time-wasting activity. In contrast, his teacher viewed it as 'an opportunity for them to get themselves calmed down after lunchtime and get focused again'. For her perhaps, this time was not primarily an opportunity to read for the potential pleasure of it, but a behaviour calming activity.

The perceived purpose of the time also influences the teacher's role. In the TaRs research we found that when teachers read alongside the class, this not only helped them to widen their repertoires of children's texts, but also provided a model of an engaged adult reader (Cremin et al., 2014). A positive relationship between teacher modelling of reading and student on-task reading behaviour during this time has been documented (Methe and Hintze, 2003), and in TaRs our observations showed that when practitioners engaged as readers, this frequently triggered informal book blether between teachers and children (Cremin et al., 2014). Some began to open up a space at the close of reading time and invited children to share an aspect of what they had just read with a friend. This included a new piece of information, a character, a sentence which was shocking or amusing or something else of their own choosing. Such opportunities for conversation about their texts served to support the development of new relationships between readers. It contributed to what we call reciprocal reading for pleasure (reciprocal RfP) (see Chapter 6) and as Skeeters et al.'s (2016) work has shown, is important for increasing children's informal social engagement in what they are reading. In contrast, in our more recent study, undertaken at a time of increased curriculum pressure, we found that only one teacher read during reading time (in school B) and children were never invited to talk about what they had been reading; rather they were required to put their books away and move on to the next activity (Hempel-Jorgensen et al., 2018).

# Reading Aloud

Reading aloud is another key strand of effective learner-led RfP pedagogy (Cremin et al., 2014). It has long been recognised as a powerful tool to support young readers, offering them access to texts they cannot yet read for themselves. Unfortunately, for many years, due to curriculum pressures and assessment, reading aloud has become somewhat marginalised in UK primary schools. Nonetheless, educators and scholars commonly assert its importance (e.g. Lockwood, 2008; Miller, 2009; Trelease, 2013) and empirical research shows that frequent reading aloud to 4–5 year olds enhances reading, maths and the cognitive skills of 8–9 year olds (Kalb and van Ours, 2013). While reading aloud in families and parent–child shared reading is frequently studied at home, close documentation of reading aloud in classrooms is rare. Arguably, expressive reading aloud to young children conditions them to associate reading with pleasure especially if the experience with parents or carers is a physically near, rich and enjoyable one. It often involves close proximity between the adult and the child, and may be associated with bedtime routines or breakfast, although just as children's choices of books and time to read are idiosyncratic, so too are families' shared reading routines (Levy, 2018). Nonetheless, its timing is less salient than its presence and nature. It may involve siblings, parents and grandparents developing family 'books in common' (Cremin et al., 2018b) that have been read aloud and enjoyed together. As these books are often repeatedly read, they may become part of a family's reading history.

However, not all children have the experience of being read to at home and in some families, reading aloud that involves school recommended books is perceived as a 'punishment' (Janes and Kermani, 2001). Recent UK publisher survey data reveals that there has been a marked decline in the number of 3–4 year olds who are read to daily/nearly daily. According to this survey, completed by over 1500 parents, in 2013, 69% of preschoolers were read aloud to, but in 2017 only 51% were read aloud to (Egmont/Nielsen, 2018). Additionally, this survey suggests that children aged 8 and older are considerably less likely to be read to at home, with only 20% of these parents reporting that they do so. When considering that 1 in 10 children aged 8–18 years old have no books at home (Clark and Teravainen, 2017b), this raises cause for concern. Reading aloud in school is thus essential in part to supplement and enlarge upon children's previous shared reading experiences.

In school, the practice of reading aloud to children takes many forms. Commonly, teachers read aloud short text extracts before engaging in follow-up written work or comprehension related to the passage. The inherent purpose of such reading aloud is to provide a context to study an explicit extract. This may involve the teaching and testing of specific skills such as inference and deduction or vocabulary expansion. It is appropriate to read aloud in this context as it can support skills teaching, but this is not reading aloud aimed at fostering volitional reading – RfP. It is reading aloud for study. Such reading may of course be an enjoyable experience for some readers (those most skilled at such follow up work for example), but the fact that it is closely associated with literacy work may have negative consequences for the learners if no other provision is offered. In one of our studies we were concerned to find that when reading aloud was tethered to literacy teaching and no opportunities for more relaxed reading aloud were offered, children expressed disinterest in their teacher reading aloud, indeed many viewed it negatively (Cremin et al., 2014: 95). Some schools practise round-robin reading of class novels, but this can put pressure on readers, some of whom may struggle to read or follow the text, whilst other more able readers can do so at speed.

In the boys dis/engagement in reading study, the adults in Schools A and C frequently stopped during reading aloud, then named individual children who were expected to answer teacher-posed questions focused mainly on inference and deduction (Hempel-Jorgensen et al., 2018). This broke up the flow of the text, and appeared to be more akin to the comprehension sessions also observed, but was positioned as reading aloud. In school A, as the sporadic reading of the text progressed, children were also required to enter new vocabulary in their 'core word books', which had been handed out at the start, suggesting the purpose of the reading was vocabulary extension. Again, this altered the nature of the experience. Children's chosen new words were discussed and defined at the close of the session. No time for meaning-making or discussion of the text as a whole was offered. It could thus be argued that the practice of reading aloud, annexed as it was to the agenda of raising standards and framed by the accountability discourse, was being misappropriated.

Reading aloud as traditionally conceived was intended to motivate and engage young readers, enabling them to gain access to a diverse range of texts and to introduce them to authors and illustrators whose work they might follow up in their own reading, thus widening their repertoires. As Meek (1992: 177–178) notes:

 'most adults who read to children keep the reading whole; they go to the end of the story or poem … As a result, children get the story as something entire, the world in a book … and the listeners are kept inside the telling or the reading for its duration'.

Listening to an expressive reading of a book offers an externalised model of fluent independent reading in one's head and helps children hear the sounds and music of the text, enabling them to process more challenging content than they could when reading alone. If the teacher reads aloud well, using maximum intonation, subtle pausing, careful pacing and pathos, the strain of making meaning through decoding is taken away and children are offered the chance to imagine and inhabit possible worlds, as well as learn about the real world. Based on studies of older readers in clinical contexts, Steenberg (2017) argues that reading aloud encourages sustained attention and concentration in part due to the embodied nature of the lived through experience. Such embodied engagement can be observed at moments of tension and relief during read aloud sessions in schools when the whole class, including the adults, are held in the text's thrall. Critically, such reading aloud offers children enjoyment in a risk-free environment. There should be no pressure to be tested on the meaning of particular words, no pressure to respond correctly to a teacher's questions and no fear of failure.

Reading aloud for the purpose of pleasure has an affective power too, as we argued in Chapter 3. It can enable a class to experience individually and collectively the fear, the wonder, the surprise, and/or the delight as characters respond to challenging contexts, as new information is revealed and as language at play is felt and heard. In an Australian study of children's views of their teachers as readers, whether their teacher read aloud to them with explicit enjoyment and emotional engagement was seen to be influential (Merga, 2016). The emotional connections voiced by some teachers convinced children that their teachers were readers. As Trelease (2013: 4) argues, teachers must read aloud to 'reassure, to entertain, to bond, to inform or explain, to arouse curiosity, to inspire'. In this way, RfP creates a context for shared enjoyment and builds a shared reading history of 'books in common' (Cremin et al., 2014) within the class, prompting later intertextual referencing and connections between the stories shared and known. However, making time for it is not easy in a pressured classroom. In the boys reading study we found a gap between professional intentions and realised practice; reading aloud was voiced as a valuable activity, but in practice it was seen as an 'optional' addition and was often side-lined (Hempel-Jorgensen et al., 2018). Whilst the teachers all identified reading aloud as part of their normal practice, and in school B it was timetabled daily, the reality was very different and no read aloud occurred in that class in the week we observed. One 30-minute session was offered in the week in schools A and D, and two sessions (of 10 and 6 minutes respectively) in school C. Half of the sessions were led by Teaching Assistants, reducing the opportunity for the teachers to create connections with the class. In school C one of the focus boys who was 'struggling with reading' according to his teacher, missed both sessions as he was taken out during one session for extra spelling and grammar practice, and attended an inter-school sports competition on the other. Yet strugglers and less interested readers are the very children who may benefit the most from experiencing reading as pleasurable in this context.

Far from being a one-sided experience, reading aloud can be interactive – packed with young children's observations, responses to the text and significant 'book blether' that emerges impromptu, not in response to teacher-focused questions. The ethos of read aloud is key; if it remains informal and social, with texts that tempt the children, it will have value. It does not have to be offered without interruption, although there is value in such, much will depend upon the text and the context. Some teachers, still reading aloud for the purpose of pleasure, offer 'read aloud plus' and respond sensitively to the text and any perceived difficulties in it, as well as the children's responses to it. It is argued that children benefit if they are in the lead, as agentic young readers who are positioned as the 'boss of the book' as one school calls it. At home or at school when sharing texts one to one, adults sensitively take their lead from the child, reading the next section when the child is ready and responding to the child's interests. In the primary classroom with 30 plus children, such responsive interaction is more difficult to handle and more reading aloud without interruption or overt voiced engagement will happen. Nonetheless, blending reading aloud and brief moments of interaction, not only prompts children to listen actively and process more challenging texts and vocabulary than they could achieve alone, it also invites them into the text more actively. This might involve encouraging them to make personal connections to people they know, places they have been, such that the text resonates for them and engagement is fostered.

Since pleasure and involvement in a text precede full understanding, opportunities to discuss the text with friends or to draw during read aloud can be useful supports for young readers. Read aloud plus activities can be offered before, during, or after the reading to engage and invite readers into the narrative, but must judiciously avoid interrupting the flow, music and meaning of the text. Reading aloud for the sole purpose of shared enjoyment thus represents a rich resource for conversation, and for making connections and relationships between readers (Cremin, 2018).

Text diversity is central to effective read aloud practice, capturing the interests of all and enabling the patterns of diverse texts to be heard. The reading aloud of novels in particular needs to be planned across the school to ensure a wide range of authors and genres are offered over the years. In one school we observed disinterest as the 9–10 year olds were read *The Witches* by Roald Dahl for the second year running (Hempel-Jorgensen et al., 2018). This challenge was compounded by the fact that the teacher had just completed reading aloud *The Twits* by the same author to her class. Sometimes dedicated time read aloud time is labelled story time on school timetables, but this implicitly denigrates the power of non-fiction and poetry. All text types offer rich possibilities for children, stretching their imaginations and arousing their curiosity. This applies to digital or non-digital texts. Many teachers scan in the pages of picture fiction texts or poems to share on the whiteboard, enabling all the class to experience these more fully. Others have class collections of a novel for example and seek to read this aloud for the purpose of fostering reading enjoyment. Planning for diversity and quality is important, ensuring a range of texts are read, shared and enjoyed across each key stage. Much classroom practice will depend upon teachers' knowledge of children's texts, which as we have noted is not strong. In order to ensure that this time is to some degree learner-led and with texts that tempt the young people themselves, teachers can offer a number of options. Practitioners can offer resumes of several World War II novels or tales of space or refugees, displaying these and a few days later inviting the class to vote. Equally children can be involved in suggesting texts for read alouds, be encouraged to read aloud themselves to each other (in pairs, to small groups or in cross age reading partners) or sign up to perform poems in small groups for the class 'poem of the week', run and led by the children. Empowering children to lead reading activities, whatever the genre and whatever the medium (e-book or print book) is key to rich read aloud practice oriented to RfP.

The Internet can usefully be applied to the goal of widening textual diversity, with many free e-books, audio books, iBooks or texts about texts (e.g. interviews with authors, illustrators). Opportunities to listen to more texts can be offered through the use of audio books (Brock, 2017), through 'All Change' reading sessions (when staff read from their favourite genres/texts to those choosing their session) and through re-reading, particularly poetry and emerging picture fiction favourites. In addition, opportunities to watch poetry performed online by diverse poets can bring new voices into the classroom. Teachers can model online reading by sharing with children how to search for appropriate texts, which keywords to use in the search engine and how to select from the texts offered. Platforms such as Storyweaver, for example, offer multimedia original stories in multiple languages, authored by users themselves. Perusing such texts can be instructional not only in terms of showcasing text diversity, but also offer the possibility of contributing to the bank of texts that the Internet has become. Story-sharing platforms, such as Unite for Literacy, Scene Speak, Story Place and others (see more examples in Kucirkova, 2018b), that explicitly encourage children's own story production, can act as sources of inspiration for preserving and sculpting text diversity.

## Book Talk, Inside-Text Talk and Recommendations

Talk about texts and making recommendations is a key strand of effective RfP pedagogy – this was strongly evidenced across the TaRs data set (Cremin et al., 2014). Chambers' (1985) original use of the term 'book talk' mostly related to explicit teaching contexts and was often teacher-initiated and framed, with attention to a particular text and children's 'likes-dislikes-puzzles and patterns' in response. Such talk has considerable value and was fostered by the TaRs teachers, but in addition opportunities for children to talk informally about their current reading were offered and learner-led talk *about* reading and *being a reader* as well as a talk in the context of *book recommendations* emerged. Embracing this broader conceptualisation of book talk and affording more space and time to simply blether about books, without needing to answer teachers' questions or write responses, appeared to release the children to engage in very considerable child-initiated book talk. Informal 'book blether' that was learner-led, informal, social and with texts that the children wanted to share and discuss (with each other and their teachers) became very high profile in project classrooms. As one teacher observed 'we hear it everywhere now, as they come in in the morning, when they're packing away or changing for PE and on the playground, there in particular, children are chatting about books and what they're reading. We've simply never heard anything like it before, there's a real book buzz and it's *not* just our able readers'. When this arose spontaneously, was linked to particular 'books in common' between friends or across the class, and involved quoting from the text in some way, we called this 'inside-text talk' (Cremin et al., 2009, 2014).

Inside-text talk involved children drawing on their shared knowledge of particular texts. Commonly, but not exclusively, these texts were those that had been read aloud by the teacher. Children began to quote lines from such texts to each other or joined in re-voicing short extracts from their poems or narratives in common. Frequently, the extracts from narratives were affectively charged and voiced as the character, often in a somewhat exaggerated manner, such as Plop the baby owl saying 'Act-u-a-ll-y I'm a barn owl', each time he meets someone new in *The Owl who was Afraid of the Dark* (Jill Tomlinson). Other kinds of inside-text talk from stories involved playing with words, for example as Dick King-Smith's character Max *The Hodgeheg* does after he bumps his head. Children in one class took particular delight in knowingly borrowing and re-voicing some of Max's phrases, such as 'hip roohay' and 'K.O' and spontaneously inventing their own. Poetry too was often re-voiced and shared amongst friends, often with the teacher's original emphasis. For instance, on observing a cat asleep just outside the school playground two 6 year olds began, without discussing it, to chant the poem 'Cats sleep anywhere any table, any chair' by Eleanor Farjeon. After five lines they were unable to recall any more so they repeated the first five lines again, delighting in the found cat, the language and each other. There was a kind of intimacy involved in this spontaneous inside-text talk; one child might begin to quote from a 'book in common' and others would join them, eyes would meet, and grins often emerged as they re-voiced extracts and verses in unison. Their pleasure in this highly relational and affective reading practice was evident. Drawing on Bakhtin's (1981) notion of multi-voicing, we argue that in borrowing and appropriating the voices of characters or poets, the children were connecting to one another as readers and as friends, and linking to the literary works they had encountered. They were not though merely imitating, they were asserting their shared text knowledge and expressing agency as they selected the lines and stylised the extract. The presence of spontaneous and collaborative revoicing of 'books in common' came to be recognised as a marker of deeply engaged reading communities (Cremin et al., 2014).

Teachers in the project often took part in the book talk in their classrooms, offered their views (drawing on their own knowledge of texts and the reading experience), and in the process found out more about the children's opinions and practices. Gradually they came to appreciate the critical significance of such apparently low-key conversations. The role of dialogue in education has long been documented (e.g. Mercer, 2000; Mercer and Littleton, 2007; Wells, 1999). As Alexander (2008: 15) notes it 'entails a meeting of minds; and it is therefore mediated through text, internet and computer screen as well as through face to face interaction'. Such interaction enabled new understandings to develop as teachers and children built on each other's contributions about particular texts and shared their views. In these conversations, whilst some readers felt the same about a character or a text, many did not and the talk shifted from being cumulative, (where productively they added to each other's knowledge and understanding about the text by sharing their ideas), to being more exploratory in nature. Mercer and Littleton (2007) note that whilst cumulative talk is focused on knowledge accumulation, exploratory talk involves constructive challenge and reasoning, and this was often in evidence in the informal book talk documented.

Initially such conversations were seen as incidental, part of the shifting social environment around reading, but gradually, through reconceptualising reading as a social process, teachers came to appreciate the significant pedagogic purposes of such interaction in children's development as readers. Children need to be enabled and encouraged to talk about texts with one another and with their teacher in an informal, incidental manner, where the comments shared, the opinions voiced and the questions asked are child-initiated and relevant to the individuals involved. In contrast to teacher-led whole class discussions about texts, such talk is arguably more personal, more focused and more salient to each child's journey as a reader. This does not denigrate the value of whole class book talk, nor focused discussions during literacy lessons or reading aloud. Rather it recognises the enduring value of spontaneous reader-to-reader interaction. Participating in discussions with children about their chosen books enabled teachers to get to know them better and the life-to-text and text-to-life connections made, strengthened the practitioners' capacity to make tailored text recommendations. Many found it was valuable to offer two or three recommendations such that the children's agency as readers was respected and they could make their own choices. Practitioners do not want children to feel obliged to read or like what they have suggested and must remain open to reading books recommended to them. This reciprocal process of text recommendations and book swaps in the TaRs project helped to enrich the interactive communities of readers that were built (Cremin et al., 2014). Wider recommendations can be shared with parents too, via reading newsletters with reviews written by staff and children.

Other research has also highlighted the value of informal text talk. In a class of 10–11 year olds, Maybin (2013) noted children's creative oral engagement and fleeting emotional and moral responses to literature. These were voiced as asides to the main task set by the teacher, yet they supported the children's understanding of the text and fostered their engagement. Such reader-to-reader talk deserves increased professional attention. In our project on extracurricular group reading, there was also evidence of informal text talk (Cremin and Swann, 2016, 2017). The discourse patterns in these groups were mainly relaxed, responsive and rarely overtly instructional. In mixed age groups, the young readers often engaged in 'book blether' as soon as they arrived and whilst later the librarian leader would draw the group together, there was no sense of checking or monitoring the young people's responses. Students were free to voice their views without attention to the assessment agenda that they perceived prevailed in their 'English' lessons, and the librarians and teachers also shared their views informally and conversationally (Cremin and Swann, 2016, 2017). The discursive stance towards reading adopted by the adults served to afford space for the readers to construct a more dialogic understanding of the literary texts, and, in some instances, of the texts of their own and each other's lives.

In a study focused on developing a love of reading in a class of 6–7 year olds in the US, informal book talk and recommendations were woven through the teacher's pedagogy (Moses and Kelly, 2018). Weekly opportunities for 'book shopping' (browsing the class library to select texts), book sharing times (when teachers and children discussed favourites), small-group literature discussions, and book parties all enabled the children to experience reading as a socially shared experience. This combined with reading aloud and reading time had positive consequences: the young became well-acquainted with children's literature, began to develop their tastes as readers, and talked freely about books (Moses and Kelly, 2018). However, in the boys' reading study, we found scant incidence of observed or reported informal text talk and all book-related talk was literacy instruction focused and of an instructional nature (Hempel-Jorgensen et al., 2018). Whilst the teachers referred to talking about texts in interview, there was no evidence that they or the children engaged in informal book talk, and only one teacher–child book recommendation was documented across the four weeks; this was in school D where the newly qualified teacher promoted one of the 100 new books. The absence of recommendations, while undoubtedly influenced by the teachers' knowledge of children's literature, is also likely to have been shaped by the teachers' conceptions of reading in schools A–C. Their understandings, framed by the assessment agenda, were predominantly of reading as technical proficiency. These were internalised by the children and influenced pedagogic practice such that the boys who were disengaged were obliged to remain so (Hempel-Jorgensen et al., 2018). Reading as a social practice remained unrecognised in these schools.

## Social Reading Environments

The creation of social reading environments is another element of an effective RfP pedagogy. In these, children are enabled to engage interactively and creatively as readers (Cremin et al., 2014); such environments are more than physical, they are the ethos in which reading time, reading aloud and book talk are experienced. Having discussed these strands however, we focus here more on the physical features of classrooms and schools which support RfP. In TaRs, the teachers were invited to reflect on the conditions in which they preferred to read, to hold up a mirror to their own reading practices and consider possible consequences for the classroom (Cremin et al., 2014). As a result, many sought to create environments that were more comfortable and social and involved the children, giving them a chance to shape and create their own reading areas and to personalise these spaces. Displays which profiled children's and teachers' reading practices quickly emerged. These included, for example, 24-hour reads, reading rivers and readers in disguise, and gave children the chance to share, showcase and collage their reading histories and current practices in creative ways (see Chapter 7 for more details). Uniqueness was evident, made manifest in considerable textual diversity, authenticity and personal differences. Teachers learnt a great deal about the young readers through these activities, and this was mutual, and talk about texts and being a reader was triggered. This talk was conversational in nature and, like the displays themselves, carried clear messages about the reading community, the children, teachers, teaching assistants and others whose reading lives were shared (Cremin et al., 2014).

Alongside newly formed reading corners co-created by children and teachers, new more transient spaces emerged, indoors and out. Many of these involved some kind of food, as the teachers themselves had noted reading with refreshment of some kind was key in their home reading environments. Subsequently, teachers involved in the ongoing Open University RfP work that builds on the TaRs research (Open University, 2019) have created space and time for stories and hot chocolate, reading cafes, reading dens (with blankets and torches under the tables), reading picnics, outdoor reading (linked to Forest school) and even a mini Hay Festival. Cognisant that the company of friends or peers (Kuzmičová et al., 2018), the physical place and the embodied nature of the experience influences our reading, these teachers offer relaxed opportunities to read (and on occasion eat and drink together) in child-owned and shaped environments. They found these support young readers' sustained engagement with texts.

In our study of extracurricular reading groups with primary and secondary aged readers, we found that the physical setting of libraries and other meeting areas made a difference to readers' interactions and engagement (Cremin and Swann, 2016, 2017). In these, nonhierarchical seating arrangements pertained, and group members and leaders typically sat together around a large table or clustered around smaller tables in relaxed postures. Freedom of movement was allowed, group members sometimes moved to join other groups of friends, food was eaten, hands were rarely raised, and conversation flowed. Parallels with research into adult reading groups can be seen where informality, comfort and openness combine to support sustained engagement and enable creative interpretations of the text (Swann, 2012). Although there is no substitute for face-to-face reading environments, actual human interaction should not be perceived as an antidote for digital contact. There could be group members who cannot join in person for personal, physical or economic reasons who could be invited to join the meeting virtually through a videoconference call. Face-to-face meetings can also be enriched with e-reading resources such as videos or podcasts with authors or the creation of a short multimedia story about the meeting that is shared with everyone (e.g. with the Storify app or the 'story' option on Instagram).

We recognise that these examples represent best, rather than typical, practice. In contrast, in the boys' reading study schools, all of whom had invested time, money and effort to develop RfP, no such informality and sociality was observed (Hempel-Jorgensen et al., 2018). Whilst reading was profiled in each classroom, no sense of readers or authors was evident. Class reading displays profiled reading as a skill and were adult-led and developed. Additionally, beyond book borrowing, minimal use was made of the designated reading areas. In school A the corner was used for time out for bad behaviour and as an extra workspace, in B no use was observed, and in C the reading shed was only used twice across the week as part of a guided reading carousel. However, in school D, the area was used for relaxation, reading and conversation. With the exception of this school, reading tended to be performed and displayed and was not participated in as a shared or sustained social practice. Reading, and particularly volitional reading, was positioned as an individual and solitary activity and informal interaction around reading was rare. Looking across our RfP studies and in line with Laurenson et al.'s (2015) research in post primary classrooms, it is clear that school environments, which invite children's involvement, are reader-led, informal and seek to foster their ownership and choice with texts that tempt, are more likely to nurture social interaction and engage young readers. Young readers feel more engaged when they have ownership of their own reading journeys and are given choice in selecting the reading materials.

## Conclusion

The four strands of RfP pedagogy are operationalised in the classroom in subtle and nuanced ways depending upon teachers' underlying conceptions of reading and being a reader. Such conceptions have consequences. They impact upon the ways in which children are enabled to interact with one another, with their teacher and with texts, and the degree of agency and ownership of their reading journeys that can exert. In addition, practitioners' knowledge of children's literature and other texts and their knowledge of children's everyday reading practices will influence the provision offered. We have argued before that:

> Without such knowledge and understanding, the establishment of reading environments, reading aloud, book talk and independent reading, might well become little more than a routine set of pedagogic procedures, void of authentic reader engagement and interaction. (Cremin et al., 2014: 151)

It is not simply a case of timetabling volitional reading sessions and reading aloud, and integrating some book-based interaction into these slots. As the maxim observes: 'it's not what you do but the way that you do it'. Principled professional planning, informed by both subject knowledge and pedagogical content knowledge, is key. Furthermore, such practice needs careful documenting to ascertain its impact on all the children's identities as readers, as we discuss in Chapter 8. In order to foster children's shared and sustained engagement in reading texts that tempt them as readers, the informal, social and learner-led nature of this complex RfP pedagogy needs to be both nurtured and lived.

# 6

# Reciprocal Reading Communities

T he concept of reciprocity is key to nurturing communities of readers. Alongside interaction, reciprocity was identified as a key characteristic of engaged reading communities in one of our studies (Cremin et al., 2014). However, in the light of Rosenblatt's (1978/1994) transactional theory of reading, it takes on additional relevance. Texts are not passive objects; they connect and guide us into reciprocal relationships with authors and with other readers. Such relationships are typified by interaction, so our focus in this chapter is on the facets of interactive and shared engagement in environments where children can interact with others around texts, both online and offline. Children's lived experience of reading needs to be acknowledged in reading communities so that more equivalent relationships around reading can be formed. In this context, we understand communities as instantiated and initiated by active members and as spaces that have features that are both contributed to by their members and embodied by them. As Williams posits:

> The making of a community is always an exploration, for consciousness cannot precede creation, and there is no formula for unknown experience. A good community, a living culture, will, because of this, not only make room for but actively encourage all and any who can contribute .... Wherever we have started from we need to listen to others who started from a different position. (Williams, 1982: 334)

Drawing on theories of reading and perspective-taking, data from our projects and practical examples of current reading platforms, we propose a definition of reciprocal reading for pleasure (reciprocal RfP). This definition emphasises the social and communal aspects of reading and hints at the relational. We begin with a theoretical synthesis of two key concepts that are salient to our emerging definition: transactions of meaning through extensive perspective-taking and the importance of dialogue in inter-thinking and knowledge transformation. Heeding the advice by Conole et al. (2004) for theoretically rigorous design of educational technology, we perceive these concepts as principles that are key to children's reading for pleasure (RfP) and use them to guide design and practice parameters. We reflect on our earlier insights regarding local and physical reading communities and the ways in which these acknowledged and celebrated diversity and difference. We also consider the ways in which new reading platforms, such as digital story hubs and digital libraries, form around social media and shape children's identities as readers through online interactions. In addition, in order to support our argument and illustrate practical ways to build ongoing and reciprocal dialogue in online communities, we include some examples of effective designs of social platforms for young people. Finally, we envision new online reading spaces and reflect on the ways in which the underpinning research-informed principles also apply to local and physical reading communities.

## Theorising Reading Reciprocity

In outlining subjectivity as a verb in Chapter 4, we described the dialogic process between readers and texts. We argued that dialogic and dialectical processes work in tension and that Vygotsky's (1978) and Bakhtin's (1981) theories of 'self' and 'other' help us to understand reading and in particular how reading has been expanded with the arrival of digital texts. In this chapter, Vygotskian and neo-Vygotskian theories provide a theoretical base for understanding how and why narratives feed reciprocity among authors, readers and texts and support the development of reading communities. With every story, there is a continuous back-and-forth between the writer's intention and the reader's interpretation. This forwards and backwards process is at the heart of Rosenblatt's (1978/1994) transactional theory of reading and writing which we introduced in Chapter 2. As she observed: 'The relation between the reader and the signs on the page proceeds in a to-and-fro spiral in which each is continually affected by what the other has contributed' (1995: 26). Rosenblatt thus saw reading as a growing and recursive exchange – between what the author wrote and what the reader (whether child or adult) – understood and later adapted or transformed.

Children, as we have stressed elsewhere, need to be enabled to draw upon their 'funds of knowledge' Moll et al. (1992) – their social, cultural and linguistic assets – to participate in this transaction which Cliff-Hodges (2016a: 57) describes as a 'kind of reciprocal engagement'. Yet when they come to school, they are frequently obliged to leave their 'virtual school bags' (Thomson, 2002) which are packed with such life knowledge at home. It is possible though to enable the young to make use of their cultural capital in order to read and to learn. If from their earliest encounters with books, they are supported to create meaning from and with the text, they will come to fill the blanks or gaps that Iser (1978) argues give the reader an integral role to play. In the transactional process of reading, the reader and the writer mutually shape, condition and define each other (Rosenblatt, 1995). This model of the flexible exchange of meanings can be mapped directly onto psychological theories of perspective-taking.

## Perspective-taking

Being able to take the perspective of another person is a critical life skill and is arguably an essential condition for participating in and co-creating a reading community. When you put yourself in another person's shoes, you place yourself into their position, see the world, albeit in the context of reading a fictional one, from their point of view. This mode of thinking is neither a given nor an automatic process, it needs to be nurtured and cultivated. Psychologists interested in perspective-taking and theory of mind, seek to connect it to children's comprehension and understanding of texts (e.g. Doherty, 2008). In this research literature, theory of mind refers to the ability to attribute a mental state to oneself and infer the mental states of others. Based on numerous experimental studies, it is now widely established that 4–5-year-old children (but rarely children of a younger age) understand that what they think might be different from what others think, and that people act based on their beliefs and thoughts (e.g. Leslie et al., 2004; Saxe et al., 2009). Some contexts, experiences and resources on and offline can facilitate the development of children's theory of mind. For instance, talking about the emotions of others (e.g. if a sibling hits another sibling), engaging in pretend play where children become characters who experience certain emotions, looking closely at character's faces at key points in a story and other language-based activities (Rosnay and Hughes, 2006).

Literary scholars (e.g. Mar, 2011; Oatley, 2016) argue that fiction, and literary fiction in particular, simulates social experiences and through this simulation, it expands perspective-taking and even empathy as we discussed in Chapter 2. Literary fiction presents us with complex characters, situations and emotions that we may or may not have experienced, so it represents a rich resource to practise perspective-taking. In young children's literature, both the text and the illustrations provide opportunities for the development of emotions, widening experience and understanding the emotions of others. Oatley (2011) argues that approximately 75% of books for pre-schoolers reference mental states in order to support their emerging understanding of both themselves and others. The narrative frame of fictional stories can arouse children's imaginations and take them to worlds that don't exist (e.g. animals that speak, witches in frozen lands) enabling them to make sense of the real world in which they live (Nikolajeva, 2002). The journey from 'what-if' to 'what-is' (Engel, 2005) is travelled daily in households and schools where children are read to and choose to read to themselves and with each other. Such children are transported emotionally into stories, and may experience these deeply, 'living through the text' in Rosenblatt's (1995) words, and learning about the lives and views of others on their travels. The perspective-taking involved supports their comprehension of the text, but also more broadly, contributes to their ability to empathise, assume moral responsibility and become democratic citizens (Wolf, 2018a).

Recognising that fictional texts play a crucial role in nurturing and propagating perspective-taking, we identify elements that support this process. In Chapter 4, we detailed the features of books that draw young children's attention to their own 'self', such as the use of personal names in personalised books or for toddlers a reflective surface (mirror) in which to see their face. In a similar vein, some text features draw children's attention to the perspective of others. A common technique used in children's books is to present traditional fairy tales from the villain's perspective. In print books, this can be achieved with so-called Upside-Down books. For example, *Snow White: The Untold Story* by Catherine Heller (illustrated by Karen Stolper) recounts the story from the stepmother's perspective and *The True Story of the 3 Little Pigs* by A. Wolf as told to Jon Scieszka (illustrated by Lane Smith), offers the reader Alexander T. Wolf's point of view. Some publishers even present stories with several perspectives in one book, as two parallel tales. For instance, in the digital book *Goldilocks and Little Bear* by Nosy Crow, the tale is re-created as two parallel stories, one for each of the key characters. Depending on how the reader tilts the iPad, they can experience the story from either Goldilocks' or Little Bear's perspective. This creates some amusing scenes where the two characters engage in parallel actions, for example while Goldilocks is in the bears' home, eating their porridge, sitting in their chairs, and sleeping in their beds, on the e-pages of the Little Bear, the little bear is in Goldilocks's family's home – eating their pancakes, wearing their clothes, and reading their books!

While these examples provide *explicit* ways of drawing children's attention to the perspective of others, since fiction is built on the notion of mental transactions between readers and authors, some perspective-taking will be triggered anyway. These mental transactions accumulate and give rise to what Rosenblatt described as cumulative meaning: 'The arousal and fulfilment – or frustration and revision – of expectations contribute to the construction of cumulative meaning' (Rosenblatt, 2005: 1371). A cumulative meaning fulfils an important role in connecting an individual literary experience and its social context, and acts, Rosenblatt argues, as a 'stimulant to the development of critical and self-critical reading, essential to citizens of a democracy' (1994: 180). It is this cumulative meaning-making, from multiple and ongoing reading experiences, that fosters the recipro-cal understanding between readers and writers, and readers and other readers.

To understand the mechanism, or process, through which reciprocal understanding occurs, we turn to a second theoretical concept: dialogue in inter-thinking.

## Dialogue in inter-thinking

So far, we have outlined how meanings 'travel' from readers to texts since a text, as 'an object of paper and ink' (Rosenblatt, 1994: 23) has no meaning until it encounters the reader who brings to bear their prior experience. In physical and virtual contexts, read-ers widen their understandings about texts as they exchange ideas through dialogue. In online reading spaces dialogue happens through written responses, when readers post their book reviews or write messages to each other. It can also happen through actions, when, for example a reader suggests a title for another reader and places an e-book on their friend's virtual bookshelf. In principle, not dissimilar dialogues can occur in physi-cal reading communities: readers discuss book titles, share their views of what they liked/disliked about particular texts or characters, and physically exchange books with one another. In both contexts, readers can engage in productive dialogue, which is essential for knowledge transformation.

The powerful role of dialogue in the development of children's thinking has been extensively documented by Mercer (1995) and his UK colleagues (e.g. Littleton, Wegeriff, Hennessy, Kershner and Warwick) in the UK and across the world (e.g. Mexico, Japan,

Singapore, Australia, USA). In most classrooms studied by Mercer et al. in the late eighties and early nineties however, the research team found a relatively narrow range of opportunities for learners to participate in dialogues with their teachers. Referring to language as a 'social model of thinking', Mercer (1995: 61) advocates for teachers to provide more opportunities for children to 'think together' with them. His resultant teaching approach, entitled 'Thinking Together' involves the guided construction of knowledge and shows that when talk is put to work, the process that ensues is 'inter-thinking' (Littleton and Mercer, 2013). Inter-thinking, these scholars argue, thrives in spaces with flexible power structures, and withers in more traditional and hierarchically organised settings.

Inter-thinking is not about the quantity of words deployed in a given interchange, but about the quality of knowledge exchanged through the dialogue. The specific words that are used to encourage responses from others are important, for example, research shows that exploratory talk (which involves why and how questions and reasoning) is the most productive form of talk in nurturing dialogue in primary schools (Mercer et al., 1999). Thinking together, research suggests, is at the core of: productive collaboration during problem-solving activities (Pino-Pasternak et al., 2018); effective argumentative writing (Morris et al., 2018); and general academic language proficiency (Uccelli et al., 2013). In these projects, the young learners and their teachers drew on 'ground rules for educational dialogues' (Edwards and Mercer, 1987/2013) which were openly stated and discussed in order to facilitate effective inter-thinking. The concept of inter-thinking maps directly on the neo-Vygotskian view of 'distributed cognition' (Cole and Engeström, 1993), that is cognition that is owned by all entities in the socio-technological environment. In distributed cognition models, knowledge and understanding is co-constructed. Thus, knowledge becomes both a resource and an action, or as Salomon (1998) describes it, both the process and object of learning. This reciprocal dynamic gives rise to knowledge transformation.

The value of dialogue in the process of knowledge transformation, together with Rosenblatt's transactional theory of reading and psychological research on perspective-taking, provides a solid basis for what we term 'reciprocal reading for pleasure'.

## Reciprocal RfP

Our suggested definition of reciprocal RfP is that: Reciprocal RfP is a dialogic process during which readers transform the meanings of texts through the volitional exchange of ideas and perspectives and find satisfaction in so doing.

In other words, we locate reciprocity in an *active* process of exchanging meanings and perspectives in relation to texts, and recognise the reader's desire to engage in this way in anticipation of satisfaction. In reciprocal RfP there is no uni-directional transfer of knowledge from a text or from any given reader of it, but rather the ongoing sharing and pollination of ideas, the generation of new perspectives and the re-negotiation of old views. These processes can give rise to knowledge transformation and are, we argue, likely to be nurtured most effectively in reading communities. Such communities draw readers together in different spaces, on and offline, since as Mercer acknowledges, 'community membership can be distributed, multiple, and complex, and based as much on common interests as common locality' (2000: 105). Children and young people today will be members of many different and changing communities and social groups. Those denoted as reading communities, need, we believe, to encompass difference and diversity, agreement and disagreement, if they are to foster reciprocal RfP and nurture readers for life. Our argument here is informed by William's (1976) conception of community as focused on notions of equality and the quality of human relationships – communitas – rather than social systems or organisational structures, though we recognise the co-existence of both.

In order to explore our theoretically derived definition of reciprocal RfP in the context of reading communities, we apply it to our previous offline research and to future online design possibilities. Initially though we connect to school, class and group reading communities documented in our studies before we turn to current and imagined online reading spaces that bring non-local and diverse communities of readers together.

## Reading Communities Online and Offline

Reading communities take many forms. They may be created on a small scale through the establishment of an afterschool reading group or a teacher book group, may be experienced in classrooms led by Reading Teachers (see Chapter 7), and may be evident across whole schools where the culture of RfP is strong. In addition, local reading festivals or events in libraries can, for a short time, create a sense of engagement and belonging, a strong connection to others also participating as readers. Some transient communities take the form of shared reading events that are 'supersized' (Fuller and Rehberg Sedo, 2017) in mass reading events across a city or region. Broadcast book programmes have been influential in this space with televised book clubs such as Richard and Judy, and Oprah's Book Club becoming very popular. Connected city-wide events often focus on a single book as the focus for a myriad of activities, with the opportunity to participate online and enhancing the reach of these.

Our socio-cultural research has focused on smaller scale reading communities in classrooms and schools, and it is on one of these that we draw here. This explored the creation of communities of readers and identified four characteristics of highly engaged communities, namely: reciprocity and interaction, difference and diversity (Cremin, 2010a,b; Cremin et al., 2009, 2012, 2014, 2015). At the start of the project, relationships around reading in the classrooms were framed by and limited to discussions of texts related to literacy learning – teacher-led discussions focused on teacher-chosen texts for the purposes of instruction, the development of reading skills and assessment. Such talk is necessary to ensure reading strategies are taught and applied effectively, but in order to foster RfP more equitable relationships around reading and being a reader needed to be established. For many schools this involved a significant cultural shift.

As teachers found out more about the children's reading preferences and practices beyond the school gate, the boundaries between reading in school and beyond began to blur. Children were enabled to bring more from their homes, cultures and histories – their 'funds of knowledge' (Moll et al., 1992) and their reading selves to school. Teachers too opened up as readers and many began authentically to share their own reading lives such that new positions were adopted, and new reading identities enacted. As a consequence, gradually diversity and difference, both in relation to texts and to readers were recognised and respected and a broader notion of what counts as reading developed. Significantly too, the nature of talk about texts shifted and became more shared, different views and ideas about texts were voiced, and these were listened to and debated within small and larger networks of readers. A different sort of reader relationship emerged as a result: one with reciprocity at the heart. This developed between teachers and children, children and children and in some cases teachers and parents and was evidenced in a degree of giving and receiving as readers. A sense of complementarity around reading was apparent in project classrooms, children's choices were honoured, their views on reading and being a reader sought and they were listened to attentively. Discussion and debate ensued. Such child-directed reading interactions became commonplace. Non-assessed and informal conversations of this kind were both less hierarchical and more reciprocal in nature and talking about reading and connecting to other readers became part of the fabric of many classrooms.

These reading communities took considerable time to build. They fostered a sense of belonging, were relationship-strong and highly interactive, and they shifted reading from being positioned as an individual private pursuit to a more collaborative social activity (Cremin et al., 2014). Tracking the children across the year indicated that they were effectively nurtured through their involvement in such richly reciprocal communities of readers. The communities involved a shared concept of what it means to be a reader in the twenty-first century; considerable teacher and child knowledge of children's literature and other texts; RfP pedagogy which acknowledged and developed diverse reader identities; new social spaces that encouraged choice and child ownership of their own RfP; informal book talk on the part of all; and a shift in the locus of control that fosters reader agency and independence. The Teachers as Readers (TaRs) research did not, however, pay extensive attention to digital texts and did not explore the possibilities of developing reading communities online. Some teachers did make use of their school websites for offering book reviews and videos of teachers reading aloud for instance and others enabled children to read online during independent reading time, but the year-long project focused predominantly on print texts.

So, in what follows, we attempt to apply our definition of reciprocal RfP to the design of current and then an imaginative online reading space that could bring together diverse communities of readers typified by interaction and reciprocity. We begin with an expose of existing online platforms and a broader discussion of the online space and its growing impact on readers. We then discuss some of the shortcomings of current digital reading platforms designed for children and reflect briefly on existing online community platforms, that while not designed explicitly for reading, have inspired our thinking.

# Online Reading Communities

## The reader in online spaces

The Internet, a giant book of articles and snippets of communication, is increasingly a space for building and sustaining diverse communities. These communities 'crowdsource' knowledge from each other and harness the potential of collective intelligence. The Internet offers a distinct opportunity to support learning communities as it can deliver information at scale and allows its users to jointly and iteratively develop knowledge. At the same time, the scale and speed of presenting online information can be lethal for knowledge-sharing and may lead to misinformation, spreading of propaganda and biased reporting. In online communities, people can follow like-minded individuals, create and share multimedia content and learn from each other. This benefits discussions of local and niche interest, as well as difficult topics, but the affordances of information exchange in online communities are not without their problems. A key problem of like-minded individuals following each other on social media is that they become too narrowly focused on their own 'bubble' of views and perspectives, arguably the antithesis of reciprocal RfP. Highlighting the double-sided arrow of online communication, Boyd (2017) points out that:

> Many in the tech world imagined that the internet would connect people in unprecedented ways, allow for divisions to be bridged and wounds to heal – a Kumbaya dream of sorts. Today, those same dreamers find it quite unsettling to watch as the tools that were designed to bring people together are used by people to magnify divisions and undermine social solidarity.

What he refers to is not the problem of editorship (traditional newspapers have always edited content and shaped opinions), but the issue of new information providers, such as Google and Facebook, that are only beginning to develop more sound models of content-sharing. The commercial nature of online information and in some countries, the political influence on recommended content, are significant issues in the digital reading landscape (Williamson, 2016). Most, if not all, information we share online is not private information, but data for companies that use it for predicting our behaviour and follow it up with commercial offers, targeted advertisements and in some countries, policy-making (ibid.). Again, offline communities can suffer from similar biases, but online communities have the added issue of recommender algorithms.

## Online reading communities and the issue of algorithms

Recommender systems are algorithms that analyse visitor usage patterns and make recommendations for content, such as news information on Google News website, or for products such as on the Amazon retail site. Recommender systems aggregate data which allow advertisement companies to tailor their advertisements, and platform providers to understand popularity and trends to dynamically adjust their services and performance (see Davies, 2019). There is no magic behind Google's personalised suggestions or Amazon's recommendation of 'if you liked Hemmingway, you might also like Scott Fitzgerald'. These recommendations are automated responses to the information users provide. Given the large amounts of information online, a recommendation system is needed to reduce this information and make it relevant to individual users. The recommendations can be for commercial, educational or entertainment purposes, or a combination. On a commercial basis, Amazon has pioneered the way such systems work for recommending book titles: if you buy a book on their website, you are shown recommendations based on your own and other users purchased items (the latter are often fictional but relate to the item you bought). The book online space Goodreads (which is run and owned by Amazon), employs the same logic for recommending books to readers for entertainment (recommended books are directly linked to the Amazon bookstore). All recommendations follow a complex matrix that combines the characteristics of the users' profiles (age, gender, job, nationality) with the characteristics of other users' book choices and books' characteristics (author, content, publisher). The data in Goodreads come from the users directly, and is based on their purchase history on Amazon, their interaction with the digital books on their virtual bookshelves, and indirectly through the users' social media contacts.

While Amazon mastered the algorithmic formula for direct sales, Google dominates information search and Facebook social media. These Internet giants are 'giants' because their primary occupation is to offer products and adverts that often employ opaque techniques to dominate the market. Readers will remember the widely cited Cambridge

Analytica scandal or numerous fines levelled at these technology giants by the European Commission for misusing their powers for private and political ends. Lack of transparency and moral guidance on these online platforms create tensions not only in online, but also offline communities. Flawed algorithms have been blamed for contributing to media bias, abuses of political power and polarisation in communities. On balance, it is fair to say that flawed algorithms thrive in systems with flawed structural and historical problems. We need to avoid treating technology giants as scapegoats for all our problems and instead ponder on societal solutions. While in offline communities the rules or conventions for exchanging ideas are well-known, in online communities these are yet to be established. Teachers' and children's voices need to be part of this development. Given that children's access to online content is global, it also requires an international perspective that would incorporate best practice on the use of children's data for educational purposes from a global viewpoint. National governments are increasingly applying tighter rules to technology giants and while these will not fix the bigger issue of surveillance and power, they are a sign that things are changing and citizens can and should be part of this.

If we conceive of reading from a broader perspective, its concept includes the challenges of recommender systems, online reading practices and the new literacy skills which are necessary for navigating an online networked environment. This is reflected in a classic definition of new literacies by Leu et al.:

> The new literacies of the Internet and other ICTs include the skills, strategies, and dispositions necessary to successfully use and adapt to the rapidly changing information and communication technologies and contexts that continuously emerge in our world and influence all areas of our personal and professional lives. These new literacies allow us to use the Internet and other ICTs to identify important questions, locate information, critically evaluate the usefulness of that information, synthesize information to answer those questions, and then communicate the answers to others. (2004: 1572)

A key step in the process of understanding and developing new literacy competencies is to adopt a reflective stance and develop critical literacy skills (see Burnett and Merchant, 2018b for a discussion of critical literacy). This should not wait until children are at secondary school – critical skills demanded by new technologies are essential skills needed for modern day-to-day life. For instructional digital books, for example, children need to understand that when they finish their reading and send their reading score to the publisher, there will be consequences for what kind of texts they will be automatically offered to read next. Teachers can talk to young readers about the benefits and limitations of online reading and help them reflect critically on the complexities of online texts. Teachers do not need to be experts in algorithms: common text questions, such as who wrote the content, for whom and for what purpose, apply in any context. There are several resources that can help in this process of educating teachers, parents and children about the often opaque ways in which information is propagated and monetised online. For example, the report *Life in Likes* by the UK's Children's Commissioner, resources on fake news by the National Literacy Trust, *News and Media Literacy* toolkit by Common Sense Media or the *What Works?* Series on the Ministry of Education website in Canada.

The rapidly evolving digital literacy environment demands awareness of the fact that all online texts, just like their analogue versions, have embedded values and points of view (Kellner and Share, 2005). This is why online reading, new literacies and literacy more broadly, are connected to the political context and discussions of democracy. And it is the notion of democracy that brings us back to RfP, not as a personal/psychological process but as a socio-cultural practice, as conceptualised in socio-cultural theories (Vygotsky, 1978) and specifically by Luke and Freebody (1997) in relation to reading.

Understanding what digital literacy is, and how to develop children's critical awareness and resilience concerning online information, are the first steps on the path to building sustainable reading communities online. The next step is making sure that the interactions that happen in the community are in the spirit of reciprocal RfP meaning-transformation. In what follows, we build on the theoretical concepts to illustrate some of the shortcomings of current digital reading platforms designed for children's use in schools. Whilst we selectively focus on reading platforms' limitations, we caution against the inference that the systems are limited overall, arguing that these drawbacks reflect other online reading platforms for children.

## Limitations of current online reading platforms

Online reading systems are paid-for subscription platforms that act as book depositories and provide customised recommendations for new book titles to individual users or groups of users. Based on a theorised and systematic review of a selection of these systems (Kucirkova and Cremin, 2017) and informal discussions with teachers, we identified some common benefits and limitations of using these systems in relation to RfP. Such systems have very considerable potential, but in relation to our discussion of identities, we argue that their current design tends to position teachers as 'librarians, curators and monitors' (Kucirkova and Cremin, 2017). Librarians in the sense that they can select books to recommend from a detailed database (e.g. main topic, author, genre, age range and text difficulty); see which books are on loan and which have been requested; and find out more about children's reading practices. Curators in the sense that they can suggest new book titles for purchase; link their classroom library to an external library and in some systems even edit the categories under which specific titles appear. And monitors since through access to administrator back-end data, these systems enable teachers to check the number of titles a child has accessed, the time spent with individual titles and more. Advantageously too, the platforms address three immediate and pressing professional problems: the curriculum, time and knowledge limitations. Curriculum constraints are addressed in that the platforms' design re-positions reading as a pleasurable and recreational activity, not simply as a functional or technical skill. Children can rate the books they like with stars, motivating and supporting each other in their book choices. Time constraints are addressed by giving children individual attention, with, for example, individualised recommendations for suitable book titles. Individual attention is difficult in large classes and this can support practitioners and librarians who typically need to provide recommendations suitable for the collective interest. The systems also address professional challenges, namely teachers' limited knowledge of children's book authors and titles (Cremin et al., 2014). No teacher can hold an entire bank of titles in her head, but digital library systems can have a potentially limitless list of titles and authors and run recommendation algorithms based on this list.

What we perceive as a key limitation of the design and technological features of digital library systems is the conceptually impoverished roles that they assign to teachers in terms of facilitating reciprocal RfP. Teachers could act as informed listeners, mentors and co-readers if these systems offered more possibilities for them to edit, curate and enrich the database of reading titles. Currently, although teachers can request data/statistical comparisons of children's reading histories, such data is presented and typically used for assessment and performance management, not for dialogue about the individual book titles, genres, authors and preferences with individual readers or groups. There are also limited opportunities for teachers to engage as co-readers and reflect upon and share their own reading identities. If there were attractive multimedia options for them to do so, teachers could showcase their own favourite titles and preferences. Adaptations to their design are needed in order to ensure that digital library systems offer interactive personalised spaces in which teachers are enabled to make connections, listen to younger readers' views and offer their own response to texts. This would enrich opportunities for dialogue and inter-thinking in this online space. Positioned as librarians, curators and monitors, teachers act as gatekeepers, mediating and transferring text knowledge in the library database to children in a largely hierarchical manner. Arguably, the design of current digital library systems perpetuates old pedagogic models of authoritative pedagogies where dialogue and reciprocity are side-lined, and hierarchical knowledge transfer is reified. This is unlikely to foster the development of reciprocal RfP and reading communities. In sum, while such systems currently respond to immediate curriculum, time and professional constraints, they do not offer a visionary outlook on how teachers could be positioned in online reading spaces to support reciprocal RfP. We argue teachers need to be re-positioned in these systems as co-readers, mentors and listeners (Kucirkova and Cremin, 2017) (see Figure 6.1).

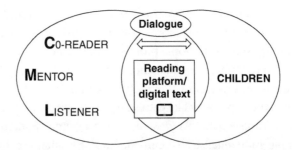

**Figure 6.1**   Teachers as co-readers, mentors and listeners: A diagram to represent networked reading communities in the context of digital library systems

In many respects, these systems illustrate wider trends in educational technology development: platforms are often designed to address immediate needs and facilitate the management of government demands on teachers' time. There are some stellar exceptions, but much educational technology is designed to stand in for teachers and positions children as autonomous, capable 'digital natives' (Prensky, 2001) who, when given the right tools, can transform their own learning (Selwyn, 2016). Whilst we support a focus on child agency (which is core to RfP), we consider that the mediating role of the teacher, online and offline, needs to be recognised. Whilst Terranova (2007: 34) argues the Internet is a site of 'disintermediation' that eradicates the middleman, this does not need to be the case with reading platforms.

To move towards more transformative design and more reciprocal approaches to online communities, we take a derivative approach and focus on four ambitious *social* online spaces which were designed to foster positive and productive engagement. Reflecting on their designs, we extrapolate features that are relevant for the kind of reciprocal RfP we envision for future generations.

## Ambitious online community spaces

Our selected online communities each focus on a different theme/topic and target different age groups, ranging from pre-schoolers to adults. We do not discuss their sustainability mechanisms or financial models, although it is worth noting that one of our examples is no longer in existence (BBC Blast) and another has been redesigned (The Club Penguin). Two (Pottermore and Instructables) are still growing and very popular at the time of writing. Although initiatives such as BBC Blast require substantial funding, it is possible to crowdsource member-based networks or monetise users' contributions to sustain platforms.

Club Penguin (www.clubpenguin.com) started as a multiplayer video game in 2005 and by 2017 had grown into an online community of 200 million users aged 6–14 years.

Shortly after its growth, the game was acquired and re-designed by Disney and currently runs as Club Penguin Island. What was interesting about the design of the original Club Penguin was how it fostered children's engagement on the platform: children could create their own penguin avatars and through advancements in the play, gain skills and resources to build houses, and purchase clothes or personal items for their penguins. In interviewing 26 children (aged 5–11) and observing 11 year olds play the game at home, Marsh (2014) concluded that the platform provided unique opportunities for children to practise their literacies, including reading and writing. She argues that when children inhabit the penguins' virtual world, it becomes a temporary reality, in which they can practise and develop life skills, such as communication as well as digital literacy skills, such as navigating online environments.

Pottermore (www.pottermore.com) describes itself as 'the digital heart of J.K. Rowling's Wizarding World' and is an online platform where users can receive news on Harry Potter and J.K. Rowling, one of the most popular fictional stories of all times with 500 million Harry Potter books sold in 2018 alone. What is interesting in the design of Pottermore is that registered users can create their own profiles, with Patronus, house and a magical wand. This gives them magical powers and makes them part of Harry Potter's fictional world. The site also includes its registered users in a 'Wizarding World Book Club', where readers can and do exchange and discuss Harry Potter stories, thus responding to texts and potentially widening their own and others' understandings of the novels through online dialogue.

BBC Blast is another inspiring example of how clever design of an online space can nurture a community of like-minded users. Designed as a network for 13–19 year olds, it ran in the UK between 2002 and 2011. The website enabled online dialogue, and users could add their own videos, audio files and comments to the online forums. In addition, dialogue happened offline, as users were invited to various BBC-supported workshops, events and meet-ups. This online–offline connection is a feature evident in our final example Instructables.

Instructables (www.instructables.com) is a community space in which members can use and share any materials or design, as long as they accompany them with a textual, pictorial or video that 'instructs' other members how to emulate the example. There are several collections members can browse through and individual projects are organised by thematic categories or users' ratings. To motivate new contributions the platform provider regularly organises contests and events, where users can contribute their designs and win prizes. Community members can discuss their ideas and questions in a dedicated forum and there is also the opportunity to learn from each other in a structured sequence, through classes that teach members specific skills, such as laser cutting, for example.

If we look at these four online spaces from the perspective of Rosenblatt's transaction theory, perspective-taking and dialogic inter-thinking, we can identify some features that are aligned with our definition of reciprocal RfP. These online spaces are not only a set of online features, but they are living communities where members are actively encouraged to take and give back, in the spirit of reciprocal listening and learning from each other. In the next section, we outline the features that strike us as particularly salient for the users' meaning-transformation and that we consider are also relevant for future online reading spaces.

## Reciprocal RfP in online reading communities

On both the Club Penguin Island and Pottermore platforms, children assume the roles of fictional characters, that is they take on the lives of various avatars and through these avatars, they connect to fellow players or readers. This, in itself, is an exercise in perspective-taking as children assume the personality of their avatars, facilitated through a playful engagement with fictional story characters. Thus, these platforms start from the premise that children can take on the perspectives of others. Whether it is an animal or Harry Potter, children are positioned as heroes in their fictional worlds, and have agency over what they look like, what they communicate to other characters and what they do with the points they earn. With challenges and problems to solve, children need to cooperate with other characters and need to understand that they too have feelings and obligations in this virtual world. In this respect, the platforms provide an interesting amalgam of role-play and book-reading and provide a playground for users to exercise their agency within the constraints of the platform structure.

As for meaning-transactions, both BBC Blast and Instructables provide multimedia space to showcase individual users' skills and knowledge, and facilitate peer learning through examples and offline workshops. They offer impressive connections between online and offline learning opportunities and facilitate dialogic interactions with moderated con-tests and user-voted competitions. The various events and competitions organised by the platform owners not only celebrate users' activity, but also allow for their presentation in a format that can be recognised and emulated by others (e.g. by awarding a badge to an avatar or watching a video).

These platforms facilitate inter-thinking in that the users are provided with multiple possibilities to express their own meaning and to access others multimodally: they can use videos, texts, images and audio files (voiceovers or sounds) to express how their avatars feel and what they think. This diversity of meaning-expression allows children to share the ways in which they envision the narratives and extends beyond the written word. In terms of adult mediation, Pottermore and Club Penguin are constructed for children's independent use, without much, or any, interference from adults. This is likely to contribute to children's feelings of agency and empowerment in their own fictional worlds and to their enjoyment. As we discussed more fully in Chapter 5, RfP is both agentic and volitional.

In sum, we consider the four platforms are inspiring representations of how stories can be exchanged in rich multimedia spaces and how users can experience and enjoy multiple meaning-transactions. In the next section, we move from existing examples to exploring an imaginary *reading* e-space online. This space demonstrates how reciprocal RfP could be actualised in the design and use of an online reading community.

# Envisioning Reading Spaces

We synthesise the theoretical concepts of meaning-transactions, perspective-taking and inter-thinking with some design solutions for possible reading communities online. The main focus in our hypothetical online reading space is reading, so unlike digital games that involve players in the game through interactivity, we aim to involve readers/non-readers through written stories. This is not to underestimate the important role video games play in reading. Many video games contain a high proportion of texts and indirectly foster children's RfP by providing children with intrinsically motivating texts (e.g. instructions on how to play a game) to share (e.g. comments to fellow players) (see Apperley and Walsh, 2012). Others, such as Pottermore, may well serve to encourage reading and re-reading of the novels offline and prompt children to read more widely within the genre.

Cognisant that our Teachers as Readers research fell short with regard to the use and value of digital texts and online reading communities (Cremin et al., 2014), we seek to envision new reading spaces online and reflect on the ways in which the underpinning research-informed principles also apply to physical reading communities. Progress in platform design and development is faster than the progress we can anticipate with our model, so we present our imaginary reading platform as a set of principles that could be adopted depending on the platform's specific audiences, needs and interests. Our focus on design features is not meant to suggest that only designers and developers of the systems can provide more visionary solutions. Quite the opposite – we aim to encourage teachers and users of online reading spaces to consider the design features as a way of auditing their current practice and advocating for potentially more valuable experiences that foster reciprocal RfP in both on and offline spaces. We begin with the design considerations that map onto meaning-transactions through extensive perspective-taking.

# Principle 1: Opportunities for extensive perspective-taking

As we have argued throughout the book, teachers need to have a wide subject knowledge of children's literature and other texts and they also need to know the young readers in their classes. Without such knowledge, they will not be in a strong position to engage in dialogue about books and reading, nor be able to connect to the young people's perspectives on the stories they read. In alignment with Vygotsky's (1987) notion of more knowledge-able others, we consider the role of adults is paramount to children's interactions online and offline, with or without books. Yet, at the same time, we contend that children too can act as more knowledgeable others in guiding their teachers (and peers) through the literature they like, in the process of inter-thinking, as Littleton and Mercer (2013) might describe it. Reading in the digital age is mediated by a range of technological tools, and these tools should neither minimise nor side-line the role of adults. In spaces designed for young readers, both adults and children are important mediators of meaning-transactions. Online, children could be involved in teaching adult users how to customise their avatars, how to place a recommended book into the e-library and other online navigation tricks. The intergenerational gap in relation to technology skills is well-documented and small steps, such as positioning children as teachers in a digital environment, can help address this. Equally offline, in physical reading environments, children can recommend books to teachers and teaching assistants, as well as their peers. Key to this is the extent to which they know these adults as readers and appreciate their reading tastes, preferences and perspectives.

In our newly envisioned reading spaces, teachers would be positioned authentically as co-readers, engaging in dialogue with children about the texts they are reading not only face to face, but also online. This would include discussing a range of texts that motivate the young and might include, for example, comics, magazines, poetry (perhaps watched online), novels, and Minecraft instructions. The young readers, acting as teachers in the example of Club Penguin advanced our understanding of how children can be positioned in online spaces in inclusive and empowering ways. Any user can have an avatar of their choice and be part of a virtual world; this is open to all children, regardless of their reading skills or background.

Avatars are popular, widely deployed as effective technological tools in human–computer interaction projects, and research reveals that children respond positively to them (Gossen et al., 2014). Avatars should not be limited to schematic representations of oneself online, but rather as an opportunity to engage children in co-creating fictional worlds. The less pre-designed and the more open-ended the possibilities for self-representation online, the more children's choices are honoured and enabled. Human–computer interaction designers call such an approach 'participatory, user-centered design' and have successfully applied it to the design of child-centred spaces. For example, Druin (2005) involved 4–9 year olds in the design of the International Children's Digital Library (www.icdlbooks.org). Their direct involvement improved, among other things, the development of the book search facility as the children suggested search categories that adults had not even considered.

The use of fictional characters is a particularly effective way of inviting participation based on reading enjoyment and ludic interactions. We could imagine the online reading space being full of character choices, related perhaps to a core of potent and contemporary texts. In such online spaces, children could be positioned as active creators, who create new imaginary characters or assume the role of a fictional character, thus removing personal markers that might re-create hierarchies and tensions in the offline world.

In physical reading spaces, time and space for children and their teachers to 'wonder and ponder' and envision and co-create story alternatives also needs to be set aside. In playful often dramatic ways, children can take on different persona and extend the known versions of narratives and their understanding of characters' perspectives.

## Principle 2: Meanings transacted through multimedia

Our second principle relates to the use of multimedia to facilitate content sharing and content production to encourage dialogue in the online community. Smartphones and tablets provide unprecedented opportunities for creating and exchanging multimedia content with the possibility to create, edit and share multimedia content embedded in one device. These opportunities could be harnessed to 'transact meanings', to borrow Rosenblatt's term, about books. We saw how the design of Instructables fosters knowledge and idea sharing through user-generated videos of products and processes. We could imagine similar mechanisms in an online reading community: individual users could share their perspectives on various books and narratives via multimedia (video, audio and textual options). Opportunities for peer learning could also be provided with regular challenges and playful activities, akin to the role-play experiences offered through the imaginary worlds of Pottermore or Club Penguin. As noted earlier in offline spaces, drama is a powerful tool for adopting roles and exploring characters' perspectives through inhabiting their world, standing in their shoes. Such 'innerstanding' can also be fostered through the use of props, toys and puppets linked to specific texts. The creation of fictional worlds through drama, small world play, tabletop role-play and animation (using digi blue cameras for instance) offer children the chance to transact meanings as they co-create and imagine together.

In the online space, teachers and children could share their perspectives on specific books, authors or stories as short vlogs and written blogs, as podcasts and voiceovers or as narratives and short text entries. For rich dialogues to develop, there needs to be an opportunity for individual users to comment, via multimedia, on each other's contributions. So, for example, a short video about a child's experience of reading a Michael Rosen book, could be attached to another child's drawing of one of his poems, a photograph of a group freeze frame depicting the theme of the poem, or a blog or review of another of his texts. The digital format can hold multiple and diverse types of content and an online reading space could thus become a thematically organised multimedia repository of diverse stories and readers' responses to stories. Such a co-created repository would afford new opportunities for children to become more involved as producers of new technologies in school, which, research evidence suggests, is relatively rare (Abrams and Merchant, 2013).

## Principle 3: Dialogue facilitating knowledge transformation

Our third principle is related to inter-thinking and ensuring that the dialogue that ensues on the reading platform and in the classroom is affectively engaging and nurtures RfP. Clearly, the way readers interact in online communities and the way providers design the platforms influence the quality of dialogue and perspective-taking that play out on platforms. In our experience of designing online learning spaces, we have noted the importance of seemingly small design choices for increasing learners' participation in online dialogue. For instance, the comment feature in online forums is often based on numerical ranking, where posts that are commented upon the most often receive higher ranking and more prominent positions on the page. Yet, we know from inter-thinking theory that it is not the quantity, but the quality of dialogue that matters for knowledge transformation. Users' comments should be ranked by their quality of insight, but current machine learning models are not powerful enough to accommodate this conception. Moreover, while in physical classroom environments individual students' contributions are rarely ignored by teachers, this can easily happen in the online system where only the most 'liked' posts get read and commented on by the community. In our experience of designing a MOOC about children's use of technology, we opted for a moderated forum, where the tutor provided constructive feedback on the different comments made by the course participants. This led to a richer dialogue among participants (in this case these were adults from around the world).

In children's online spaces, the need for moderation is inevitable and should be secured through direct adult involvement and regular monitoring. The positioning of the adult as a guide rather than authoritative monitor is, however, crucial to ensure that the community's appeal to children is not lost. On the Club Penguin platform, adult moderation was carefully hidden and security measures were pre-programmed (e.g. the removal of swear words from the online forum). The provider's clear articulation of the security measures gained many parents' trust in the platform's appropriateness for their children. The positioning of the adult as a co-reader can be accomplished with a non-hierarchical user-interface, where all users are given equal rights for content sharing. To ensure there is reciprocity and mutual dependency rather than control or dominancy in the dialogue/meaning-transaction process, such an online reading community needs to have a non-hierarchical structure of participation. As we evidenced in the TaRs study, when teachers engaged as fellow readers they were less hierarchically positioned in school and were but 'one voice amongst many' (Nystrand et al., 2003) in dialogues around books. Listening to others' views, they did not seek to impose their own on the young people but to engage authentically as interested readers. In this way, online or offline, diverse perspectives and reading experiences can be debated, challenged and celebrated, so that all readers (both children and adults) become aware of others' perspectives in order that they can re-consider their own.

## Conclusion

We acknowledge that this envisioning of online reading spaces, whilst informed by our empirical research into school reading communities, is largely theoretical with regard to online ones. We also accept that publishers and providers face considerable practical constraints in designing effective online spaces, and that the examples of design features we use might be obsolete at the time this book is published. However, by defining reciprocal RfP and drawing on concrete examples of existing communities we sought to discern the principles which underpin it. We consider that all stakeholders involved in the use of digital reading systems need to push forward in ways that foster greater innovation and enable reciprocity between readers and creators, paying more attention to literature in the process. While Rosenblatt's (1995) notion of the transaction of meaning has long influenced professional understanding and reader-response is part of much classroom practice, we suggest that publishers and designers of contemporary online reading spaces also consider its application in order to realise new reading platforms. Inter-thinking too can be applied to understand the process of knowledge exchange in classrooms, and in digital learning spaces and online communities.

We argue that more opportunities for child engagement in a range of open-ended online activities need to be offered and that these need to be blended with well-aligned offline reading opportunities, such that a stronger sense of engagement, motivation and delight in the reading experience can be fostered and vibrant communities of readers built. In these communities, reciprocal RfP can and should take priority.

# 7

# Readers'
# Identities

R eaders' identities matter. As we have discussed throughout the book, reading encompasses motivational and behavioural characteristics alongside cognitive ones and whether children identify themselves as readers is important. Yet as teachers negotiate high accountability policy environments, children's identities as readers are often neither acknowledged nor nurtured (Comber, 2012). How teachers conceive of reading and construct notions of readers in their classrooms has a significant and differential effect on young people's engagement and sense of self as readers. Parents' perceptions and attitudes to reading also serve to frame and shape their reader identities. Nonetheless children are agentic and may take up or reject the subject positions which they are offered as readers (Hall, 2010; Hempel-Jorgensen and Cremin, forthcoming; Moje and Dillon, 2006).

In this chapter, drawing on multiple studies and connecting to the facets of personalised and interactive engagement in reading for pleasure (RfP) (Kucirkova et al., 2016), we consider how young readers' identities are shaped and formed within and beyond school, and what it might mean to be positioned or to position oneself as a certain kind of reader (e.g. 'good', 'struggling') in different contexts. We also focus our lens upon teachers, who can decide how to position themselves as readers in the classroom: adopting institutionalised positions as teachers of reading instruction and/or adopting more personally engaged positions as fellow-readers. We consider evidence which suggests that when teachers consider the diversity of their own and the children's reading lives, and position themselves as Reading Teachers (teachers who read and readers who teach), classroom practice changes and becomes more aligned with RfP principles (e.g. Cremin, 2010; Cremin et al., 2014; Merga, 2016). Finally, we explore ways in which practitioners can learn more about the identities and individualities of the readers in their classes, widening their understanding of each unique child reader and using this to support their reading journeys.


## Readers' Identities

Literacy plays a significant role in young people's identity construction (Collier, 2010; McCarthey and Moje, 2002). How literacy is viewed influences the way identity is viewed and vice versa (Moje et al., 2009). In our work, we conceive of literacy and identity as positional, relational, and therefore multiple, enacted in interaction (Holland and Lave, 2001; Holland et al., 1998). In other words, we recognise that children's and adults' identities as readers are thus not fixed or immutable, but are context-dependent and fluid, constantly shaped and enacted through interaction with others in response to different situational contexts. This raises questions about how a culture of reading in the home and school will affect the development of young people's identities and also how this connects to Discourses. By Discourses we mean the 'ways of being in the world ... a sort of identity kit', as Gee (2011: 127) describes them. He argues that humans are apprenticed early in life to Primary Discourses which operate as a kind of baseline within which later Discourses are acquired or resisted. These Primary Discourses 'form our initial taken-for-granted understandings of who we are and who people "like us" are, as well as what sorts of things we ("people like us") do, value, and believe when we are not "in public"' (2011: 137).

Secondary Discourses, Gee argues, are formed outside the home and include for example school, church, particular group memberships, gangs, offices and so on. He suggests that Secondary Discourses 'constitute the recognisability and meaningfulness of our "public" (more formal) acts' (2011: 137).

Gee's (2011) Discourses are a useful analytic tool for researchers, but also for teachers interested in understanding how and why children develop 'taken for granted understandings' of themselves as readers in the home, influenced by their parents, siblings, grandparents and significant others. A family's attitudes to reading, and the reading practices and interactions around texts that take place in their home and community serve to position children in particular ways as readers, even before they attend school. Their home practices may or may not be affirmed in the classroom, although it is argued that home-based recreational reading practices 'may allow individuals to more easily develop a Discourse valued in schools' (Knoester and Plikuhn, 2016: 480).

Teachers' attitudes and understanding of what counts as reading, alongside their practice and the opportunities for interaction around texts that they offer also shape the way children view themselves as readers. Children have their own personal interests and inclinations and may actively position themselves as certain kinds of readers depending on the opportunities offered and their sense of self as readers. For example, some may seek to join an emerging reading network in class and position themselves as motivated readers among their peers, by volunteering for instance to read aloud, lead small group book recommendations, take the playground picture book box out at lunchtimes or be a library monitor. Others, due to particular peer relationships, pedagogic practice, labelling and/or their previous experience of reading at home and school, may refrain from offering in this way, not wanting perhaps to be viewed in their peer group as 'too keen' a reader. How children are identified by those around them has been referred to as their *discursive identities* (Gee, 2011). Such socially constructed identities are shaped by other children's, parents', teachers' and teaching assistants' interactions with them as individuals, and by how they construe those interactions in relation to the models of being a reader that are available to them in a particular community. It is important that teachers are aware of, and reflect on, the ways in which discursive identities are formed inside and outside of classrooms and how they impact children's reader identities. We emphasise this point because it is essential for understanding what a good reader is and what a good reader does.

The definition of a 'good reader' is highly context dependent and is constructed, negotiated and instantiated through interaction. In this sense each reader is always in the process of becoming a reader or learning how to be a reader in different contexts, actively shaping and reshaping their identity and also being positioned as a particular kind of reader by others. Literary scholars refer to these context-dependent, always changing, reader identities as the 'transient nature of identities'. For example, Blommaert (2005: 232) captures the transient nature of identities in commenting that it is:

... not a matter of articulating *one* identity, but of the mobilisation of a whole *repertoire* of identity features converted into complex and subtle moment-to-moment speaking positions.

Children's sense of themselves as readers is also constructed and re-constructed by the literacy activities in which they are required to engage, either at home (e.g. homework), or school (e.g. reading comprehension). While children's wider literacy identities are constructed holistically in all contexts and interactions (see Parry and Taylor, 2018), for the purpose of this book we focus on their reader identities alone, beginning at home.

## Being a Reader at Home

From birth children learn to participate in different environments and relationships and are apprenticed into particular Primary Discourses (Gee, 2011) as we noted earlier. Through their families and the communities in which they live, they have access to different 'funds of knowledge' (Gonzalez et al., 2005) which include information, ways of thinking and learning, and approaches to learning. Children's experience of reading and being a reader in the home, their knowledge and interests about particular areas of life will be shaped by these funds of knowledge and by their parents' interests and occupations, such that one child may be fascinated by texts on fishing, another by ferrets, still others by dinosaurs or donkeys. Diversity will abound as will access to and ownership of books in the home. Indeed, a longitudinal study with 27 countries found that the availability of books at home is as influential on a child's reading attainment as their parents' educational level (Evans et al., 2010). Even as few as 20 books made a difference. In a meta-analysis of such research, Lindsay (2010) also found that access to print materials in the home not only improves children's reading performance but it also encourages children to read more and for longer periods. It follows that issues of book access and book ownership contribute to educational inequalities. This is why a number of literacy organisations and book charities, such as Reach Out and Read in the USA or BookTrust in the UK, actively promote children's book ownership through various campaigns and book-gifting schemes.

Nonetheless, when children come to school with their funds of knowledge or what Thomson (2002) called 'virtual school bags' of personal interests, skills and knowledge, they may not be encouraged to open these and make use of their contents to develop as readers. Much will depend upon the culture of the school and the individual teacher's support. Children's experience of being a reader in home and community contexts will also be influenced by their parents' attitudes to and beliefs about the purposes of reading and how children learn to read. For example, in one study those children whose parents viewed reading as a source of enjoyment were more motivated to read than those whose parents held less positive views (Baker and Scher, 2002). Parents' attitudes influence not only whether and how much children read at home but also the types of books they have access to. Studies with Canadian (Strouse and Ganea, 2017b), British (Kucirkova and Littleton, 2016) and Australian (Nicolas and Paatsch, 2018) parents show that they strongly prefer print books as opposed to digital books. Collectively, these studies show that parents perceive digital books as unsuitable for bedtime reading routines and they purposefully choose print and not digital books when selecting books for home libraries and their children's reading at home.

Research also indicates there is marked heterogeneity amongst parents and that within different ethnic and class groups they may have very different perceptions of the nature of reading and use it differently in their own lives. Many parents encourage positive dispositions towards a wide range of texts, including comics, poetry or short novels, and support their children in reading at home and outside school (Gregory and Williams, 2000). But while many parents understand the importance of diverse contents of children's reading, they are less aware of the importance of diverse formats of children's reading. Yet, as we noted in the introductory chapter, digital books add an important dimension to children's contemporary reading experiences. They introduce children to new authors, motivate reluctant readers to read and can be especially helpful to readers struggling with language or literacy.

Social interactions with grandparents and siblings also play a key role in children developing the habit of recreational reading and their sense of self as readers (Gregory, 2001; Knoester and Plikuhn, 2016). Whilst reading in various forms and for multiple purposes is a feature in many families' practices and routines (Levy et al., 2018), the nature of children's home reading experiences is often unknown to teachers, and may be viewed less than positively due to the persistence of deficit discourses about certain homes and parents' perceived skills and attitudes to reading. In addition, government policies tend to homogenise class, race and gender differences and many practitioners' attempts at involving parents in reading are 'school-centric' in nature. Many literacy scholars view such interactions as requiring families to support reading as conceived and practised in school, rather than teachers learning about and building on the children's and their families' home reading practices (see, for example, Cremin et al., 2015; Williams, 2009).

In order to foster more positive reader identities in the young generation, we argue for developing new understandings about the shared social space that exists between children's, parents' and teachers' reading lives. As depicted in Figure 7.1, such a shared space recognises diversity and areas of commonality in children's, parents' and teachers' reading lives and practices. In an optimal shared space, more equivalent reading relationships between home and school can be developed, potentially enabling children to bridge more effectively between their Primary (home) Discourse and school-based Secondary Discourses.

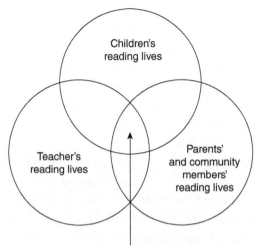

This shared social space needs expansion
to support young readers
in the 21st century

**Figure 7.1**   A model for the development of shared reading lives: Diversity and collaboration (Cremin et al., 2014: 159)

## Being a Reader at School

As children engage in reading in school, they interact with others in response to the literacy practices offered to them. This dynamic process of identity construction and enactment is also influenced by their own and their teachers' conceptions of reading and being a reader. Several of the studies that document this process reveal the complexities of interactions involved, particularly for less assured readers. In the next section, we present some of the conclusions reached by researchers studying these complexities.

### Being positioned or positioning oneself as a less than assured reader

The well-documented association between reading motivation, frequency and volume and higher reading attainment is often described as the Matthew effect (Stanovich, 1986) and has consequences for children's experiences and positions as readers in school. Those children viewed as 'good' readers are more likely to read recreationally outside school, be placed in higher 'ability' sets at school (Fletcher et al., 2012) and be offered more opportunities to engage personally, aesthetically and critically with literary texts than the less assured readers. Conversely, those perceived as 'poor' readers typically come from poorer socio-economic backgrounds, are often placed in lower 'ability' sets and offered more opportunities to practise discrete reading skills from simple texts (Allen, 2015; Westbrook et al., 2018). Studies suggest that lower achieving teenagers report continual reductions in their desire to read and a lowering of their self-concept as readers (Vaknin-Nusbaum et al., 2018). If teachers are supported to change the practice and expectations of less assured readers, they can address the Matthew effect. For example, teachers can offer less assured readers richly engaging and challenging whole texts that motivate their desire to comprehend (Westbrook et al., 2018). Such texts may entice them to read more, influencing the frequency with which they engage in volitional reading.

Other studies affirm that teachers' conceptions of reading and specific readers may result in reduced opportunities and impoverished reading experiences, particularly for those readers who struggle (e.g. Hall, 2010; Hempel-Jorgensen and Cremin, forthcoming; Hempel-Jorgensen et al., 2018). In Hall's (2010) study with US teachers, the teachers repeatedly made it clear to their classes that good readers were those who applied specific comprehension strategies, who read ('practised at home') and asked questions about texts. The teachers' views of reading influenced the types of reading tasks and instruction they offered, and the children, acutely aware of these models of identity, mainly sought to work towards becoming 'good' readers. As a consequence, those who perceived they were 'bad' or 'poor' readers interacted in particular ways in order to avoid their peers identifying them as struggling readers. For example, they held back from participating in discussions or reading aloud, and kept their heads down, despite not understanding the texts. Hall (2010) shows that the young people engaged in behaviours that they knew would prevent them from improving as readers; they were obliged to maintain their struggling reader status.

In a not dissimilar manner, our UK-based study also revealed that teachers' conceptions of reading as proficiency and their categorisation of children as 'good', 'struggling' or 'below/above standard' readers had consequences for the kinds of instruction and support they offered individuals (Hempel-Jorgensen et al., 2018). In this research, despite the teachers' awareness of the potential of RfP, this was side-lined in practice and narrow schooled definitions of reading were embraced by all but one of the practitioners. Limited characterisations of reading linked to assessment discourses and the national 'reading domains' (DfE, 2014) held sway; the teachers stressed comprehension as well as phonic knowledge, fluency, decoding and punctuation. Struggling readers were seen by both teachers and children in this study as those who received low reading scores in tests and who lacked the skills to achieve a technically 'correct performance' in relation to the characteristics. As we discussed in Chapter 5, the teachers' resultant pedagogy was highly performative (Bernstein, 2000); the assessment agenda drove practice and activities such as reading aloud, and independent reading time were appropriated to the service of the reading as proficiency agenda. Children's volition and social interaction around texts was not encouraged, so once again struggling readers were obliged to remain so. They were caught in a hermetically sealed circle of impoverished practice (Hempel-Jorgensen et al., 2018).

In both these studies there was no sense of teachers questioning the identity models of readers that they held. These were, we argue, underpinned by an autonomous model of literacy (Street, 1984, 2008) which fails to recognise that the 'ways in which people address reading and writing are themselves rooted in conceptions of knowledge, identity, being' (Street, 2008: 7). In both studies, narrow ways of describing readers were deployed by children and teachers in a manner akin to labelling. Children in the UK-based study described good readers as those who read 'nicely', answer questions and are on a 'high book bands' (Hempel-Jorgensen et al., 2018). Limited definitions of readers and reader identities were made particularly visible through the practice of ability grouping, with the top reading group in one classroom named after Charles Dickens, and the bottom Roald Dahl. Children in different 'ability' groups experienced significantly different reading opportunities, with the less assured, mainly the boys, being offered a more impoverished reading diet. These studies demonstrate the indispensable role that teachers play in forming and re-forming children's reader identities in the school context – and beyond.

## Gendered reading identities

There is a significant gender gap in reading performance, with girls consistently outperforming boys in many countries (e.g. McGrane et al., 2017; OECD, 2017a, 2017b, 2018). Some scholars argue that the nature of masculine gender identities mitigate against boys engaging as readers, since reading may not be seen to support positive performances of dominant masculine gender identities (McGeown et al., 2012b; Smith et al., 2012). Others posit that boys may have different reading interests to girls and that these are not considered in school in part due to the predominantly female workforce and feminisation (DfE, 2012; Repaskey et al., 2017). Whilst these arguments are worth our consideration, they not only fail to recognise the role of teachers and schools in producing gendered reader identities through classroom interaction and the reading practices and positions offered, but also, as Moss (2011) argues, fail to acknowledge that reader identities are shaped by wider gender discourses at play in the reading curriculum. It is from this more nuanced perspective that we consider gendered reader identities in this chapter.

In an ethnographic study which documented classroom practice, Moss's (2007) work showed that boys respond differently to the reader positions made available at school in comparison with girls. The boys were influenced by school practices framed by accountability measures and in order to avoid being labelled by the hierarchically organised fiction book boxes, they chose to read non-fiction books. The non-fiction books, unlike the fiction texts, were not banded according to the level of skill required to read them. The girls in choosing to read fiction, placed themselves on the school journey to become 'free' readers. Such readers could choose their own books unconstrained by any colour-coded selection. By selecting non-fiction, the boys resisted being visibly labelled as particular kinds of readers – more or less able – and were still able to engage. The study highlights the complex difficulties that arise from classroom contexts that categorise readers. The implications for individual children's perceptions of themselves as readers of a certain category have long-term, sometimes life-long implications. Teachers need to work to ensure that any ascribed reading levels and categories are perceived as guideposts, not as an end in themselves.

Underscoring this point, in a case study of reluctant boy readers from USA, Sarroub and Pernicek (2016) found that low achievements in earlier schooling had led to their negative attitudes and low self-perceptions. This was compounded by the boys' high-school reading lacking any personal purpose for them; they experienced low level, low interest texts and scant opportunities to participate in meaningful text discussions. The researchers argue that this narrowing of their curriculum, and the gap between the boys' self-selected reading materials and those prescribed for them, ensured that the boys disliked reading. They view this as a form of unintended 'readicide' (Gallagher, 2009).

In analysing the experiences and subjectivities of disengaged boy readers, we found that the discourses of gender and reading 'ability' were particularly strongly intertwined in two schools (Hempel-Jorgensen and Cremin, forthcoming). The teachers held binary ideas about gender; they believed boys were fundamentally less able readers than girls. As one noted, the 'girls in my class do read, they never let me down with reading' but 'boys are hard to engage [with reading]'. Although in both classrooms some girls were positioned as 'struggling' readers, they were in much smaller numbers than boys. Additionally, the teachers perceived that desirable reading behaviours, such as choosing reading in 'filler' time and getting parental signatures of reading at home were more typically shown by girls. One publicly criticised a boy for 'letting me and our class down' by not having secured regular parental signatures and noted that 'he was letting himself down too of course, but I don't think he cares about that, he doesn't like reading, so he doesn't do it or press his mum. He's a real challenge'. This perception aligns with Jones and Myhill's (2004) work: they found that teachers held highly gendered perceptions of girls as more compliant than 'troublesome' boys in responding to their requirements.

In addition, our analysis revealed that teachers' perceptions of boys' intersecting gender, social class and ethnic identities can have a negative effect on the reader subjectivities that are made available in schools, particularly when these combine with discourses of 'reading ability' (Hempel-Jorgensen and Cremin, forthcoming). In one school for instance, boy readers were almost compelled by their teacher and peers into taking up particular subjectivities, such as 'struggling' working-class boy readers of colour. This had negative consequences for their engagement in reading both at home and at school. As we noted at the opening of this chapter, identity construction is an ongoing, lifelong process that is relational and situational in shared reading spaces. Yet, out study noted the limited and limiting nature of the reader identities and subjectivities in the schools. Our work shows that there is real cause for concern. It indicates that:

 reader subjectivities which are formed in teacher discourses connect with wider institutional, policy and dominant social discourses and are then instantiated within pedagogical practices when boys, their peers and the teacher negotiate the subjectivities which different children can take up. (Hempel-Jorgensen and Cremin, forthcoming)

This had negative consequences for the boys' engagement in reading.

It is important therefore for teachers to reflect upon the ways in which they view different children and the discourses they use to make judgments about them, considering in particular how these influence their classroom practice. Developing wider recognition of the prevalence of reading 'ability' discourse, so often enshrined in national curricula, is also important. Such considerations could help teachers challenge any gendered or other discourses and practices which disadvantage particular children as readers.

## Being positioned or positioning oneself as an assured reader

A key focus of educational research is on documenting and responding to challenges both individual and systemic (see Chapter 8 for details), so there are fewer studies of the identities and practices of assured than non-assured readers. We highlight three that can serve as inspirational examples for other classroom contexts.

In examining the pleasure in free reading experienced by Australian adolescents who self-identified as engaged and assured readers, Wilhelm (2016) found that their reading materials varied, but significantly, they included genres that are typically pushed to the margins in school, for instance vampire, horror, fantasy, dystopia and romance. Thus, their free choice reading was 'unofficial' in nature, often linked to popular culture and unlikely to be perceived as appropriate literature in school. Yet, the young people derived considerable enjoyment from such texts and positioned themselves in school as keen readers. Five kinds of pleasure were identified: the immersive pleasure of play, intellectual pleasure, social pleasure, the pleasure of functional work, and the pleasure of inner work (Wilhelm, 2016). It was noted however, that only intellectual pleasure was nurtured in school through studying texts. In addition, the young people distinguished between school reading, where correct answers were required, and 'real reading' that they saw as meaningful and engaging to them and connected to all five kinds of pleasure. These pleasures sustained and supported these assured readers, creating what Britton (1977) aptly described as a 'legacy of past satisfactions'. It is these satisfactions that underpin positive reader identities and motivate young people to read more frequently, and in the process build up their reading stamina, volume and comprehension, prompting increased interaction with other readers.

In examining the personal reading histories of experienced and able adolescent readers in the UK, Cliff-Hodges (2016a, 2018) found that parents and grandparents were seen as highly influential on the students' younger reading selves, 'since they were keen readers' as one student typically expressed it (2018: 68) and read aloud to them, often offering repeated readings. These appeared to have helped build familial bonds and reading routines which supported the development of positive reader identities in childhood. In addition, she notes the role of series fiction in helping them develop the habit of reading and the potency of comics and magazines in many of the young people's current and past lives as readers despite the reality that this was rarely viewed as official or acceptable literature in school. Whilst they sustained this early self-identification as readers into their teenage years, no two readers journeys were the same:

> There is no point – from spatial and historical perspectives – either in making simple judgments about any individual reader on the basis of what they appear to be doing or be able to do at any single moment in time or in drawing equally simplistic conclusions about their potential. (Cliff-Hodges, 2016a: 68)

This highlights again the need to sustain support for readers' identities, even those who position themselves as assured and able. In another of our studies, this time of extracurricular reading groups, we found young people positioning themselves and being positioned firmly as keen readers (Cremin and Swann, 2016, 2017). The groups met after school or in lunchtimes to read and discuss texts that had been shortlisted for the Carnegie and Kate Greenaway medals. Frequently in mixed-age (10–16 years) and gender groups, the young people commonly chose to attend, and whilst they did not all initially see themselves as able readers, over the 3 months of the award shadowing they came to position themselves more clearly as both competent and eager. We sought to understand the particular reader identity positions adopted by and made available to the students and to the adults involved (librarians and teachers). Group leaders highlighted extracurricular reading as pleasurable and social, and contrasted it with the dominant perception of reading in school as something for 'geeks' or 'boffins'. Such a conception of readers has also been found in a large scale survey by Clark et al. (2008: 17) as they noted that a third of the upper primary/lower secondary students saw readers as 'boring, geeks' or 'nerds'. In our case study of extracurricular reading groups, one teacher noted:

I would say there is quite a lot of negativity towards reading, and if you are a reader that you are a bit of a 'boffin' – that term 'boffin' comes up quite a lot. (Cremin and Swann, 2017: 17)

It goes without saying that such a view is radically at odds with the satisfactions experienced by the engaged and assured readers studied by Wilhelm (2016). The reading group members in our study though, whilst aware that they were labelled for attending, disregarded others' negative reactions to their interest in reading (Cremin and Swann, 2017). They took time on occasions to discuss this and laughed together about their 'minority' status as keen readers in their schools. In one group, following a 13 year old's observation that 'We're all boffins together in here', laughter ensued, and a chant began of 'Boffins us – Boffins now – Yes!' It appeared that the strong relatively non-hierarchical relationships within these small reading communities, and the non-assessed text discussions which involved both adults and students, supported and consolidated their positive reader identities.

## Reading Teachers

As we explained earlier, the identities teachers enact, consciously and unconsciously, will vary in response to context, the presence of others and in relation to their teaching and learning intentions. When teachers construct their reader identities in the classroom, they do so in relation to others – namely in relation to children, other teachers, head teachers, teaching assistants, volunteer helpers and parents, for example. How teachers both perceive themselves and are perceived by others, including children, as readers is important. Their readerly engagement enables them to model the value and satisfaction of being a reader in their lives and induct children into the pleasures and thinking involved. Some will position themselves as reading teachers – teachers who read and readers who teach – in the words of Commeyras et al. (2003: 3). However, our research shows that this identity position encompasses far more than simply being a reader outside school and teaching reading in school (Cremin et al., 2014). The complex layered identity of a Reading Teacher (which we denote with a capital R, capital T), is more appropriately ascribed to those professionals who not only read, but who continuously reflect upon their own reading journeys, preferences, practices and experiences as readers *and* who consider the consequences for classroom practice (Cremin, 2019a). To support the development of young people's identities as readers, it is arguably advantageous if practitioners adopt this more personal readerly stance.

Nonetheless, international research suggests that student teachers may not be keen readers themselves, as shown for example in the US (Nathanson et al., 2008; Sulentic-Dowell et al., 2016), in Canada (Benevides and Peterson, 2010), in Scotland (Farrar, 2019) and in Singapore (Garces-Bacsal et al., 2018). In this last study, only 27% of the 146 student teachers who participated in the survey, reported reading primarily for pleasure, and perhaps more worryingly, they perceived that their lack of interest, motivation and desire to read had no relevance for their roles as teachers. They saw themselves as disciplinary experts (needing knowledge of decoding and comprehension), not literary experts (with rich repertoires of children's texts) or readers (Garces-Bacsal et al., 2018). Furthermore,

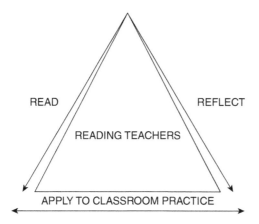

**Figure 7.2**  A schematic representation of Reading Teachers, as defined by Cremin, 2019a

they took no responsibility for fostering readers for life, marking it 'not applicable' on the survey. As other studies have shown, pre-service teachers' literacy histories impact upon their repertoires, and if in school or university they viewed reading as simply a tool to achieve higher grades, this is likely to limit their practice (McPhee and Sanden, 2016).

Studies with teachers in England have shown that whilst teachers do see themselves as readers in their own lives, and read regularly (Cremin et al., 2008a), they have limited knowledge of children's texts (as we discussed in Chapter 5) and they draw heavily, as their American peers do also, on a narrow range of classics, 'celebrity' authors and childhood favourites (Akins et al., 2018; Clark and Teravainen, 2015; Cremin et al., 2008b). This creates difficulties in relation to fostering positive reader identities in the young. There is limited time for teachers to read so they may turn to digital library systems for support. Such systems have very considerable potential, but in relation to our discussion of identities, we argue that they tend to position teachers as 'librarians, curators and monitors' (Kucirkova and Cremin, 2017), as discussed in detail in Chapter 6.

Reader-to-reader sharing was frequently observed in our study of extracurricular reading where librarians and teachers referred to being 'on a level' with young people (Cremin and Swann, 2016, 2017). English teachers often juxtaposed this with the identity positions they enacted in class. For example, one teacher shared with us the conflicting identity experienced in this process:

> I come [to the extracurricular group] in part because in this group I can be a reader – you know one of the group, whereas in class I have to be the leader and the teacher. Here it's different, I can be me.
>
> It's vastly different and I enjoy this so much more because with Carnegie they tell me about the book, rather than me asking questions, and sometimes I've not read it and even if I have, it's different and we're more equal. (Cremin and Swann, 2016: 287)

The opportunity to discuss texts with young people as co-readers in informal and convivial spaces appeared to reduce the more traditional and hierarchical relationships observed in the English classrooms in this research and enabled teachers to participate more fully, perhaps less as interrogators of children's comprehension and more as joint meaning makers and explorers. Some of the young people also noted that in these groups their teachers were 'different', 'more relaxed'. One observed:

> She treats us ... like friends, like, someone that we can talk to, we can talk about the books and have our own opinion whereas like in drama if say, we say something like, we didn't like what we are doing, we would be made to do it anyway. (Cremin and Swann, 2016: 287)

However, some teachers felt their English teacher identity with its associated focus on tasks, objectives and assessment created tensions, preventing them from engaging as readers in the group. For these practitioners, the identity positions of English teacher and group member were hard to reconcile. In the Teachers as Readers (TaRs) study (Cremin et al., 2014) it was the same: some teachers voiced concerns that reflecting on and sharing their own identities as readers might not result in raised reading standards which they saw as the long-term goal. Others voiced discomfort in positioning themselves as fellow readers, commenting:

> How far should we/could we allow our personal lives into the classroom? (Teacher, Barking and Dagenham)
>
> Surely as a professional I shouldn't be talking about my reading life, I need to focus on the children (Teacher, Kent). (Cremin et al., 2014: 71)

At the close of the TaRs study, a diversity of practice existed with some teachers adopting a more positive disposition towards reading in their classrooms, whilst others became more fully fledged Reading Teachers: reflective practitioners who sought to understand more about reading and being a reader in order to support their children's developing identities as readers (Cremin et al., 2014). In recent years we have worked alongside members of the profession exploring their experiences as Reading Teachers and the consequences for young readers (e.g. Cremin et al., 2018b, 2019, 2020). In the process we have come to conceptualise a Reading Teacher continuum (see Figure 7.3).

| Teachers who read and offer a positive disposition as a reading role model. | Teachers who read, offer a positive disposition and reflect upon and share their reading lives and practices as a reading role model. They get to know the children as readers and their practices beyond the classroom. | Teachers who read, offer a positive disposition and reflect upon and share their reading lives and practices as reading role models. They get to know the children as readers and their practices beyond the classroom. They explore the possible pedagogical consequences of their understanding of reading in order to support children as lifelong readers. |

**Figure 7.3**   A Reading Teacher continuum

The continuum indicates that some teachers who read and find some pleasure in the process share their positive dispositions in school as reading role models. They may, if they read children's texts, also be able to make informed recommendations, but without moving towards the mid-point on the continuum, and learning about the children's practices and preferences as readers, such teachers will not be able to tailor their text recommendations sufficiently to support younger readers. The midpoint on the continuum highlights the significance of teachers reflecting on their reading lives in order to recognise diversity and uniqueness and inviting children to do likewise. The far right of the continuum reflects the position of a more fully developed Reading Teacher, who is not only a positive reading role model, but who reflects upon their own and the children's reading lives and identities and the factors which influence these. Purposively, such Reading Teachers also consider possible pedagogical changes based on any new understandings. It should be noted that teachers will find their positions shift and oscillate according to their intentions. At times they may adopt more conforming identities as reading instructors yet still demonstrate they are positive reading role models, and at others they may enact more liberating identities as Reading Teachers – as sophisticated and reflective adult readers and pedagogues.

Significantly, those teachers who developed most fully as Reading Teachers in the TaRs research made a more marked and more positive impact upon children as readers (Cremin, 2010; Cremin et al., 2014). In particular they influenced the children's attitudes to and frequency of reading at home and school and increased the young people's knowledge of authors. They also positively shaped the children's perceptions of their teachers as readers. In particular, children in the classes of teachers who purposively enacted the position of Reading Teacher were able to offer considerable detail about their teachers' practices and preferences as readers. These children also had stronger reader-to-reader relationships with both their teacher and their peers than those in classrooms where teachers tended simply to share an enthusiasm for reading. Through considering their own reading lives and practices, many of the TaRs practitioners and those involved in classroom studies more recently, have transformed their understanding of the nature of reading, as demonstrated by a number of our studies and collaborations since 2014 (Cremin et al., 2014; Cremin, 2018b, 2019a, 2019b, 2020). Through sharing their reading lives and reflecting upon their own reading practices and preferences, teachers have come to widen their conceptions of what it means to be a reader in the twenty-first century and considered the potential consequences for practice. Many now take a broader, more social view of reading and being a reader, and through their own extensive engagement as readers, help build reciprocal and interactive communities of readers of which they, as Reading Teachers, are fully signed-up members.

Primary children are attentive to their teachers' attitudes and reading behaviours as an Australian study has also shown (Merga, 2016). In this survey, children reported that some teachers talked about books and shared recommendations and/or read aloud to the class with enjoyment, emotional engagement and expression, and that some teachers always had reading materials to hand. Both practices were associated with a desire to read in the classroom. Such overt modelling is advantageous to young readers, though, unlike the TaRs research, Merga (2016) did not track the consequences for children as readers or their reader-to-reader relationships. Mindful of the complexity of the reading experience and seeking to avoid any sense of conformity or imitation (a 'do as I do' mindset), Reading Teachers recognise and welcome diversity and difference in readers, young and old (Cremin, 2019a, 2019b). Nonetheless, challenges remain for those practitioners who wish to teach from a reader's point of view, especially in accountability contexts where reader relationships are pushed into the side-lines and the standards agenda persists in the spotlight. In such cultures of performativity, readers' identities are rarely known to teachers.

# Exploring Readers' Practices and Identities

In schools of high-stakes testing and a culture of performativity, teachers tend to lack in-depth knowledge of the children they teach – of their individual lives, interests, funds of knowledge and ways of learning outside school (Comber, 2012; Cremin et al., 2015; Hall, 2010; Mottram and Hall, 2009). This lack of knowledge of children's social and cultural capital seriously constrains the professional capacity to foster learning and support reader development and may impact upon the positions afforded to young readers. As Mottram and Hall assert:

> The priority was to use standardised forms of assessment and to identify each child's under-achievement as defined by national norms. The teachers worked extremely hard to understand the children's deficits rather than any assets they might have acquired.
>
> (Mottram and Hall, 2009: 104)

In order to learn more about children as readers, their social and cultural assets, their practices and identities, a number of strategies can be deployed. Exploring reading histories can be of value, with the teacher sharing visuals of their favourite childhood reading and inviting the children to do likewise: considering who was involved, which texts were salient and why, and where they used to read at home or in the community. Adult examples of such histories include works by Spufford (2002), Mackey (2016) and Mangan (2018), each of which demonstrate in myriad fascinating ways the shaping influence of early texts and contexts, of fictional characters as well as family members on our reading lives. They also highlight the embodied experience of reading and being a reader. Children too find considerable pleasure in revisiting their early reading and exploring boxes of books from younger classes. Such experiences can trigger informal book discussions, remind them of well-loved authors and texts, re-make connections and help them identify as readers.

## Practical strategies

Undertaking a 24-hour read in which everything that is read over this period is documented as a collage frequently demonstrates diversity and difference, as well as areas of commonality across the classroom and the generations. Contrasting what is read over 24 hours during term-time and in the holidays can also help teachers observe any differences in their own reading practices. One noted that reading predominantly as a teacher in term time, she tended to tackle short school-focused texts, quickly and for set purposes, whereas in the holidays, she tended to read more leisurely, incidentally, and for her own pleasure (Cremin et al., 2018b). Such explorations have value with children too as we note in Chapter 8.

Creating Reading Rivers (collage creations of one's reading over any agreed period of time, for example, summer holidays, half term, a weekend) can also help to reveal the range of places, spaces and texts encountered. This can trigger a re-consideration of reading not as a book bound activity, tied to school reading schemes or colour-coded books, but as a rich and layered social practice which is every day in nature, diverse in form and feature and linked to the reader's own purposes, interests and life. The original concept of reading rivers was created by Cliff-Hodges (2010b) while working with 12–13-year-old committed readers. The TaRs study used the technique differently, to document everyday reading practices with younger children and their teachers (Cremin et al., 2014). Since then it has been developed further by teachers creating family reading rivers, enabling a sense of collective looking back, discussion and remembering the family's 'books in common' (Biddle, 2018).

Analysis of the information gathered from reading histories, 24 hour reads or reading rivers is key to the effective use of these practical strategies. It is essential to understand the responses and work with children to explore the insights gained, both about individuals and more broadly as we emphasise in Chapter 8 also. Professional conceptions of reading are not only framed by notions of reading as proficiency within the standards agenda, but may also be book bound (Burnett and Merchant, 2018). Researchers have documented teachers' identity crises in response to the changing nature of literacy in this media age (McDougall, 2009). Analysing children's reading practices can help challenge such narrow views. Some of our research has focused on researching children's literacy lives, and involved teachers undertaking Learner Visits to young people's homes. In these visits a degree of 'digital blindness' was in evidence; the teachers neither recognised nor documented the children's engagement in digital texts as part of their literacy (Cremin et al., 2015). Whilst this may have been due to the ubiquitous nature of technology and limited conceptions of reading, it indicates, as Genrrich and Janks (2013) also argue, that there is limited professional recognition of the wide range of children's digital reading, and the breadth of media in which children engage in on a daily basis. This can create an unhelpful divide between home and school reading, between their own desired reading material and that provided by the system.

If as Reading Teachers, practitioners consider their own digital literacy histories and identities, this can foster enhanced awareness of the salience of their own and the children's digital life-worlds and avoid the ambivalence or consternation so often reported regarding societal attitudes to newer forms of reading. To foster reader identities, teachers need to be aware of the fact that many young people prefer to read digitally rather than on paper. In a national survey of 56,905 children and young people aged 9 to 18 in the UK, the National Literacy Trust (Clark and Picton, 2019) found that about a fifth of respondents read non-fiction and magazines exclusively on screens. To support diverse reading preferences, it is therefore important that teachers offer diverse reading choices to young people. To do this well, teachers need to know about the various digital reading experiences available to young people. Teachers who are 'playful social teachers', have much to share with colleagues; made explicit, their digital literacy stories enable them to draw on their own 'funds of knowledge' about digital worlds (Gonzalez et al., 2005: ix). Shared with others, these experiences might well help develop understandings about the digital worlds of their pupils (Graham, 2008: 17).

Other practices such as inviting children to draw themselves as readers or send postcards to their teacher or parents about their current reading, offer additional routes for children to reflect upon their identities as readers. Reading journals (notebooks to reflect on the text at times to suit and in response to self-chosen passages or information) can also help readers consider not just what they are reading, but their response to it. Some of these ideas are revisited in Chapter 8 where we examine their potential as tools to document children's emerging identities as readers. When young readers select texts with little understanding about how or why they made particular choices, seizing a book almost at random to fill the allocated time in school, they will be unlikely to follow through and less willing to negotiate the unknown as the text unfolds. But supported by a well-informed Reading Teacher and aware of their own (and their friends') reading preferences, favourite authors and poets for instance, they will be better able to make more discerning choices that offer satisfaction. Reading offers the opportunity to explore one's sense of self, as Rothbauer's (2004) work indicates, and we discuss more fully in Chapter 4. Yet, such exploration is only possible if the texts the children encounter reflect their own life realities.

By and large, however, there is little text diversity in terms of content that represents a wide range of story characters. In England for instance, of the 9115 UK children's books published in 2017, only 4% featured BAME characters and only 1% had a BAME main character. In order for children to be able to select reading materials that indicate their preferences and interests and mobilise their identities, teachers need to provide a wide enough range of reading material that allow choice and opportunities to discuss what they read with interested others. In order to foster personal and social reader identities, it is important that children see themselves reflected in the books they read, and this can be supported in part by teachers encouraging children to participate in book creation. Various book-making applications, such as for example Book Creator™, offer the possibility for children to make their own books, with story characters of their own choice.

The time invested in finding out about children as readers and their interests and practices beyond school is time well spent; it not only offers the teacher new knowledge and understanding, but can challenge what counts as reading in school and enable the young to come to know themselves better as readers. Personal knowledge about individual students needs to be developed through conversation and reciprocity; it cannot be circumvented by the substitution of 'routinised' and formulaic lists that overshadow the authenticity of personal relationships. While lists in digital library systems offer practical storage and curation possibilities for personal data, such authenticity can get lost with digital tools that collect data about individual students. For example, the widely popular software program Class Dojo (www.classdojo.com/) is currently used in 180 countries as a tool to document individual students' progress and home-school interests. The software's main benefit resides in classroom management and systematic behaviour tracking, which has been highlighted as practically beneficial to teachers by the software developers. However, at the same time, the emphasis on personal qualities and individual progress could be criticised for surveilling individuals and through this surveillance, modifying their behaviour to suit that envisaged as desirable by the developers – which in the case of Class Dojo is the Silicon Valley's imposition of continuously 'performing your best' (Williamson, 2017). The extent to which the 'knowledge' gathered and propagated through technology-based personal management systems such as Class Dojo is authentic and indeed helpful for fostering reader identities, remains to be demonstrated.

In contrast, when teachers engage in conversation with their students and establish their personal interests through dialogue, they support the children's identification as readers, their confidence and motivation and their awareness of their rights as readers (a point we discussed in Chapter 5). These reflexive strategies are not merely tools to think about reading in accordance with set curricula or teachers' criteria; rather, they seek to enable children to draw on and share their personal cultural practices and interests, and effectively perform their identities as readers of different texts in different contexts. Self-awareness developed through reflexive engagement is supportive of all learners as research into metacognition has shown (Dent and Koenka, 2016). For young children, such awareness can help widen their own views of what counts as reading and enable them to view themselves positively as readers who can and do choose to read for pleasure, for their own personal purposes and for those assigned to them.

## Conclusion

In seeking to foster children's pleasure in reading, teachers need to be attentive to young people's sense of identity as readers, recognising that this is fluid and malleable and will change over time in response to opportunities to engage as readers and interact with other readers within and beyond school. Children's literacy histories, their everyday reading practices and others' perceptions of them as readers, as well as the school-based interactions around reading with peers, friends and adults, influence their attitudes to and understanding of what it might mean to be a reader in particular contexts. In this way their identities and subjectivities as readers are shaped and re-shaped over time.

Adopting an identity lens can help teachers recognise, value and find out about children's previous, current and emerging reader identities. This will widen their understanding of each unique child reader, expanding this beyond knowledge about their particular skills as measured by limited national assessments. Such a lens can also prompt Reading Teachers to engage reflexively, widening their own understanding of the lived experience of reading and being a reader, and changing their professional practice as a consequence. Developing positive reader identities in education is a professional responsibility and a key strand of building reading communities of reciprocity and interaction.

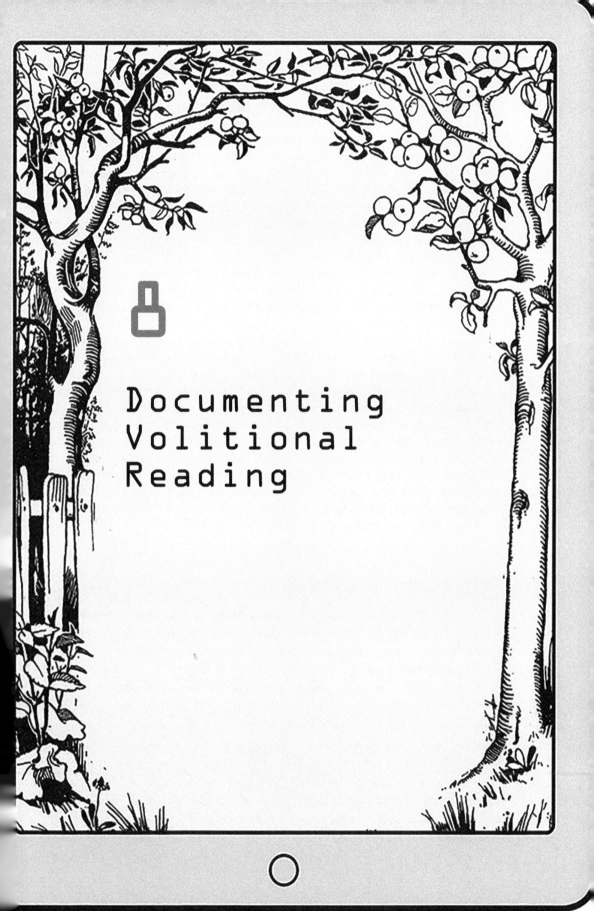

# Documenting
# Volitional
# Reading

E ducational research, a rich area of study, has been an active field since the nineteenth century (Denton, 2019) with scholars engaged in qualitatively and quantitatively oriented projects, some close to practice and some more invested in basic research and 'pure' science. A dual heritage child, educational research has two parents: psychology and sociology (Nisbet, 2008), which has always created tensions between positivist and interpretivist views. While the natural sciences adopt a positivist view and consider objective methods make measurements value-free, human sciences hold an interpretivist view that recognises ambiguity and subjectivity. These two schools of thought employ different methods: experiments, interventions and performance assessments tend to be adopted by reading researchers from the natural sciences, whereas researchers in the humanities tend to observe and/or engage with teachers and children in their natural environments, deploying an ethnographic perspective on reading. There is considerable overlap, however, and mixed methods are also common; it is rarely the case that researchers draw only on one research technique or a single data source to make inferences about children's volitional reading.

We assert the value of both teachers and researchers documenting children's journeys as readers and their reading for pleasure (RfP), but are insistent that this tracking should not be reduced to formal assessments or surveys that seek to quantify changes over time without the use of additional context-sensitive methods. We cannot measure the children's pleasure, but we can seek to map young people's engagement in reading in order both to contribute to knowledge and understanding, and to create responsive curricula that offer them appropriate support. In this chapter initially we focus on methods and methodologies, the principles and procedures followed by researchers engaged in studying RfP. Personally, as we adopt an expansive view of RfP, our research projects have tended to employ mixed methods and interdisciplinary approaches, mostly from a socio-cultural perspective. We also consider the consequences of these approaches for teachers and offer a range of tools and techniques that the profession can employ to document children's volitional reading within and beyond school.

## Educational Research

Educational research can be described as predominantly practice-relevant, policy-integrated scholarship, and is often pragmatically oriented. Since many education researchers are former or current teachers and many scholars work directly with and in schools, educational practice is in the DNA of this 'discipline'. In addition, the application of research findings to practice is high on the agenda of many funding bodies. In high accountability contexts such as those in the US, UK and Australia for instance, there is considerable investment in research that seeks to measure the effectiveness of interventions that focus on raising standards in reading. These studies mainly involve large-scale Randomised Control Trials (RCTs) in order to ensure the replicability of any successful interventions. Whilst as we discuss later, this approach is celebrated by some as a potential means of addressing inequality of opportunity, there are also opposing voices, highlighting that more attention needs to be paid to the classroom context in which programmes are implemented, and expressing concerns about the increased 'datafication' of education (e.g. Hilton, 2006; Koutsouris and Norwich, 2018). The numbers culture does not align well with education researchers who study multiple realities, subjectivities and complexities. These researchers tend to foreground learning situations that are side-lined by the current regime, including RfP, and often challenge the one-size fits all mentality (see Taylor, 2016 for an extended critique). Nonetheless funding constraints influence the research methods chosen, just as teachers' time constraints influence the tools that they use to document children's RfP.

Professional awareness of this wider policy context and the normalisation of numbers as purportedly offering the most salient or valid knowledge is important. Researchers and teachers alike need to ensure that children's reading practices and identities are not reduced to a tick-box exercise. In the current test-driven culture, the choice of research methods and theoretical orientations becomes more than a methodological decision; it becomes a political statement (see Pérez and McCarthy, 2004).

## Theories and Methods

Methods are tools to collect data, while methodologies are understood more broadly, as involving the theoretical underpinnings, data collection, analysis and interpretation employed (Silverman, 2006). Researchers' choice of methods are dictated by their research questions and these are guided by their theoretical framework. By the way of example, a socio-cultural perspective, represented by theorists and philosophers such as Vygotsky (1987) or Dewey (1916), directs attention to the importance of the reading context, which is influenced by the learners and their teachers and which influences the learners and teachers. This implies the use of methods such as observations or group interviews that can take into account the views and behaviours of all social agents and the environment in which they interact. For another example, we can look at the post-humanist perspective, which puts forward the argument that there is no division between human and non-human entities; objects and people are entangled in co-constructing a joint reality (Kuby and Rowsell, 2017). It follows that the documentation and interpretation of the reality of children's RfP necessitates new methods that are suited to the post-humanist focus on new phenomena. For example, exploring the role of sound or touch in reading as an under-researched area of children's literacies (Hackett and Somerville, 2017).

We offer an overview of the four main methods/research techniques that have been used to document and understand RfP in homes and schools: observations, interviews, surveys and experimental methods. Part of our vision for future research on children's reading is to ensure a balanced approach to the physical, social, material and affective aspects of RfP, so we include methods that afford equal attention to these, acknowledging nonetheless that some studies foreground the social (such as the role of teachers), and some the material aspects (such as the effect of a specific book-based intervention). We highlight in particular the use of multiple research tools which can serve, when analysed separately and then combined, to strengthen the validity of the findings.

The choice of a research technique depends on the study's research questions. If researchers are interested in establishing what causes particular children's disinterest in print books for instance, they may choose to investigate possible causal mechanisms or seek to identify possible associations. They may wish to know more about the children's demographic characteristics (e.g. gender, age, socio-economic background) and/or process and context variables such as reading experiences (e.g. the quality of home/school learning environment, teachers' knowledge and influence). Causality can potentially be established through experimental methods, such as the use of an RCT or by studying the development of specific patterns over time in a longitudinal design. In contrast, correlations or associations can potentially be established through observational methods, interviews or survey data, which offer insights into individual variables at the time of the study. The four research techniques that follow – observations, interviews, surveys and experiments – are widely used tools for ascertaining causal and correlational relations in children's RfP.

In addition, in documenting children's volitional reading, teachers and children can be invited to participate as researchers – as co-participant researchers – such that the research is not carried out 'on' or 'about' the teachers or the children but *with* them. Co-research techniques apprentice teachers and children, inviting them to share and negotiate meaning with researchers. These techniques, which include for example video stimulated review and the use of puppets to teach the researcher about RfP, which we examine later, seek to position teachers and children, as co-creators of research, rather than subjects or consumers of it. Many teachers also undertake their own research studies for interest and for further study, often deploying observations to which we now turn.

## Research Techniques

### Observations

Several RfP studies use observation to explore, describe and generate interpretations through studying the dynamics between teachers, parents, children, resources and the wider learning environment. Researchers may position themselves as non-participant observers, seeking to remain silent whilst observing, making notes or recording situations. Or researchers may be participant observers, involved not as teachers, but with teachers and children, engaging with the young people in response to request and in order to understand more fully their behaviours and attitudes. Researchers observe during various reading events, collecting data on occurrences, processes and relationships connected to RfP. For example, Moss and McDonald (2004) documented children's reader networks by observing them in classroom and library contexts and by examining library reading records. Such participant research observations are often undertaken in the spirit of reciprocity as Jorgensen notes.

> Direct involvement in the here and now of people's daily lives provides both a point of reference for the logic and process of participant observational inquiry, and a strategy for gaining access to phenomena that commonly are obscured from the standpoint of a non-participant. (Jorgensen, 2015: 15)

Nonetheless non-participant observation also offers a way to observe and document reading practices. In Chapter 4, we reflected on one of our studies on personalised digital books and children's early interest in reading (Kucirkova, 2019b). In this, the researcher observed children's engagement with the books with the aim of identifying parent–child behaviours that support learning with digital technology. This was a single-case study, suitable for a case that has not been investigated in much detail before such as children's digital personalised books. Case studies examine 'the complex dynamic and unfolding interactions of events, human relationships and other factors in a unique instance' (Cohen et al., 2000: 181). Whilst not generalisable to the wider population, case studies can, if they follow rigorous theoretical propositions and encompass 'thick descriptions' (Geertz, 1973), in effect multi-layered interpretations, offer the potential for application in other contexts. This case study consisted of seven families living in the Greater Manchester and London areas. Four boys and three girls (aged 3-years old) and their seven mothers participated. Our observations took place in the homes of the participating families in the mornings or afternoons, depending on their preference. The number of and length of visits varied from six to two visits per family and from 4.5 hours to 30 minutes, depending on the children's willingness to read the digital books and the mothers' availability. We sought to ensure the observations were as natural as possible, corresponding to the families' usual reading engagement. Interactions were filmed with a handheld camera, positioned such that it captured the sounds, bodies, facial expressions, movement and the interactions happening on the iPad screen. We audio-recorded sessions and took field notes, capturing particular impressions and highlights. Seeking to minimise her influence on the interactions, the researcher positioned herself as a non-participant observer.

   In a not dissimilar manner in our study of dis/engaged boy readers, the research team also positioned themselves as non-participant observers (Hempel-Jorgensen et al., 2018). Four researchers each spent a school week watching, listening and audio-recording interactions in four different classrooms of 9–10 year olds. This multiple case study sought to understand the processes by which reader subjectivities were produced and the pedagogy associated with this. Primary schools from different parts of England were selected according to set criteria relating to: high numbers of Free School Meals (used as a proxy for poverty), ethnic diversity and the schools' professed use of three of the four strands of pedagogical practice known to effectively support RfP (Cremin et al., 2014). Data collection encompassed lesson observations across the curriculum, although only those that focused on literacy were designated as RfP sessions (e.g. independent reading) and were transcribed. In addition, semi-structured interviews with class teachers and the focus group of three children (two boys and a girl who the teacher deemed to be 'struggling') were undertaken, as well as book audits and artefactual analysis of reading-related resources (e.g. home–school reading records, reading scores, book bands, photographs). An observation schedule was employed to ensure consistency across the team. It included strands such as how the lessons were framed (e.g. by learning objectives), seating arrangements, use of 'ability' grouping, differentiation, and teacher talk to the class and individuals. In each class there was a primary focus on boys, observations of whom were prioritised.

## Analysis of observational data

Analytic techniques for observational data are typically determined by the researchers' theoretical lens as well as the nature of the data gathered (e.g. multimedia available for re-watching or in the form of field notes). Planned analysis of observational data involves either deductively examining the predictions of the theory which guided the study, or exploring the key patterns bottom-up in a more data-driven unplanned inductive analysis (Rosenbaum, 2010).

   In some of our research which involved observing children reading print and digital books, we used multimodal analysis to explore how different modes of communication, as well as language are selected and work together during interaction (Kucirkova et al., 2013). Gaze, gesture, body orientation, movement, images, sounds and talk are all integral to meaning-making, and silent modes too express meaning. Multimodal analysis considers how these multiple semiotic resources, or modes of communication, work together to communicate meaning (Kress et al., 2001). In our study, this analytic method allowed us to more fully understand the expressed, as well as the potential, meanings of the participating child. Again, we used a case study approach to study a mother's interaction with her 33-month-old daughter around a digital story that they co-created together on an iPad. The video of their interaction was analysed to identify all the communication modes used and the modes embedded in the digital book (text, pictures, interactivity). Close analysis of these verbal and non-verbal modes enabled us to conclude that personalised digital stories, which are co-produced by the participants and include direct references to them, can contribute to positive reading exchanges. The exchange was characterised by an attunement of multiple modes: shared eye contact, coordinated gestures, frequent smiles and a harmonious conversation (Kucirkova et al., 2013).

Often observation is combined with other research methods, so that the process of analysis involves drawing together multiple insights and patterns across complementary data sources. For instance, in one of our studies of extracurricular group reading (Cremin and Swann, 2017), in order to understand the young people's experience of these groups, we observed their engagement, audio-recorded their interactions and interviewed members (adults and young people). This work involved case studying seven groups across the UK which were selected to ensure as diverse a range as possible along several dimensions: geographical location; a social and cultural mix; the inclusion of boys as well as girls; and a range of abilities. We visited each reading group several times, and also observed and took field notes in the classrooms of some of the teachers who attended the groups. We sought in particular to explore the reader identity positions adopted by and made available to the students (aged 10–16 years old), and to the adults involved (librarians and teachers). In addition, we mapped the physical spaces where the groups took place, we made diagrams and took photographs and collected other evidence (e.g. posters, student book reviews posted to a website).

The technique of combining different types or sources of data to refine and strengthen interpretations is known as 'triangulation' (Ragin and Amoroso, 2011), and it supports the identification of themes and underlying patterns. Through coding the observed and transcribed data inductively, and then grouping these into broader categories or levels of code, we were able to identify major themes. We followed Braun and Clark's (2006) process of thematic analysis, familiarising ourselves with the full set of evidence collected prior to coding. We also involved an independent researcher to cross moderate our perspectives to enhance the potential trustworthiness of our decisions (Lincoln and Guba, 1985).

## Interviews

Interviews which can be structured or semi-structured, are frequently used to explore children's RfP. They allow for unexpected insights contributed by participants, are particularly well-suited for researching personal topics (Gratton and Jones, 2014) and can help researchers find out about young people's, parents' and teachers' attitudes and perceptions of reading. As noted earlier, they are often combined with observational methods.

In the Teachers as Readers (TaRs) study for example, the 43 teachers were invited to identify three 'focus' children in their classes (Cremin et al., 2014), using Moss's (2000) threefold characterisation of readers: readers who *can and do* read freely; readers who *can but don't* read freely, and readers who *can't yet and don't* read freely (2000: 102). The teachers selected three young readers from the second characterisation – those who, whilst able to read and adequately undertake most class reading tasks, were disinterested. They appeared to find little pleasure or satisfaction in the experience, sought to avoid it, and did not choose of their own volition to read over any other available activity in school. As such it was agreed they were not RfP. These children, who were mainly boys and aged between 6–11 years old (most were 10–11 year olds), were interviewed by the research team three times in groups of three across the year of the project and were observed on three separate occasions during reading sessions in their classrooms. In addition, the teachers completed termly observations (on schedules, provided by the research team). To understand the children's perspectives, they were invited to explain how they felt about reading in their own words, were offered the use of smiley, sad and indifferent faces to communicate their views on some questions and also completed a short questionnaire on reading. What surprised the teachers and the researchers was that the data indicated that some of these 'disaffected' readers were engaged in consider-able volitional, free choice reading at home. They described a range of reading materials and activities outside school, yet demonstrated disaffection and disinterest in relation to reading in school. A number of possible reasons for this intriguing insight were explored, including the range of reading material available, the ways in which reading was framed in classrooms and the influence of peers on their reader identity positioning (Cremin et al., 2014: 131).

Younger children, particularly pre-schoolers, are less commonly positioned as inter-viewees and active study informants, although Levy's (2008, 2009) studies indicate this is possible. In the former, a case study of five 3–4 year olds, Levy used games and activities to find out about the children's attitudes towards reading at home and in school. Similarly, in the latter study, age-appropriate research activities were used to gain insights into chil-dren's reading habits directly from the children (Levy, 2009). For example, instead of asking children directly about their reading habits, she asked them about what they liked doing at home and what their favourite toys or TV shows were. Follow-up 'interviews' were conducted with a puppet (called Charlie Chick) who asked them questions such as 'What is reading?'; 'Can you read?' and then the puppet conveyed their responses to the researcher. This reduced the hierarchy between the adult researcher and the child inter-viewees and was supplemented by the use of pictures, photographs (so that the children could point to a picture to express their views non-verbally), and small world play sce-narios (these enabled children to role play their home and school reading experiences) (Levy, 2009).

In the TaRs study, children were invited to 'draw a reader' at the close of the year – this represents another tool for exploring their conceptions (Cremin et al., 2014). The team found many drew multiple readers and when invited to explain their pictures, they connected to the social and relational nature of reading, noting for example: 'We're all readers in here, Miss is too' and 'I couldn't draw one, there isn't just one – there's loads of readers in this class'. These examples show the value of adapting interviews and using additional activities to ascertain young people's perspectives. We explore more of these in a later section on creative approaches.

## Video-stimulated review

Video-stimulated review, a form of interview, is often used to stimulate professional conversations between the teacher and the researcher who observed and filmed their practice. The technique involves the use of selected video clips as prompts for reflection and discussion and although we are not aware of any RfP studies which have employed this method, we have used it in studies concerned with children's possibility thinking and teachers identities as writers (e.g. Cremin and Baker, 2010; Cremin et al., 2006). We believe it could help teachers to consider their RfP pedagogy, enabling closer attention to individual child readers' responses and to their volitional reading. In our previous studies, as part of in-depth interviews, teachers selected critical incidents, key extracts that they considered to be examples of children's engagement in possibility thinking or their own engagement as writers in the classroom. As researchers we acted as co-learners, scrutinising these video extracts with the teachers and reflecting with them on their practice and its consequences. They reported valuing the opportunity to look and listen closely to the children. In this way, video-stimulated review can provide 'the means by which teachers-as-professionals and teachers-as-researchers can reinterpret their professional practice' (Cremin et al., 2006: 120).

In another of our projects, focused on children's storytelling and story acting, we noticed similar patterns: the participating teachers recognised children's abilities and capabilities through the process of re-viewing video extracts and facilitated reflection (Cremin et al., 2017). The teachers commented for example on how, over the course of the class's participation in this narrative-based approach, some of the shyest children became more open about their inner worlds through the stories they shared. The approach, combined with the video-stimulated review, provided the teachers with an opportunity to attend to, record and evaluate the development of children's narratives. It enabled both teachers and researchers to notice details that might have been missed in direct interaction, such as a child's eye-gaze while recounting a story, for instance. The method afforded space for slow thinking and dialogue and as a result, the teachers became aware of the subtle multi-modal nature of interactions around literacy, and the multiple intertextual references on which the children drew, from the world of children's literature, popular culture and their own lives. In this way, by being positioned as co-participant researchers, the teachers were potentially enabled to reinterpret their teaching, a process which Weiser (2018: 7) argues, can 'transform ... the professional self'.

## Analysis of interview data

Interview data are typically analysed as we noted earlier by looking for patterns, using content or thematic analysis to establish the main themes in participants' accounts and move from data description to data interpretation. Both forms of analysis (content and thematic) involve identifying the main 'threads' in the data and then drawing on these to interpret it (Vaismoradi et al., 2013). They differ though in the analytic phase as content analysis has three steps – preparation, organising and reporting – while thematic analysis involves data familiarisation, the generation of codes via several levels of coding, then defining and naming the final themes. Researchers commonly use software packages (e.g. NVivo, Dedoose) to input their interview transcripts as these support the process of coding and analysis.

## Surveys

Surveys and questionnaires are considered by many researchers as a vital tool for cost-effective assessment of children's perceptions and attitudes towards reading. Unlike questionnaires which tend to be smaller scale, surveys allow for more participants and thus can encompass a wider range of perspectives. Surveys require careful piloting to ensure the instrument is able to ascertain information about readers' attitudes, knowledge or beliefs. The highly influential PIRLS and PISA surveys, which we initially discussed in Chapter 2, provide benchmarks of education in a wide range of countries. These assessments have different objectives: PISA focuses on the reading, mathematics and science literacy of 15 year olds to 'determine the "yield" of education systems, or what skills and competencies students have acquired and can apply in these subjects to real-world contexts' (Stephens and Coleman, 2007: 2–3). In 2021, 'creative thinking' is to be added to the suite of PISA tests. In contrast, PIRLS is about the reading and literacy curriculum achievement of 10 year olds in approximately 60–70 countries and nation states every five years. Policy-makers draw on these surveys to evaluate their country's literacy/reading levels and the perceived success or otherwise of their policies or the education system more generally. However, children often have no choice but to participate in these assessments, which is partly why critics of PIRLS and PISA (e.g. Hilton, 2006) have described the surveys as indicative of schools' complicit participation in an examination culture, and why they have questioned the cultural validity of the surveys. In addition, surveys tend to receive very low response rates, unless there is a tangible benefit for the respondents (Jones et al., 2013) or, as in the case of PIRLS and PISA, responses are 'required'.

Nonetheless, researchers pay attention to international trends in such data, for example in Chapter 7 we noted that PISA and PIRLS data continuously report higher reading levels for girls than boys. We discussed how this notion of gendered reader identities can be misrepresented as inherent to gender rather than wider social influences. Researchers also mine these large-scale data sets, as Jerrim and Moss (2019) did with the 2009 PISA data in order to investigate if the frequency with which 15 year olds read different text types is linked to their reading skills. As we noted, in examining the results of 35 OECD countries they found a strong 'fiction effect'. National data gathered through PIRLS are also commonly examined, with McGrane et al. (2017), for instance, finding that children in England who report having more books at home also report much higher levels of enjoyment in reading. Of those with 10 or fewer books in their homes, 42% report that they do not like reading, compared to just 12% of pupils who have more than 200 books in their home. In addition, researchers aggregate data from several countries, for example Park (2008) evaluated the extent to which home literacy environments influence children's reading performance in 25 countries. She found that measures of early literacy activities, parental attitudes toward reading, and the number of books at home, positively affected children's reading performance, but that this association worked in different ways across countries.

International and national surveys can offer useful depth and detail, for example several recent studies found that national, immigrant/native, school and socio-economic contexts make a difference to the association between RfP and reading achievement (e.g. Chema, 2018; Miyamoto et al., 2018). Such survey insights can influence policy-making. Our own TaRs phase I survey, completed by 1200 teachers in 11 local authorities across England (none of whom were English leaders in their schools), explored teachers' personal reading habits and preferences, their knowledge and use of children's literature in the classroom and the extent of their involvement in local area/school library services (Cremin et al., 2008a, 2008b). As previously noted, it highlighted weak subject knowledge of children's literature and in so doing drew policy-makers and practitioners' attention to this issue.

Capturing policy-makers' interest is somewhat easier with a survey when the figures represent cause for concern (e.g. 24% of the teachers could not or did not name a picture fiction creator) or when the survey is conducted year on year and is able to show trends (e.g. the National Literacy Trust reading survey in the UK). It is widely recognised that it is harder to gain policy traction with smaller scale closely observed qualitative studies. In another of our national surveys, we collaborated with the UK charity BookTrust to find out about young children's use of digital media and e-books (Kucirkova and Littleton, 2016). The survey was aimed at parents' perceptions of RfP with print and digital books at home with their children aged between 0 and 8 years. In total, 1511 parents completed the survey online or by telephone. The findings allowed us to understand several issues, including why e-books for young children are unpopular in many families – 92% of surveyed parents had some or many concerns about children's e-books.

## Analysis of survey data

Survey data is typically analysed quantitatively, using descriptive techniques that organise data into tables, graphs or charts and with advanced statistical analyses that allow inferences concerning associations and strength of relationships between one or more variables. Researchers who analyse PIRLS data tend to use progressive statistical methods to establish their country's performance in relation to international averages and the suitability of the scale for national context. For example, Cheung et al. (2016) analysed the PIRLS data of Chinese children to estimate its suitability for the Chinese context and concluded that the relationship between home-related practices and children's reading achievement is applicable to all Chinese communities, including Hong Kong, Taiwan, Singapore and mainland cities.

## Experimental methods

Classically experimental research methods can be divided into three areas: true experimental, quasi-experimental and single subject experiments. In a 'true' experiment, researchers randomly assign participants to a treatment or control condition and as such, they are able to determine whether there is a causal influence of the treatment condition on the participants or not. Quasi-experimental and single case experiments do not assign participants to the treatment (intervention) and control conditions, but involve stringent experimental methods and are often used to draw causal inferences (Suter, 2011). Nevertheless, it is only with randomisation that researchers can conclude that no pre-existing differences between an intervention and control group exist and that therefore, the effects between a pre- and post-test administered to both groups, can be attributed to the intervention. However, we argue that creating change in educational practice and outcomes is a highly complex process (particularly in relation to volitional reading), and that many initiatives in education do not achieve the changes expected. If an intervention in reading that seeks to foster RfP is unsuccessful, it may be that the causal chain from the reading intervention to improved student outcomes is more indirect, with a range of mediating factors which need to be considered, and more time for teachers to embed new ways of working. If the focus is on teacher professional development for example, one mediating factor may be the extent to which this generates sufficient explicit pedagogical knowledge to be transferred to classrooms in order to alter the experience of young readers.

In health research and in many parts of educational research, the 'gold standard' of experimental designs is an RCT which always involves randomisation. Given its standing in clinical research, RCTs are increasingly favoured in educational policy, and often referred to as the most reliable form of scientific evidence that can remove bias and establish causality (Bulpitt, 2012). However, many scholars argue that RCTs are unfairly prioritised over other types of evidence-based practice (e.g. Hanley et al., 2016). They assert that the medical model of testing the effectiveness of a single drug or treatment method cannot be directly applied to the educational context which includes unique school settings and complex interactions between family and school communities, particularly around reading (e.g. Biesta, 2010). We agree that educational change is not a simple, unidirectional mechanism, and a RCT does not account for the way in which elements of change are highly subject to disruption by a range of contextual factors, including for example pupil characteristics, teacher effectiveness, school assessment regimes, national expectations about reading standards and so forth. As we discussed in Chapters 5 and 7, such factors shape teachers' pedagogy and can serve to limit children's identities as readers (e.g. Cremin, 2020; Hall, 2012).

Despite the controversy surrounding the use of RCTs in educational research, major centres and organisations concerned with effective education, such as the Education Endowment Foundation in England, deploy them to evaluate interventions, including those focused on reading. For example, an RCT was used to determine the value and appropriateness of BookTrust's and Pearson's Booktime Pack for 4–5 year olds in Northern Ireland (Connolly et al., 2012). It aimed to establish the effect of the scheme on children's and parents' reading and literacy habits. Five indices were measured: the frequency of shared reading between parents and children at home; relationships between parents and schools regarding the child's reading; parents' attitudes to reading for themselves; parents' use of their local libraries; and children's use of their local libraries. Thirty schools were randomly assigned to either the intervention group or the control group (15 schools per group) and while the intervention group received the packs, the control group continued as normal, without them. The study found no added value of the intervention on the children's or parents' outcomes that it set out to measure. While there was some enthusiasm noted by the teachers and children receiving the packs, this interest did not in this case translate into the learning benefits investigated by the researchers. This is worth knowing, but it could be that the intervention had an effect on outcomes that were not part of the RCT assessment, or that the approach worked better in some homes/schools than others. As Koutsouris and Norwich (2018: 939) acknowledge:

> a focus on the different ways that programmes work under different circumstances, and when implemented by different people, is a more useful perspective. This might not provide the certainty that policy-makers would likely opt for, but it captures better the complexity associated with teaching programme evaluation.

We perceive, as we have highlighted throughout this chapter, that combining diverse sources of data is helpful, and suggest that RCTs need to be accompanied by robust qualitative data collection. Through combining statistical and qualitative data together, a more nuanced and productive understanding is generated, which in researching children's volitional reading is more appropriate. Arguably, such research is not about generating generalisable data about 'what works' for RfP since 'what works' in some contexts may not in others. Much will depend upon the readers, the context, its history and the practitioners' subject and pedagogical content knowledge. Combined approaches may also lead to the exploration of context-led modifications that might enable increased impact and the identification of future research questions. In addition, combined approaches permit the broader picture and trends regarding RfP and possible associations to be established statistically, whilst at the same time enabling close attention to individual readers and recognition of their difference and diversity.

## Creative Methods and Technologies

The research methods reviewed thus far are commonly deployed to understand more about children's attitudes to reading, their practices, reading motivations, behaviours and shifting identities as readers. Nonetheless, some retooling of current methods and methodologies may be needed to fit the contemporary reality of children's reading off and on screen. A judicious balance between old and new and potentially more creative methods is necessary to broaden and deepen our understanding of children's RfP in diverse contexts and with contemporary digital texts. Therefore, in alignment with theories of reading and the turn towards a 'transdisciplinary model of embodied, textual reading accounting for its psychological, ergonomic, technological, social, cultural and evolutionary aspects' (Mangen and van der Weel, 2016: 116), we suggest that innovative research methods, which take account of children's multi-faceted and subjective engagement with texts, should be considered.

The use of digital apps for instance to measure and evaluate children's behaviour and attitudes is increasing in research (Turner et al., 2015) but it is still not common. Researchers have studied how children use tablet/smartphone apps to expand their literacy (Beschorner and Hutchison, 2013) and their art-making (Harwood, 2017). Falloon (2017) was one of the first researchers to use iPad apps for collecting data about children's activities in the science classroom. We may have been the first research team to use a story-making app for prompting children's reflections and perceptions. The app that we used is called *Our Story* (http://wels.open.ac.uk/our_story). It was developed at The Open University by child psychologists to support young children's engagement with self-made stories. It works on any touch-screen device and is freely available as a public download for smartphones or tablets. With *Our Story*, children can choose to tell their stories with digital pictures (taken with the inbuilt camera or downloaded from a website), and by adding their own texts or audio-recordings. The app thus contains multiple possibilities in that it does not provide pre-established templates or in any other way constrain children's content. It consists of two elements: a gallery of pictures and a storyboard. For each picture in their gallery, children can add text (words, sentences or whole paragraphs) and/ or their own recorded sounds. The storyboard (filmstrip at the bottom of the gallery of pictures) enables children to put their pictures together in a sequence, making up a story with a beginning and an end. The app requires no previous proficiency in picture editing or screen writing; it is intuitive to use and was developed for children and young users. Figure 8.1 shows the app's deliberately child-friendly user-interface.

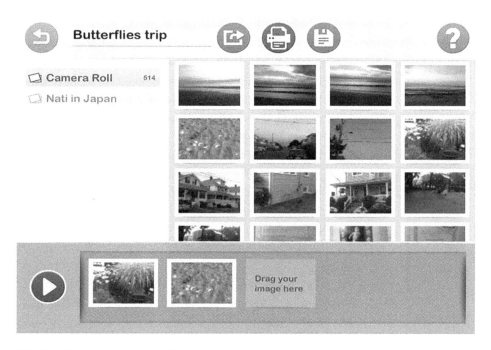

Figure 8.1    *Our Story* app user interface

During our storytelling and story-acting research, we interviewed all the case study children in pairs using the *Our Story* app to prompt their reflections on their experience of this approach (Cremin et al., 2018a). The children were aged between 3–6 years old. The app was pre-loaded with pictures depicting the children, or their peers, acting out their own stories in the classroom. The multimedia options in the app meant that the children could share their stories not only in photographs and text, but also with sounds and voiceovers. Some enjoyed the option of recording animal sounds to accompany the pictures and some took great care to record their story, and engaged in the process of recording, listening back, evaluating, and then recording again. We do not have comparative data with which we could assess children's reflections with and without the app, but we know from literature and previous experience that young children are often reluctant to share their views and feelings with researchers. With the use of *Our Story*, however, the children enthusiastically told us about their stories, recounted a new story, or told us about their classmates' tales, many of which drew intertextually on books known to the children. We consider their eagerness may have been triggered by the app's design with the integration of multimedia helping them create an authentic account of their experiences. Thus far, we know very little about how different technologies might influence the content of children's responses to researchers, but multimedia apps that allow children to reflect and to create multimedia responses represent an interesting new research option.

We do not claim that technology per se can make a difference to the quality of participants' reflections, but that its use might prompt richer reflections, and, in our case, it might have contributed to the children's willingness to share their personal stories. Other researchers have also found that the presence of visual and audio stimulation significantly influences children's engagement in sharing their stories. Research by Caton and Hackett (2019), framed in post-humanist terms, suggests that young children can discern the different ways in which cameras and apps record their stories and behaviours. Given the choice of different recording tools to document their participation in the classroom, the children voiced strong preferences for small cameras that they controlled and carried, instead of head-mounted or researcher-operated cameras. These 'roaming cameras' enhanced their willingness to share their views with the researchers. They used the cameras, as in our story-based work, not only to document their experiences, but to generate new ones, for example, some older children used the cameras to film their own vlogs, thus contributing extra data to the project.

The use of technologies to prompt children's responses can serve to disrupt a narrow focus on children's reading proficiency, as it repositions them as agentic and offers greater space for their voices. However, sophisticated technologies are not needed; for example, in the Teachers as Readers study, children in some classes were invited to capture their own and their families' reading practices with the use of the schools' digi-blue cameras (Cremin et al., 2014). Teachers and teaching assistants also took photographs in their own homes and shared these with the children. The resultant montages initially appeared to reflect considerable textual diversity, but when they were analysed by the teachers for recurring patterns, it was clear that print books were dominant and fiction books prevailed. Some children even staged photographs of pets 'reading' appropriate fiction (e.g. a dog bent over a copy of *Hairy MacClary from Donaldson's Dairy* by Lynley Dodd). In their photographs, teachers and children were arguably enacting or performing their identities as readers, what they perceived to be the desired identity – one of a keen fiction reader. At the close of the year-long project, some classes repeated this activity. The teachers were interested to discern a wider vision of texts: non-fiction, newspapers, poetry, magazines, comics, iPads showing Internet sites and other media were included. Placing this information alongside the teachers' observations, and evidence from the research team (in the form of surveys, observations and interviews), we argued that these children and their teachers were developing a broader view of what 'counts as reading' at home and in school (Cremin et al., 2014).

In another case study, Cliff-Hodges (2010b) invited keen adolescent readers to interview their parents or grandparents about their reading, offering them agency and a role as co-researchers in the process. In addition, she conducted her own interviews and activities with the young people and prompted them to create 'reading rivers' – critical incident collages which connected strongly to notions of space, time and history, and represented an innovative research method that enabled the young people to reflect on their journeys as habitual readers. Their reading rivers 'chartered formative events in their personal reading histories' (Cliff-Hodges, 2016b: 56) and were later used as the basis of interviews. They served to open up the students' development as readers seen through their own eyes. Their collages showed traces of social relationships and cultural practices related to reading, which were developed differently in and by their families over time. In our own research with primary-aged learners, we built on this idea and children created reading rivers to reflect their everyday reading lives and practices (Cremin et al., 2014) (see Chapter 7). This approach helped the young people (and their teachers) recognise diversity in texts, modes and media.

While traditional methods such as surveys and interviews can inform practitioners about children's reported attitudes to reading and the satisfactions they derive from it, creative collaborative methods can offer another lens on children's volitional reading, potentially revealing more of its affective, social and relational nature. We thus encourage researchers to integrate traditional methods with other methods which involve and engage the young, and include technologies in their data collection toolkits. Teachers too can be creative as they seek to document children's RfP.

## Documenting RfP Within and Beyond School

Historically, teachers have always been expected to track children's progress as readers, and focus in particular on their phonic knowledge, their decoding and comprehension skills, and vocabulary. Documenting children's reading habits, their emerging and sustained interests in different genres or the work of particular authors and their desire to read, however, has been afforded far less attention. Yet, practitioners have a professional responsibility to understand and to support the development of positive attitudes to reading and reading behaviours and want to nurture children's confidence and motivation as readers. In order to document the subtle shifts in children's attitudes and identities as readers over time and to track their reading habits, teachers will want to employ a number of tools. These should enable them to get to know the children as readers, their preferences and practices in order to tailor their support. Developing a broad picture of a class as readers, and a closer more in-depth knowledge of the unique individuals which comprise this potential reading community, is vital. Their views need to be sought, heard and attended to, since as Scherer (2016: 172) observes, in neo-liberal cultures we need to 'make visible the silent power that policy exerts on children', through targets, ability groups for reading and other forms of reading hierarchies. Children's RfP is too often constrained.

Gathering a sense of children's attitudes and behaviours at the start of the year is useful for formative purposes, enabling targeted development to ensue in response to the particular needs or challenges identified. This also ensures children's voices and views about different dimensions of RfP practice are heard and acted upon. For example, if independent reading time is being refined and developed, a discussion or written survey of children's views, alongside observation and brief notes of their engagement before, during and after any changes are put in place, is invaluable. Involving the young people in the changed pedagogic practice is also key, ensuring that this is learner-led, informal, social and with texts that tempt, in alignment with a RfP pedagogy LIST as we discussed in Chapter 5. Documenting children's views in several ways, pre and post any changes, enable new pedagogic practices directed at supporting children's RfP to be evaluated and reshaped in response to the information gathered. Teaching staff, school leaders and parents' perspectives may also be valuable depending on the focus of development. It is not enough to introduce new RfP activities in the hope that these will impact on children's engagement and pleasure; as professionals teachers need to know and adjust their practice accordingly. It can be productive to track the impact on a few children at a time, perhaps prioritising those who are disinterested or disaffected yet able to read, the 'can but don't readers' as Moss (2000) describes this group.

Many of the methods detailed already and used in externally funded research projects are more than possible to adapt and use in school. Informal observations are key – these might be of children browsing and choosing texts, and of their behaviour during reading aloud, reading time, or book talk activities. Equally observing children in the cloakroom before school and at break or in the library can be revealing, availing opportunities to note their informal reader networks or the absence of these. Paying close attention to their interactions around texts and reader relationships can inform professional judgments and identify possible ways to nurture their pleasure in reading. Making incidental notes (akin to field notes) of reading behaviours, views offered, or surprising engagement observed for instance can help to build a more rounded picture of particular child readers. Their dispositions towards reading will be reflected in their reading behaviours, so through observation teachers can see how particular children enact their identities as readers in school. This may be shown for example in their inability to settle during reading time, constant book swapping, making informal recommendations to friends, inside-text talk and bringing in texts from home. In one of our projects, teachers found undertaking Learner Visits to children's homes to understand more about their everyday literacy lives very revealing and these influenced their subsequent practice in school (Cremin et al., 2015).

Taking time to listen to children's views in informal conversational contexts (rather than interviews) is also valuable. In termly reader-to-reader conferences, their reading habits, preferences, practices and interests at home/school can be explored, as well as a sense of themselves as readers. What is critical here is the extent to which children perceive such conversations are framed by their teacher as an assessor or as a fellow reader. The latter will open up space for more authentic reader-to-reader conversations and if organised in small groups, this can enable teachers to discern more depth and detail about individual's reading habits and motivations. Discussion at parent evenings can widen professional knowledge of reading at home, alongside home–school reading records and informal conversations in the playground with parents.

Surveys can also be used at the start and close of the year. However, their use needs to be combined with other tools as such instruments are too readily used as the sole evidence source, due in part to the allure of numbers in accountability cultures. Understanding children's identities and practices as readers demands more than the presentation of crude percentage shifts in their reported pleasure in reading. Nonetheless, if the responses are carefully analysed and combined with other sources, surveys can help teachers identify concerns, such as the number of children who report disliking reading, who prefer reading at home or who have narrow repertoires (for KS1, KS2 and parent surveys and tools to summarise these see https://www.researchrichpedagogies.org/research/reading-for-pleasure). It needs to be borne in mind, however, that survey respondents of whatever age tend to over-inflate their responses in the direction they perceive is desired, so understanding their qualitative comments on surveys is key. For instance, when analysing children's reasons for reporting that they enjoy reading, do their reasons reflect extrinsic motivations – such as 'I want to get a good job when I'm older', 'I want to do well at school', 'I'm going to get the Best Reader in Class award' (all of which have been seen on such surveys) – or do their responses reflect intrinsic motivation in reading? Examples we have seen include 'because stories make me buzz', 'reading makes me happy inside' and 'It gives your imagination muscles and takes you to a whole different world'. Knowing that research shows that RfP is more closely associated with intrinsic not extrinsic motivation is also helpful (e.g. McGeown et al., 2012a; Orkin et al., 2018).

Exploring more creative approaches can also help to ascertain children's conceptions of reading. They could be invited to undertake their own reading rivers or 24 hour reads (see Chapter 7), or reflect upon and co-construct ideas about reading through the use of a 'We are Readers' graffiti wall on which their comments, responses and conceptions about reading can be captured. Drawings of teachers as readers, or of a 'good reader' can also be revealing as can offering questions about reading that prompt their reflective engagement. The resultant discussions can enable teachers to understand for instance what the class, or a small group, think 'makes a good reader', 'what reading is good for', and what they feel about the statement 'reading is a silent solitary activity'. In addition to recording the books children enjoy reading most, exploring the range of texts they read and enabling them to keep track of their growing repertoires can be helpful. The class might create an A–Z of authors or personal 'bookshelves' (a named space on a wall display to showcase the spines of texts they have read). Equally, library or book borrowing records, print and/or digital, offer useful information to help teachers discern children's favourites, the frequency of their reading, their reading stamina, and the breadth of their repertoires. Such records enable teachers to engage in book discussions with children. In addition, opportunities for children to browse themed Book Blankets (collections of texts covering all the tables) can afford time for teachers to watch what individual readers do when browsing non-fiction texts, poetry or the class's collection, and also offer time for focused conversations about their choices.

Using a mixture of these tools, including observation and remaining alert to subtle shifts and differences, teachers can reflect upon and document children's practices, motivations and engagement as readers. Such ongoing evidence gathering enables practitioners to make more informed and supportive contributions to each reader's journey.

## Conclusion

Documenting the complex nature of children's volitional reading and their shifting identities as readers is not straightforward. Factors related to personal agency and social mediation in RfP are not uni-dimensional and research studies need to acknowledge their interrelationship in relation to particular contexts, texts and readers. Such studies are difficult to design, especially if we want to preserve the interdisciplinary orientation and authentic nature of children's choice-led engagement in reading. We caution against uncritically accepting the conclusions from current research without reflecting on the complexity of the researched phenomenon, and argue that recognising the strengths and limitations of particular research tools helps us to qualify the claims that are possible to make.

We also recognise that ways to research digital book reading are in their infancy, as their development has somewhat outstripped research. Nonetheless, exploring alternative methods and technologies can widen the toolkit available to researchers and to teachers who wish to investigate aspects of children's volitional reading of print and digital books. Documenting children's RfP within and beyond school is not only a professional responsibility, it is also an area for professional growth, but as we have asserted throughout, teachers cannot measure children's pleasure, nor require them to love reading. They can however seek to thoughtfully and carefully build communities of readers, tracking the children's journeys as they travel in order to enrich and support the development of positive reader identities and enhance their pleasure in reading.

# 9

# Revisiting the Journey

O ur concluding chapter is somewhat different from the arc of logic traced to this point in the book, in which we mapped key facets of reader engagement with diverse texts. Here, we make some space to reflect on the lessons learnt on the journey and look forwards, asking questions about possible future avenues and emerging research and practice vistas. We conclude by reflecting on our work, as writers and as publicly engaged scholars working in partnership with the education profession to effect change and to support the growth of motivated and engaged young readers.

Through this text, we have brought together several mutually amplifying contrasts: insights from theory and practice in reading for pleasure (RfP), quantitative studies in the tradition of developmental psychology and qualitative insights from ethnographic educational research focused on children's reading with print and digital books. In the context of RfP, the components of each pair – theory and practice, quantitative and qualitative, print and digital – are not opposites but are interrelated in dynamic ways that both reflect and reveal the complexities of understanding and developing young readers' engagement.

Our interdisciplinary approach to the theory and practice of RfP means that we combine scholarly voices with voices from the field (teachers, early years practitioners and professionals), as well as literary critics, authors and app designers, and of course children themselves. We emphasise the inseparable entanglement between readers' active meaning-making with texts, and the wider social context in which texts are read, experienced and produced. Whilst research into early reading and comprehension enjoys a rich and long-established empirical base, relatively less attention has been paid to motivational, behavioural and contextual factors involved in fostering children's RfP, and even less to studies with children's e-books and digital texts.

In bringing children's contemporary reading experiences to the fore we sought to focus on the experience of reading and young readers' engagement, enabling us to highlight the subtle and diverse ways in which individuals and communities of readers engage with RfP on and off-screen. In discussing RfP as it is experienced by young children growing up today, we have highlighted the generative possibilities of digital texts, e-books and apps, as well as print literature, in enriching children's learning. There is no doubt that RfP has changed with the advent of interactive multimedia texts, but we argue that by focusing on narrative, through which humans make sense of experience, key facets of reader engagement that are common to both print and digital books can be identified. Throughout the book we have exemplified these in action whilst examining the international research literature and drawing on our own studies of volitional reading. The facets thus far examined include: affective, personalised, sustained, shared, and interactive engagement (Kucirkova et al., 2016). The final facet of creative engagement is woven through all of these and is also expanded further in this final chapter.

Our theoretical framework of reader engagements built on Craft's (2011) conceptualisation of four underlying dimensions of twenty-first century digital childhoods: participation, pluralisation, possibility awareness and playfulness. It is to these four dimensions, these ways of being in the digital age, that we now turn, to synthesise our contribution and to structure our thinking about possible avenues for future RfP enquiries.

# Playfulness

Playfulness – what Craft (2011) conceived of as 'the exploratory drive' – is important for cultivating a sense of a shared past and common ground with children. We were all playful children once and this dimension of life persists into adulthood in many different forms, including in and through our engagement in RfP. Our memories, history of engaging with texts and experience of discussing texts with others, connect us to the texts of the present and the future. We are not the only active meaning-makers however, since the texts themselves as material objects can enable or constrain this process. In Chapter 8, we reflected on how post-humanist methodologies combine with socio-cultural understandings to consider texts as active players in meaning-making. Well-designed digital and print texts can be particularly helpful in inviting young children to adopt a playful approach to reading, and through their interactive features, such texts can elicit distinct affective engagement. In Chapter 3 we also explored how emotions become the common ground that connects readers to themselves, to others known to them and to the lives of still others real or imagined, vicariously or virtually across the world. Affective connections fuel readers' memories and may prompt a desire to re-read childhood favourites or classic texts, even as adults. As the contemporary children's author Katherine Rundell (2019) notes in a book entitled *Why You Should Read Children's Books, Even Though You Are So Old and Wise*: It's to children's fiction that you turn if you want to feel awe and hunger and longing for justice: to make the old warhorse heart stamp again in its stall (2019: 39).

Her allusive connection to Michael Morpurgo's book *Warhorse,* reminds us of the power of affective and interactive engagement that guides us into reciprocal relationships with texts and their authors, illustrators and designers and through this connection, to our own reader identities. Couching the characteristics of digital books in the language of affect, is a potent way to connect to all readers, with their diverse preferences, proficiency levels and expectations around texts. Currently, the dominant educational framing of reading as merely proficiency keeps teachers and parents tethered to the past, to narrow conceptions of reading as a set of skills that are print-bound and learning focused. Notions of literary heritage also play out in the official framing of traditional children's literature, in contrast to the unofficial framing of children's everyday reading lives and practices. Yet today's children grow up surrounded by texts that are far more diverse than those their older siblings or adult co-readers encountered in childhood. Such contemporary texts both demand and enable playfulness, and require open-minded attitudes towards what is possible.

Looking to the future, and drawing on our arguments in Chapters 2 and 6, we believe that to explore the playful possibilities of texts, adults need to be open to engage in children's texts personally and affectively themselves. Such engagement is key to developing increased understanding of children's literature and to an enhanced awareness of the unique features of children's digital books. Our observations of meaning-transactions in which various narrative texts engaged young readers show the playful exploration involved. In Vygotskian theory, imagination and play are seen as leading children's emotional, social and cognitive development, creating zones of proximal development where children can temporarily fulfil their desires tempered by the social rules they rehearse in playful contexts. The kind of imaginative activity described by Vygotsky (1978) has also been associated with the reading and experience of fiction, which, Meek (2002) suggests, like play, is a dialogue with a child's future and has the capacity to enrich their realist thinking, as well as stretch the bounds of their imagination. Thus, children's playful and creative engagement in texts, confirms and enhances their sense of 'what is' as well as providing a window into 'what if' worlds. It is through such affective, interactive and creative engagement that we can foster children's personal and authentic responses to texts, in all their forms and formats. Such responses can, and will, over time, shape unique reader identities that enrich the old reading canon with a collaborative playfulness that stimulates new thinking.

## Participation

Participation, framed by Craft (2011) as 'all welcome through democratic, dialogic voice', embraces creativity with attention to readers' shared and sustained engagement. Participation relates to the wider social context in which reading takes place. In western-speaking countries, the current neoliberal agenda that emphasises accountability has led to an instrumental approach to teaching and learning reading. Such an approach, as we have noted, fails to recognise that learning is an act of participation and reading a highly complex, socio-cultural practice. Participation also connects to the key theoretical frameworks that we have drawn upon in this book: Rosenblatt's focus on the shared meaning-making between authors and readers which 'involves both the author's text and what the reader brings to it' (1994: 14), and Vygotsky's (1978) and Bakhtin's (1981) attention to dialogue. Dialogue represents a powerful resource for educational professionals focused on developing children's reading futures.

We highlighted four strands of RfP pedagogy that are central to inviting children's participation as readers and enabling interaction with their teachers, parents and other co-readers located at home, in the classroom or elsewhere in the world. Drawing on the Teachers as Readers project, we highlighted the significance of social reading environments that are characterised by intersecting pedagogical practices: reading aloud, child-led reading time, and informal text talk and recommendations (Cremin et al., 2014). These informal practices can enable children to exercise both agency and ownership of their reading journeys. Pedagogy for volitional child-led reading can also be fostered on a micro-scale, through purposefully designed books and e-books. Our examples of personalised e-book designs show that children can be in the flow of the reading experience and immersed in the story plot, while paying attention to other co-readers.

Critically, teachers and parents need to know which texts (digital and print) tempt particular individuals and which resonate with them – this knowledge can be fostered through adult explorations of children's literature, the recognition of one's affective response to texts and the salience of one's identity as a reader. Knowledge of children's literature can also be fostered through online reading recommendation platforms that operate to scale and with remarkable diversity. Online reading spaces can bring together large groups of readers from across the world and connect them around a shared reading interest, providing tailored recommendations and automatically scaffolding their progress with individualised feedback and adjusted levels of reading difficulty. While extremely helpful for independent reading, the current design of many popular reading platforms however is not participatory: didactic rather than student-led, they position children as autonomous readers and are led not by teachers or librarians, but by technology companies. In Chapters 4 and 5, we suggested ways to re-design online reading platforms in the spirit of online communities, where all members' contributions are valued and enabled. Thinking about participatory futures for RfP, we argue that sustained and shared reader engagement can thrive only through the principled commitment of all the stakeholders involved in the authorship, design and use of children's texts.


# Pluralisation

In our original conceptualisation of the key facets of reading engagement, we positioned personalised engagement at the intersection with pluralisation (see Figure 2.2). We perceive the two dimensions are always entangled: the personal cannot exist without the social, and the 'self' is always influenced by, and always influences, the 'other'. Given that personalisation and pluralisation are inseparable, and operate in 'synergistic interaction' (Kucirkova, 2017a), we cannot sequence them, or assert for example that a personal response to text emerges prior to the shared context. Understanding narrative texts, whether print or digital, requires understanding the perspectives of others, which is why we elaborated on the mechanisms of perspective-taking, inter-thinking and empathy in Chapters 2 and 6. We also introduced the new conceptual construct of reciprocal reading for pleasure (reciprocal RfP) that connects personal and shared response to narrative and unites psychological and socio-cultural research on children's choice-led reading. This definition, in emphasising the personal and the social/communal aspects of reading, also hints at the relational, and recognises that young people's motivation to read is influenced by their interactions around reading with peers and adults. Thus, the nature of their reader relationships shape the experience and their sense of identity as readers.

Reciprocal RfP recognises that personalised engagement is not begotten by subjectivity alone; it is present and it becomes mature through others' reading practices and perceptions. Everyday home and school-based interactions around reading with families, friends and teachers contribute to the construction of readers' discursive identities. Readers are always positioned in certain ways and also position themselves, thus connecting to Craft's (2011) framing of the 'plurality of identities (people, places, activities, literacies)'. This further resonates with our examination of Reading Teachers who recognise themselves as readers, and welcome diversity and difference in the children as readers. Reciprocal RfP within the theoretical context of personalisation–pluralisation (Kucirkova, 2017a) is a deliberate reminder for the teaching profession to expand the restricted lens of national curricula focused on reading as a set of skills to be acquired and measured (decoding, comprehension, vocabulary) to reading as a social practice, and a uniquely human way of connecting with others. This connection happens on the mental and verbal level but, as we discuss in Chapters 2 and 5, it is also embodied and sensorial.

While the extent to which the five human senses are represented varies in different book formats, the involvement of the senses in a reading experience is another way of tapping into the personal–plural connection to texts. Each act of reading is a physical and spatial experience, an embodied and situated one that shapes the reader's creative engagement. Creativity uniquely contributes to the act of reading by diversifying the reader's response and the possibilities for its modification, which gives rise to new understandings, new texts, new narratives.

## Possibility Awareness

While all Craft's (2011) 4Ps of children's digital childhood are rooted in creativity, it is possibility awareness that maps most directly onto creative reading engagement. Craft's research positioned possibility thinking at the heart of creativity, and conceived of possibility awareness as 'what might be invented, of access options, of learning by doing and of active engagement' (2011: 33). The nature of reading is generative, heightening the readers' awareness of other possible worlds, fictional and real. Within these, problems are found and potentially solved through envisioning alternative ways forward, imagining potential endings to familiar situations, and even transforming unwanted situations into more desirable ones.

At its core, reading is thinking about meaning and being open to the text's possible connections to self, to others and to other texts. Thus, it capitalises upon the readers' active engagement in this meaning-transaction (Rosenblatt, 1994). As we consider our personal and shared journeys as the authors of this text, possibility awareness in RfP is very useful. In the year following acceptance of our proposal, we shared ideas and possible arguments in more depth, debated these and created new options, and then started drafting, refining and shaping the text through dialogue, reading, commenting and editing each other's writing. With a lens towards creativity we acknowledge our own role as writers shaping your own possibility awareness concerning children's RfP. Being open to questioning the terrain travelled and contemplating new paths for future research and practice, engages us all creatively and imaginatively.

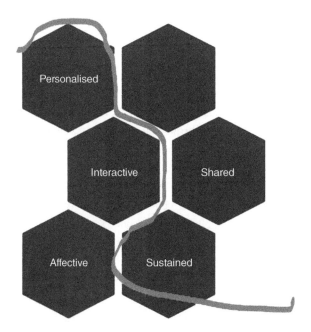

**Figure 9.1**   A diagram to represent the red thread of creative engagement connecting the facets of reader engagement

Looking back, we believe that creative engagement is the red thread running through all the chapters in this book (see Figure 9.1), connecting all the facets of reader engagement and connecting us to our readers – all of whom by definition are members of the wider RfP research and practice community. Possibility awareness has the potential to expand the facets and weave through their intersections. Like the hexagons in a beehive, which are able to store pollen, honey and queen bee's eggs, due to the gaps in the honeycomb, so too small gaps exist between the facets, ready to be creatively filled with new threads of enquiry into volitional reading.

# Conclusion

Even as we draw this text to a close, we find ourselves still discussing features of digital texts, such as augmented reality for example, that will be far more advanced by the time this book reaches your hands. As Meek (2011: 12) observes 'literacy becomes different as times change'; the pace of change, which is accelerating, will always herald new forms of texts and new ways of processing them, affecting both reading formats and content. In parallel to the increased use of portable screens and the fast-paced lifestyle they propagate, there have been changes to reading content, such as a recent surge of shorter reading materials. These encompass potted versions of novels in the form of novellas, bitesize courses, and introductions to major subjects available in pocket-size paperbacks and as quick e-reader downloads. We acknowledge that the possibility of digital and print books becoming blurred, might itself be superseded by new forms that, as yet, do not exist. Thanks to the largest book in the world, the Internet, narratives are already distributed in time and space, and represented through bodies inter-connected with objects, with the textual possibilities of the Internet of Things expanding daily. As scholars of digital literacies remind us though (Lankshear and Knobel, 2011), past conventions offer no surety as to future representations and it is counterproductive for us to try to anticipate them.

Nonetheless, new and critical digital literacies offer an alternative vision to the politicisation of teaching and learning (see Clark et al., 2014) and a means of bringing together communities of like-minded professionals. In our work too we seek to establish communities of educationalists who, conscious of the dehumanising trend in education so prevalent in recent years, gather around the shared goal of nurturing young people's pleasure in reading print and digital books. As academics committed to public engagement, we have co-created with teachers a professional research and practice website, which seeks to share the findings of a number of Open University RfP studies (https://researchrichpedagogies.org/research/reading-for-pleasure).

The space was designed as a community website, with and for the profession, and at the time of writing, the website hosts several hundred examples of teachers' research-informed practice, developed as a consequence of their engagement with the research and their desire to share their practice and inspire others. In addition, there are a range of resources including: audits, practical classroom strategies, research summaries, resources for whole school development, PowerPoints for professional development, videoed interviews with teachers and researchers, classroom film clips evidencing learner-led practice, monthly Top Texts and Authors, blogs by teachers and academics and a monthly newsletter.

The site has also spawned several hundred linked Teacher Reading Groups, which are local communities of teachers and librarians who engage in yearlong professional development for children's and teachers' RfP. Other possibilities have been created by working in partnership with the UK Literacy Association (a subject association), Coram Beanstalk (a national reading volunteer organisation) and the publisher Egmont. The last partnership involves national RfP Awards that profile the work of practitioners and schools who create vibrant research-informed RfP cultures. In addition, we work with Higher Education partners to support the development of positive reader identities in the next generation of teachers.

Through our active engagement in the building of digital and face-to-face reading communities, academic blogging and presence on social media, we have come to appreciate the possibilities of new reading spaces. These will expand further if you – our readers – become involved. So do join us on this journey of reciprocal RfP which values and intentionally integrates diverse narratives that map both past and future reading roads.

# REFERENCES

Abelson, R.P. (1987) Artificial intelligence and literary appreciation: How big is the gap? *Literary Discourse: Aspects of Cognitive and Social Psychological Approaches*, 1–37.

Abrams, S. and Merchant, G. (2013) The digital challenge. In K. Hall, T. Cremin, B. Comber and L. Moll (eds), *International Handbook of Research on Children's Literacy, Learning, and Culture*. Oxford: Wiley Blackwell. pp. 319–332.

Akins, M., Tichenor, M., Heins, E. and Piechura, K. (2018) Teacher's knowledge of children's literature: What genres do teachers read? *Reading Improvement*, 55(2), 63–65.

Al-Yaqout, G. and Nikolajeva, M. (2015) Re-conceptualising picturebook theory in the digital age. *Barnelitterært Forskningstidsskrift*, 6(1).

Alexander, R. (2008) *Towards Dialogic Teaching: Rethinking Classroom Talk*. Cambridge: Dialogos.

Allen, R. (2015) *Missing Talent*, Research Brief Edition 5, The Sutton Trust. Available at www.suttontrust.com/wp-content/uploads/2015/06/Missing-Talent-final-june.pdf. (accessed 27 November 2018).

Allington, R.L. (2014) How reading volume affects both reading fluency and reading achievement. *International Electronic Journal of Elementary Education*, 7(1), 13–26.

Allyn, P. (2009) *What to Read When: The Books and Stories to Read with Your Child and All the Best Times to Read Them*. London: Penguin.

Anderson, R., Wilson, P.T. and Fielding, L.G. (1988) Growth in reading and how children spend their time outside of school. *Reading Research Quarterly*, 23(3), 85–303.

Apperley, T. and Walsh, C. (2012) What digital games and literacy have in common: A heuristic for understanding pupils' gaming literacy. *Literacy*, 46(3), 115–122.

Appleyard, J.A. (1990) *Becoming a Reader: The Experience of Fiction from Childhood to Adulthood*. Cambridge: Cambridge University Press.

Archambault, L. and Crippen, K. (2009) Examining TPACK among K-12 online distance educators in the United States. *Contemporary Issues in Technology and Teacher Education*, 9(1), 71–88.

Arizpe, E., Farrell, M. and McAdam, J. (2013) Opening the classroom door to children's literature: A review of research. In K. Hall, T. Cremin, B. Comber and L. Moll, *The Wiley Blackwell International Research Handbook of Children's Literacy, Learning and Culture*. Oxford: Wiley Blackwell. pp. 241–257.

Arizpe, E., Colomer, T. and Martínez-Roldán, C. (2014) *Visual Journeys Through Wordless Narratives*. London: Bloomsbury Academic.

Baker, L. and Scher, D. (2002) Beginning readers' motivation for reading in relation to parental beliefs and home reading experiences. *Reading Psychology, 23*, 239–269.

Bakhtin, M. (1981) *The Dialogic Imagination: Four Essays* (ed. M. Holquist; trans. C. Emerson and M. Holquist). Austin, TX: University of Texas Press.

Baron, N.S. (2008) *Always On: Language in an Online and Mobile World*. Oxford, New York: Oxford University Press.

Baron, N.S. (2015) *Words Onscreen: The Fate of Reading in a Digital World*. New York: Oxford University Press.

Baron, N. (forthcoming) *How We Read Now: Effective Strategies for Print, Digital, and Audio*. Oxford: Oxford University Press.

Barthes, R. (1975) *The Pleasure of Text* (trans. R. Miller). New York: Hill and Wang.

Barthes, R. (1977) *Image, Music, Text*. New York: Hill and Wang.

Bearne, E. (2003) Rethinking literacy: Communication, representation and text. *Reading Literacy and Language, 37*(3), 98–103.

Benedetto, S., Drai-Zerbib, V., Pedrotti, M., Tissier, G. and Baccino, T. (2013) E-readers and visual fatigue. *PLoS ONE, 8*(12).

Benevides, T. and Peterson, S.S. (2010) Literacy attitudes, habits and achievements of future teachers. *Journal of Education for Teaching, 36*(3), 291–302.

Bennett, J. (2001) *The Enchantment of Modern Life: Attachments, Crossings and Ethics*. Princeton: Princetown University Press.

Bernstein, B.B. (2000) *Pedagogy, Symbolic Control, and Identity: Theory, Research, Critique*. Lanham, MD: Rowman & Littlefield.

Beschorner, B. and Hutchison, A. (2013) iPads as a literacy teaching tool in early childhood. *International Journal of Education in Mathematics Science and Technology, 1*(1), 16–24.

Biddle, J. (2018) *Reading Rivers*. Available at: https://researchrichpedagogies.org/research/example/reading-rivers (accessed 16 September 2019).

Biesta, G. (2010) Why 'what works' still won't work: From evidence-based education to value-based education. *Studies in Philosophy and Education, 29*(5), 491–503.

Blommaert, J. (2005) *Discourse: A Critical Introduction*. Cambridge: Cambridge University Press.

Botelho, M. and Rudman, M. (2009) *Critical Multicultural Analysis of Children's Literature: Mirrors, Windows and Doors*. New York: Routledge.

Boyd, D. (2017) Self-segregation: How a personalized world is dividing Americans. *The Guardian*, 13 January. Available at: www.theguardian.com/technology/2017/jan/13/self-segregation-military-facebook-college-diversity (accessed 20 December 2019).

Braun, V. and Clarke, V. (2006) Using thematic analysis in psychology. *Qualitative Research in Psychology, 3*(2), 77–101.

Britton, J. (1977) The third area where we are more ourselves: The role of fantasy and the nature of a reader's satisfaction and response to literature. In M. Meek, A. Warlow and G. Barton (eds), *The Cool Web*. London: Bodley Head.

Brock, R. (2017) How audio books support literacy. In J. Court (ed.), *Reading by Right*. London: Facet. pp. 169–187.

Bruner, J. (1986) *Actual Minds, Possible Worlds*. Cambridge, MA: Harvard University Press.

Bruner, J. (1990a) *Acts of Meaning*. Cambridge, MA: Harvard University Press.

Bruner, J. (1990b) Culture and human development: A new look. *Human Development*, *33*(6), 344–355.

Bruner, J. (1991) The narrative construction of reality. *Critical Inquiry*, *18*, 1–21.

Bulpitt, C.J. (2012) *Randomised Controlled Clinical Trials*. Boston, MA: Springer Science & Business Media.

Burnett, C. (2010) Technology and literacy in early childhood educational settings: A review of research. *Journal of Early Childhood Literacy*, *10*, 247–270.

Burnett, C. and Merchant, G. (2018a) Affective encounters: Enchantment and the possibility of reading for pleasure. *Literacy*, *52*(2), 62–69.

Burnett, C. and Merchant, G. (2018b) *New Media in the Classroom: Rethinking Primary Literacy*. London: Sage.

Calinescu, M. (1993) Orality in literacy: Some historical paradoxes of reading. *The Yale Journal of Criticism*, *6*(2), 175.

Caton, L. and Hackett, A. (2019) The methodological potentials of a GoPro camera and ontological possibilities for doing visual research with child participants differently. In N. Kucirkova, J. Rowsell and G. Falloon (eds), *The Routledge International Handbook of Learning with Technology in Early Childhood*. London: Routledge. pp. 362–377.

Centre for Literacy in Primary Education (2018) *Reflecting Realities: Survey of Ethnic Representation Within UK Children's Literature 2017*. London: CLPE.

Chaiklin, S. (2003) The zone of proximal development in Vygotsky's analysis of learning and instruction. *Vygotsky's Educational Theory in Cultural Context*, *1*, 39–64.

Chambers, A. (1985) *Booktalk: Occasional Writing on Literature and Children*. London: Bodley Head.

Chema, J. (2018) Adolescents' enjoyment of reading as a predictor of reading achievement: New evidence from a cross-country survey. *Journal of Research in Reading*, *41*(S1), S149–S162.

Cheung, W.M., Lam, J.W., Au, D.W., Tsang, H.W. and Chan, S.W. (2016) Examining factor structure of the Chinese version of the PIRLS 2011 Home Questionnaire. *Education Research International*. Available at: http://dx.doi.org/10.1155/2016/7574107 (accessed 13 January 2020).

Clark, C. and Picton, I. (2019) *Children, Young People and Digital Reading*. London: National Literacy Trust.

Clark, C. and Rumbold, K. (2006) *Reading for Pleasure: A Research Overview*. London: National Literacy Trust.

Clark, C. and Teravainen, A. (2015) *Teachers and Literacy: Their Perceptions, Understanding, Confidence and Awareness*. London: National Literacy Trust.

Clark, C. and Teravainen, A. (2017a) *What it Means to be a Reader at Age 11: Valuing Skills, Affective Components and Behavioural Processes – An Outline of the Evidence*. London: National Literacy Trust.

Clark, C. and Teravainen, A. (2017b) *Celebrating Reading for Enjoyment: Findings from our Annual Literacy Survey 2016*. London: National Literacy Trust.

Clark, C., Osborne, S. and Akerman, R. (2008) *Young People's Self-perceptions as Readers: An Investigation Including Family, Peer and School Influence*. London: National Literacy Trust.

Clark, J.S., Heron-Hruby, A. and Landon-Hays, M. (2014) In closing – The potential of current grassroots efforts for effecting sustainable change: A socio-historical perspective on making a difference. In A. Heron-Hruby and M. Landon-Hays (eds), *Digital Networking for School Reform: The Online Grassroots Efforts of Parent and Teacher Activists*. New York: Palgrave Macmillan. pp. 63–74.

Clay, M.M. (1977) *Reading: The Patterning of Complex Behaviour*. Exeter, NH: Heinemann Educational Books.

Cliff–Hodges, G. (2010a) Reasons for reading: Why literature matters. *Literacy*, 44(2), 60–68.

Cliff–Hodges, G. (2010b) Rivers of reading: Using critical incident collages to learn about adolescent readers and their readership. *English in Education*, 44(3), 180–199.

Cliff–Hodges, G. (2016a) Reimagining reading. In P. Rothbauer, K.L. Skjerdingstad, L. McKechnie and K. Oterholm (eds), *Plotting the Reading Experience: Theory/Practice/ Politics*. Ontario: Wilfrid Laurier University Press. pp. 55–71.

Cliff–Hodges, G. (2016b) *Researching and Teaching Reading: Developing Pedagogy Through Critical Enquiry*. Oxon: Routledge.

Cliff–Hodges, G. (2018) Rivers of reading: A research method to explore young adults' personal reading histories. In A. Arizpe and G. Cliff-Hodges, *Young People Reading: Empirical Research Across International Contexts*. London: Routledge. pp. 55–70.

Cohen, L., Manion, L. and Morrison, K. (2003) *Research Methods in Education*, 5th edn. London: Routledge Falmer.

Cole, M. and Engeström, Y. (1993) A cultural-historical approach to distributed cognition. In G. Salomon (ed.), *Distributed Cognitions: Psychological and Educational Considerations*. New York: Cambridge University Press. pp. 1–46.

Cole, M. and Wertsch, J.V. (1996) Beyond the individual-social antinomy in discussions of Piaget and Vygotsky. *Human Development*, 39(5), 250–256.

Collier, D.R. (2010) Journey to becoming a writer: Review of research about children's identities as writers. *Language and Literacy: An e-journal*, 12(1), 1–18. Available at: http://ejournals.library.ualberta.ca/index.php/langandlit/article/view/9348 (accessed 29 December 2019).

Comber, B. (2012) Mandated literacy assessment and the reorganisation of teachers' work: Federal policy, local effects. *Critical Studies in Education*, 53, 119–136.

Comber, B. and Kamler, B. (2005) *Turn-around Pedagogies: Literacy Interventions for At-risk Students*. Metro, NSW: PETA.

Commeyras, M., Bisplinhoff, B.S. and Olson, J. (2003) *Teachers as Readers: Perspectives on the Importance of Reading in Teachers' Classrooms and Lives*. Newark: International Reading Association.

Common Sense Media (2019) *The New Normal: Parents, Teens and Devices Around the World*. Available at: www.commonsensemedia.org/research/the-new-normal-parents-teens-and-devices-around-the-world (accessed 16 December 2019).

Condon, M. and Harrison, C. (2007) *Using Real E-books in Real E-classrooms in the US, UK, and South Africa*. Paper presented at the annual meeting of the International Reading Association, Toronto, ON, Canada. Available at: http://extendboundariesof literacy.pbworks.com/w/page/9077041/FrontPage (accessed 19 December 2019).

Congleton, A.R. and Rajaram, S. (2014) Collaboration changes both the content and the structure of memory. *Journal of Experimental Psychology: General, 143*(4), 1570–1584.

Connelly, F.M. and Clandinin, D.J. (1990) Stories of experience and narrative inquiry. *Educational Researcher, 19*(5), 2–14.

Connolly, P., O'Hare, L. and Mitchell, D. (2012) *A Cluster Randomised Controlled Trial Evaluation of Booktime Northern Ireland: A Book Gifting Intervention for Children in Their First Year of Primary School*. Belfast: Centre for Effective Education, Queen's University Belfast.

Conole, G., Dyke, M., Oliver, M. and Seale, J. (2004) Mapping pedagogy and tools for effective learning design. *Computers & Education, 43*(1–2), 17–33.

Cordova, D.I. and Lepper, M.R. (1996) Intrinsic motivation and the process of learning: Beneficial effects of contextualization, personalization, and choice. *Journal of Educational Psychology, 88*(4), 715.

Courage, M.L. (2019) From print to digital: The medium is only part of the message. In J.E. Kim and B. Hassinger-Das (eds), *Reading in the Digital Age: Young Children's Experiences with E-Books*. Cham: Springer. pp. 23–43.

Courtney, M. (2019) Diverse literature in school libraries: Reflected realities. *The School Librarian, 67*(3), 133–135.

Craft, A. (2011) *Creativity and Education Futures*. Stoke On Trent: Trentham.

Cremin, T. (2010a) Reconceptualising reading in the 21st century. In T. McCannon (ed.), *Reading in the 21st Century*. Dublin: Reading Association of Ireland.

Cremin, T. (2010b) Poetry teachers: Teachers who read and readers who teach poetry. In M. Styles and M. Rosen (eds), *Poetry and Childhood*. London: Trentham. pp. 219–227.

Cremin, T. (2016) *Reading For Pleasure: Just Window Dressing?* Cambridge Primary Review Trust. Available at: https://cprtrust.org.uk/cprt-blog/reading-for-pleasure-just-window-dressing/.

Cremin, T. (2018) *Reading Communities and Books in Common*. National Association of Advisers of English. Available at: www.naae.org.uk/reading-communities-and-books-in-common/ (accessed 21 October 2019).

Cremin, T. (2019a) Teachers as readers and writers. In V. Bowers, *Debates in Primary Education*. London: Routledge.

Cremin, T. (2019b) The personal in the professional. In S. Ogier and T. Eaude, *The Broad and Balanced Curriculum*. London: Sage.

Cremin, T. (2020) Reading for pleasure: Tensions and challenges. In C. Daly and J. Davison, *Debates in English Teaching*. London: Routledge.

Cremin, T. and Baker, S. (2010) Exploring teacher-writer identities in the classroom: Conceptualising the struggle. *English Teaching: Practice and Critique, 9*(3), 8–25.

Cremin, T., Bearne, E., Mottram, M. and Goodwin, P. (2008b) Primary teachers as readers. *English in Education, 42*(1), 1–16.

Cremin, T., Craft, A. and Burnard, P. (2006) Pedagogy and possibility thinking in the early years. *Journal of Thinking Skills and Creativity, 1*(2), 108–119.

Cremin, T., Flewitt, R., Mardell, B. and Swann, J. (eds) (2017) *Storytelling in Early Childhood: Language, Literacy, and Classroom Culture*. London and New York: Routledge.

Cremin, T., Harris, B. and Birchall, L. (2020) Reading for pleasure pedagogy for non-fiction. *English 4–11, 69*.

Cremin, T., Mottram, M., Bearne, E. and Goodwin, P. (2008a) Exploring teachers' knowledge of children's literature. *Cambridge Journal of Education, 38*(4), 449–464.

Cremin, T., Mottram, M., Collins, F., Powell, S. and Drury, R. (2012) Building communities: Teachers researching literacy lives. *Improving Schools, 15*(2), 101–115.

Cremin, T., Mottram, M., Collins, F., Powell, S. and Safford, K. (2009) Teachers as readers: Building communities of readers. *Literacy, 43*(1), 11–19.

Cremin, T., Mottram, M., Powell, S., Collins, R. and Drury, R. (2015) *Researching Literacy Lives: Building Home School Communities*. London and New York: Routledge.

Cremin, T., Mottram, M., Powell, S., Collins, R. and Safford, K. (2014) *Building Communities of Engaged Readers: Reading for Pleasure*. London and New York: Routledge.

Cremin, T., Thomson, B., Williams, C. and Davies, S. (2018b) Reading Teachers. *English 4–11, 62*.

Cremin, T. and Swann, J. (2016) Literature in common: Reading for pleasure in school reading groups. In P. Rothbauer, K.I. Skjerdingstad, L. McKechnie and K. Oterholm (eds), *Plotting the Reading Experience: Theory/Practice/Politics*. Ontario: Wilfrid Laurier University Press. pp. 279–300.

Cremin, T. and Swann, J. (2017) School librarians as facilitators of extracurricular reading groups. In J. Pihl, K. Skinstad van der Kooij and T.C. Carlsten (eds), *Teacher and Librarian Partnerships in Literacy Education in the 21st Century*. Oslo: Sense Publishers. pp. 118–137.

Cremin, T., Swann, J., Flewitt, R., Faulkner, D. and Kucirkova, N. (2018a) Storytelling and story acting: Co-construction in action. *Journal of Early Childhood Research, 16*(1), 3–17.

Cremin, T., Williams, C. and Denby, R. (2019) Reading Teachers: Exploring non-fiction. *English 4–11, 68.*

Crone, E.A. and Dahl, R.E. (2012) Understanding adolescence as a period of social–affective engagement and goal flexibility. *Nature Reviews Neuroscience, 13*(9), 636–650.

Crum, M. (2015) Sorry, ebooks. These 9 studies show why print is better. *Huffington Post,* 27 February. Available at: www.huffpost.com/entry/print-ebooks-studies_n_6762674 (accessed 16 December 2019).

Czarniawska, B. (2004) *Narratives in Social Science Research.* London: Sage.

Davies, W. (2019) The political economy of pulse: Techno-somatic rhythm and real-time data. *Ephemera, 19*(3), 513–536.

Dent, A. and Koenka, A. (2016) The relation between self-regulated learning and academic achievement across childhood and adolesence: A meta analysis. *Educational Psychology Review, 28*(4), 425–474.

Denton, J. (2019) Mixing methodologies: A sliding continuum or an iterative cycle? In V. Reyes, J. Charteris, A. Nye and S. Mavropoulou (eds), *Educational Research in the Age of Anthropocene.* Hershey, PA: IGI Global. pp. 84–109.

Department for Education (2012) All Party Parliamentary Literacy Group, *Boys Reading Commission,* Final report compiled by the National Literacy Trust. Available at: www.literacytrust.org.uk/assets/0001/4056/Boys_Commission_Report.pdf (accessed 1 December 2012).

Department for Education (2014) *The National Curriculum.* London: DFE.

Department for Education (2018) *Schools, Pupils and their Characteristics.* London: DfE.

Dewey, J. (1916) *Democracy and Education. An Introduction to the Philosophy of Education.* New York: Macmillan Company.

Djikic, M., Oatley, K. and Moldoveanu, M.C. (2013) Reading other minds: Effects of literature on empathy. *Scientific Study of Literature, 3,* 28–47.

Doherty, M. (2008) *Theory of Mind: How Children Understand Others' Thoughts and Feelings.* London: Psychology Press.

Dreher, M.J. (2002) Motivating teachers to read. *The Reading Teacher, 56*(4), 338–340.

Dresang, E.T. and Koh, K. (2009) Radical change theory, youth information behavior, and school libraries. *Library Trends, 58*(1), 26–50.

Druin, A. (2005) What children can teach us: Developing digital libraries for children with children. *The Library Quarterly, 75*(1), 20–41.

Dyson, A.H. (1995) Writing children: Reinventing the development of childhood literacy. *Written Communication, 12*(1), 4–46.

Edwards, D. and Mercer, N. (1987/2013) *Common Knowledge (Routledge Revivals): The Development of Understanding in the Classroom.* London: Routledge.

Egmont/Nielsen (2018) *Understanding the Children's Book Consumer.* Available at: www.egmont.co.uk/research/creating-readers-for-the-future/ (accessed 29 September 2019).

Engel, S. (2005) The narrative worlds of *what-is and what-if*. *Cognitive Development, 20*, 514–525.

English, E., Hargreaves, L. and Hislam, J. (2002) Pedagogical dilemmas in the National Literacy Strategy. *Cambridge Journal of Education, 32*(1), 9–26.

Ensor, J. (2013) Children's progress hindered by e-books and Kindles, charity warns. *The Telegraph*, 16 May. Available at: www.telegraph.co.uk/education/education-news/10059820/Childrens-progress-hindered-by-e-books-and-Kindles-charity-warns.html (accessed 13 January 2020).

Evans, M.D.R., Kelley, J., Sikora, J. and Treiman, D.J. (2010) Family scholarly culture and educational success: Books and schooling in 27 nations. *Research in Social Stratification and Mobility, 28*, 171–197.

Ezell, H.K. and Justice, L.M. (2005) *Shared Storybook Reading*. Baltimore, MD: Brookes.

Falloon, G. (2017) Mobile devices and apps as scaffolds to science learning in the primary classroom. *Journal of Science Education and Technology, 26*(6), 613–628.

Farrar, J. (2019) *Student Teachers' Knowledge of Children's Literature*. Presentation at UKLA Higher Education Special Interest Group conference, 22 February, OU Camden.

Fleer, M. (2017) Digital playworlds in an Australian context: Supporting double subjectivity. In T. Brice, P. Hakkarainen and M. Bredikyte (eds), *The Routledge International Handbook of Early Childhood Play*. London: Routledge. p. 289.

Fleming, L. (2013) Expanding learning opportunities with transmedia practices: Inanimate Alice as an exemplar. *Journal of Media Literacy Education, 5*(2). Available at: http://digitalcommons.uri.edu/jmle/vol5/iss2/3 (accessed 19 December 2019).

Fletcher, J., Grimley, M., Greenwood, J. and Parkhill, F. (2012) Motivating and improving attitudes to reading in the final years of primary schooling in five New Zealand schools. *Literacy, 46*(1), 3–16.

Flewitt, R., Messer, D. and Kucirkova, N. (2015) New directions for early literacy in a digital age: The iPad. *Journal of Early Childhood Literacy, 15*(3), 289–310.

Flynn, N. (2007) What do effective teachers of literacy do? Subject knowledge and pedagogical choices for literacy. *Literacy, 41*(3), 137–146.

Fuller, D. and Rehberg Sedo, D. (2017) Fun … and other reasons for sharing reading with strangers: Mass reading events and the possibilities of pleasure. In P. Rothbauer, K.I. Skjerdingstad, L. McKechnie and K. Oterholm (eds), *Plotting the Reading Experience: Theory/Practice/ Politics*. Ontario: Wilfrid Laurier University Press. pp. 133–147.

Gallagher, K. (2009) *Readicide: How Schools are Killing Reading and What You Can Do About It*. Portland, ME: Stenhouse.

Garces-Bacsal, R., Tupas, R., Kaur, S., Paculdar, A. and Baja, E. (2018) Reading for pleasure: Whose job is it to build lifelong readers in the classroom? *Literacy, 52*(2), 95–102.

Garvis, S., Ødegaard, E.E. and Lemon, N. (2015) *Beyond Observations: Narratives and Young Children*. New York: Brill Sense.

Gee, J.P. (2011) *An Introduction to Discourse Analysis: Theory and Method*, 3rd edn. Routledge: Abingdon.

Geertz, C. (1973) *The Interpretation of Cultures: Selected Essays*. New York: Basic Books.

Gennrich, T. and Janks, H. (2013) Teachers' literate identities. In K. Hall, T. Cremin, B. Comber and L. Moll (eds), *The Wiley Blackwell International Research Handbook of Children's Literacy, Learning and Culture*. Oxford: Wiley Blackwell. pp. 456–468.

Gerrig, R.J. (1993) *Experiencing Narrative Worlds: On the Psychological Activities of Reading*. New Haven: Yale University Press.

Gonzalez, N., Moll, L. and Amanti, C. (2005) *Funds of Knowledge: Theorizing Practices in Households, Communities and Classrooms*. London: Lawrence Erlbaum.

Gopalakrishnan, A. (2011) *Multicultural Children's Literature: A Critical Issues Approach*. London: Sage.

Gossen, T., Müller, R., Stober, S. and Nürnberger, A. (2014) *Search Result Visualization with Characters for Children*. Paper presented at the Proceedings of the 2014 conference on Interaction Design and Children.

Gottschall, J. (2012) *The Storytelling Animal: How Stories Make us Human*. New York: Houghton Mifflin Harcourt.

Graesser, A.C., Olde, B. and Klettke, B. (2002) How does the mind construct and represent stories? In M.C. Green, J.J. Strange and T.C. Brock (eds), *Narrative Impact: Social and Cognitive Foundations*. Mahwah, NJ: Lawrence Erlbaum. pp. 229–262.

Graham, L. (2008) Teachers are digikids too: The digital histories and digital lives of young teachers in English primary schools. *Literacy, 42*(1), 10–18.

Grainger, T., Goouch, K. and Lambirth, A. (2005) *Creativity and Writing: Developing Voice and Verve in the Classroom*. London: Routledge.

Gratton, C. and Jones, I. (2014) *Research Methods for Sports Studies*. London: Routledge.

Graves, L. (2019) A is for Activist: why children's books are getting political. *The Guardian*, 2 May. Available at: www.theguardian.com/books/2019/may/02/childrens-books-political-diversity-shift (accessed 19 December 2019).

Gregory, E. (2001) Sisters and brothers as language and literacy teachers: Synergy between siblings playing and working together. *Journal of Early Childhood Literacy, 1*, 301–322.

Gregory, E. and Williams, A. (2000) *City Literacies: Learning to Read Across Generation and Cultures*. London: Routledge.

Guernsey, L. and Levine, M.H. (2015) *Tap, Click, Read: Growing Readers in a World of Screens*. Oxford: John Wiley & Sons.

Hackett, A. and Somerville, M. (2017) Posthuman literacies: Young children moving in time, place and more-than-human worlds. *Journal of Early Childhood Literacy, 17*(3), 374–391.

Hall, L.A. (2010) The negative consequences of becoming a good reader: Identity theory as a lens for understanding struggling readers, teachers, and reading instruction. *Teachers' College Record, 112*(7), 1792–1829.

Hall, L.A. (2012) Rewriting identities: Creating spaces for students and teachers to challenge the norms of what it means to be a reader in school. *Journal of Adolescent and Adult Literacy, 55*, 368–373.

Han, S.S. (2012) Morning reading movement that changed children's lives. In *Morning Reading for 10 Minutes that Changed our Classroom*. Happy Morning Reading. pp. 12–30.

Hanley, P., Chambers, B. and Haslam, J. (2016) Reassessing RCTs as the 'gold standard': Synergy not separatism in evaluation designs. *International Journal of Research & Method in Education, 39*(3), 287–298.

Hardy, B. (1977) Towards a poetics of fiction: An approach through narrative. In M. Meek, A. Warlow and G. Barton (eds), *The Cool Web*. London: Bodley Head.

Harris, P.L. (2000) *The Work of the Imagination*. Oxford: Blackwell Publishers.

Hartman, D.S. (1995) Eight readers reading: The intertextual links of proficient readers reading multiple passages. *Reading Research Quarterly, 30*(3), 520–561.

Harwood, D. (2017) *Crayons and iPads: Learning and Teaching of Young Children in the Digital World*. London: Sage.

Haug, K.H. and Jamissen, G. (2015) *Se Min Fortelling: Digital Historiefortelling i Barnehagen*. Oslo: Cappelen Damm Akademisk.

Heath, S.B. (1983) *Ways with Words: Language, Life and Work in Communities and Classrooms*. Cambridge: Cambridge University Press.

Hempel-Jorgensen, A. and Cremin, T. (forthcoming) An intersectionality approach to understanding boys' (dis)engagement with reading. *Gender and Education*.

Hempel-Jorgensen, A., Cremin, T., Harris, D. and Chamberlain, L. (2018) Pedagogy for reading for pleasure in low socio-economic primary schools: Beyond 'pedagogy of poverty'? *Literacy, 52*(2), 86–94.

Hewitt, J. and Scardamalia, M. (1998) Design principles for distributed knowledge building processes. *Educational Psychology Review, 10*(1), 75–96.

Hilton, M. (2006) Measuring standards in primary English: Issues of validity and accountability with respect to PIRLS and National Curriculum test scores. *British Educational Research Journal, 32*(6), 817–837.

Hogan, P.C. (2003) *The Mind and its Stories: Narrative Universals and Human Emotion*. Cambridge: Cambridge University Press.

Holland, D. and Lave, J. (2001) History in person. In D. Holland and J. Lave, *Enduring Struggles: Contentious Practice, Intimate Identities*. Santa Fe: School of American Research Press. pp. 1–32.

Holland, D., Lachicotte, W., Skinner, D. and Cain, C. (1998) *Identity and Agency in Cultural Worlds*. Cambridge, MA: Harvard.

Hopper, R. (2005) What are teenagers reading? Adolescent fiction reading habits and reading choices. *Literacy, 39*(3), 113–120.

Horning, K.T. (2014) Still an all-white world? *School Library Journal, 60*(5), 18.

Hymes, D. (2003) *'Now I Only Know So Far': Essays in Ethnopoetics*. Lincoln: University of Nebraska Press.

Iser, W. (1978) *The Act of Reading: A Theory of Aesthetic Response*. Baltimore: Johns Hopkins.

Janes, H. and Kermani, H. (2001) Caregivers' story reading to young children in family literacy programs: Pleasure or punishment? *Journal of Adolescent & Adult Literacy*, *44*(5), 458–466.

Jerrim, J. and Moss, G. (2018) The link between fiction and teenagers' reading skills: International evidence from the OECD PISA study. *British Educational Research Journal*, *45*(1), 161–181.

Johnson, D.R. (2013) Transportation into literary fiction reduces prejudice against and increases empathy for Arab-Muslims. *Scientific Study of Literature*, *3*(1), 77–92.

Jones, S. and Myhill, D. (2004).'Troublesome boys' and 'compliant girls': Gender identity and perceptions of achievement and underachievement. *British Journal of Sociology of Education*, *25*(5), 547–561.

Jones, T.L., Baxter, M.A.J. and Khanduja, V. (2013) A quick guide to survey research. *The Annals of The Royal College of Surgeons of England*, *95*(1), 5–7.

Jorgensen, D.L. (2015) Participant observation. *Emerging Trends in the Social and Behavioral Sciences*. Available at: https://doi.org/10.1002/9781118900772.etrds0247 (accessed 3 January 2020).

Kabali, H.K., Irigoyen, M.M., Nunez-Davis, R., Budacki, J.G., Mohanty, S.H., Leister, K.P. and Bonner, R.L. (2015) Exposure and use of mobile media devices by young children. *Pediatrics*, *136*(6), 1044–1050.

Kalb, G. and van Ours, J.C. (2013) *Reading to Children: A Head-start in Life?* Melbourne Institute of Applied Economic and Social Research Working Paper 17/13. Available at: http://ftp.iza.org/dp7416.pdf (accessed 2 January 2020).

Kellner, D. and Share, J. (2005) Toward critical media literacy: Core concepts, debates, organizations, and policy. *Discourse: Studies in the Cultural Politics of Education*, *26*(3), 369–386.

Kidd, C.D. and Castano, E. (2013) Reading literary fiction improves theory of the mind. *Science*, *342*(6156), 377–380.

Kinzer, C., Leu, D. and Peters, M.A. (2016) New literacies and new literacies within changing digital environments. In M.A. Peters (ed.), *The Encyclopedia of Educational Philosophy and Theory*. London: Springer.

Klass, P. (2019) Reading to your toddler? Print books are better than digital ones. *New York Times*, 25 March. Available at: www.nytimes.com/2019/03/25/well/family/reading-to-your-toddler-print-books-are-better-than-digital-ones.html#commentsContainer&commentsContainer%3Fregister=google (accessed 18 December 2019).

Knoester, M. (2010) Independent reading and the 'social turn': How adolescent reading habits and motivation may be related to cultivating social relationships. *Networks: An Online Journal for Teacher Research*, *12*(1), 1–13.

Knoester, M. and Plikuhn, M. (2016) Influence of siblings on out-of-school reading practices. *Journal of Research in Reading, 39*(4), 469–485.

Koopman, E.M. (2015) Effects of 'literariness' on emotions and on empathy and reflection after reading. *Psychology of Aesthetics, Creativity, and the Arts, 10*(1), 82–98.

Korat, O. (2010) Reading electronic books as a support for vocabulary, story comprehension and word reading in kindergarten and first grade. *Computers & Education, 55*(1), 24–31.

Korat, O. and Falk, Y. (2019) Ten years after: Revisiting the question of e-book quality as early language and literacy support. *Journal of Early Childhood Literacy, 19*(2), 206–223.

Koutsouris, G. and Norwich, B. (2018) What exactly do RCT findings tell us in education research? *British Educational Research Journal, 44*(6), 939–959.

Krashen, S. (2004) *The Power of Reading: Insights from the Research.* Portsmouth, NH: Heinemann.

Krcmar, M. and Cingel, D.P. (2014) Parent–child joint reading in traditional and electronic formats. *Media Psychology, 17*(3), 262–281.

Kress, G., Jewitt, C., Ogborn, J. and Tsatsarelis, C. (2001) *Multimodal Teaching and Learning: The Rhetorics of the Science Classroom.* London: Continuum Books.

Kuby, C.R. and Rowsell, J. (2017) Early literacy and the posthuman: Pedagogies and methodologies. *Journal of Early Childhood Literacy.* Available at: https://doi.org/10.1177/1468798417715720 (accessed 3 January 2020).

Kucirkova, N. (2016) Personalisation: A theoretical possibility to reinvigorate children's interest in storybook reading and facilitate greater book diversity. *Contemporary Issues in Early Childhood, 17*(3), 304–316.

Kucirkova, N. (2017a) *Digital Personalization in Early Childhood: Impact on Childhood.* London: Bloomsbury Publishing.

Kucirkova, N. (2017b) Pop-ups and pull-outs: How digital books offer children an experience of 'materiality'. *LSE Blogs.* Available from: https://blogs.lse.ac.uk/parenting4digitalfuture/2017/07/05/pop-ups-and-pull-outs-how-digital-books-offer-children-an-experience-of-materiality/

Kucirkova, N. (2018a) A taxonomy and research framework for personalization in children's literacy apps. *Educational Media International, 55*(3), 255–272.

Kucirkova, N. (2018b) *How and Why to Read and Create Children's Digital Books: A Guide for Primary Practitioners.* London: UCL Press.

Kucirkova, N. (2019a) How could children's storybooks promote empathy? A conceptual framework based on developmental psychology and literary theory. *Frontiers in Psychology, 10.*

Kucirkova, N. (2019b) Children's agency and reading with story-apps: Considerations of design, behavioural and social dimensions. *Qualitative Research in Psychology.* Available at: https://doi.org/10.1080/14780887.2018.1545065 (accessed 19 December 2019).

Kucirkova, N. and Cremin, T. (2017) Personalised reading for pleasure with digital libraries: Towards a pedagogy of practice and design. *Cambridge Journal of Education*, *48*(5). Available at: http://dx.doi.org/10.1080/0305764X.2017.1375458 (accessed 29 December 2019).

Kucirkova, N. and Littleton, K. (2016) *The Digital Reading Habits of Children: A National Survey of Parents' Perceptions of and Practices in Relation to Children's Reading for Pleasure with Print and Digital Books*. London: Book Trust.

Kucirkova, N., Littleton, K. and Cremin. T. (2017) Reading for pleasure and digital books. *Cambridge Journal of Education, 47*(1), 67–84.

Kucirkova, N., Messer, D., Sheehy, K. and Flewitt, R. (2013) Sharing personalised stories on iPads: A close look at one parent–child interaction. *Literacy, 47*(3), 115–122.

Kucirkova, N., Sheehy, K. and Messer, D. (2015) A Vygotskian perspective on parent–child talk during iPad story sharing. *Journal of Research in Reading, 38*(4), 428–441.

Kuzmičová, A. (2019) *Sensory Images, Memories and Reading*. Available at: https://researchrich-pedagogies.org/_downloads/Sensory_images_memories_and_reading_.pdf (accessed 20 October 2019).

Kuzmičová, A. and Bálint, K. (2019) Personal relevance in story reading: A research review. *Poetics Today*, *40*(3), 429–451.

Kuzmičová, A., Dias, P., Cepic, A.V., Albrechtslund, A.B., Casado, A., Topic, N., Lopez, X., Nilsson, S. and Teixeira-Botelho, I. (2018) Reading and company: Embodiment and social spaces in silent reading practices. *Literacy, 52*(2), 70–77.

Kwek, D., Albright, J. and Kramer-Dahl, A. (2007) Building teachers' creative capabilities in Singapore's English classrooms: A way of contesting pedagogical instrumentality. *Literacy, 42*(1).

Landry, S.H., Miller-Loncar, C.L., Smith, K.E. and Swank, P.R. (2002) The role of early parenting in children's development of executive processes. *Developmental Neuropsychology, 21*, 15– 41.

Langer, S.K. (1953) *Feeling and Form*. London: Routledge and Kegan Paul.

Lankshear, C. and Knobel, M. (2011) *New Literacies*. London: McGraw-Hill Education (UK).

Larsen, S.F. and László, J. (1990) Cultural–historical knowledge and personal experience in appreciation of literature. *European Journal of Social Psychology, 20*(5), 425–440.

Laurenson, P., Mcdermott, K., Sadlier, K. and Meade, D. (2015) From national policy to classroom practice: Promoting reading for pleasure in post-primary English classrooms. *English in Education, 49*(1), 5–24.

Lauricella, A.R., Barr, R. and Calvert, S.L. (2014) Parent–child interactions during traditional and computer storybook reading for children's comprehension: Implications for electronic storybook design. *International Journal of Child-Computer Interaction, 2*(1), 17–25.

Lerkkanen, M.-K., Kiuru, N., Pakarinen, E., Viljaranta, J., Poikkeus, A.-M., Rasku-Puttonen, H. and Nurmi, J.-E. (2012) The role of teaching practices in the development of children's interest in reading and mathematics in kindergarten. *Contemporary Educational Psychology*, *37*, 266–279.

Leslie, A.M., Friedman, O. and German, T.P. (2004) Core mechanisms in 'theory of mind'. *Trends in Cognitive Sciences*, *8*(12), 528–533.

Leu, D.J., Kinzer, C.K., Coiro, J.L. and Cammack, D.W. (2004) Toward a theory of new literacies emerging from the Internet and other information and communication technologies. *Theoretical Models and Processes of Reading*, *5*(1), 1570–1613.

Levinson, S.C. and Bowerman, M. (2001) *Language Acquisition and Conceptual Development* (No. 3). Cambridge: Cambridge University Press.

Levy, R. (2008) 'Third spaces' are interesting places: Applying 'third space theory' to nursery-aged children's constructions of themselves as readers. *Journal of Early Childhood Literacy*, *8*(1), 43–66.

Levy, R. (2009) Children's perceptions of reading and the use of reading scheme texts. *Cambridge Journal of Education*, *39*(3), 361–377.

Levy, R., Hall, M. and Preece, J. (2018) Examining the links between parents' relationships with reading and shared reading with their pre-school children. *International Journal of Educational Psychology*, *7*(2), 123–150.

Lewis, C.S. (1966/1982) *Of Other Worlds: Essays and Stories*. London: Bles.

Lim, J.W. (2018) Exploring post sixteen literature in English in a Malaysian classroom. In E. Arizpe and G. Cliff-Hodges (eds), *Young People Reading: Empirical Research Across International Contexts*. London: Routledge. pp. 149–165.

Lincoln, Y.S. and Guba, E.G. (1985) *Naturalistic Inquiry*. Beverley Hills, CA: Sage.

Lindsay, J. (2010) *Children's Access to Print Material and Education-Related Outcomes: Findings From a Meta-Analytic Review*. Naperville, IL: Learning Point Associates.

Littleton, K. and Mercer, N. (2013) *Interthinking: Putting Talk to Work*. London: Routledge.

Livingstone, S., Haddon, L., Görzig, A. and Ólafsson, K. (2011) *EU Kids Online: Final Report 2011*. Available at: www.lse.ac.uk/collections/EUKidsOnline/ (accessed 18 December 2019).

Lockwood, M. (2008) *Promoting Reading for Pleasure in the Primary School*. London: Sage.

Luke, A. and Freebody, P. (1997) The social practices of reading. In S. Muspratt, A. Luke and P. Freebody (eds), *Constructing Critical Literacies: Teaching and Learning Textual Practice*. Cresskill, NJ: Hampton.

Lupo, S., Jang, B. and McKenna, M. (2017) The relationship between reading achievement and attitudes toward print and digital texts in adolescent readers. *Literacy Research: Theory, Method, and Practice*, *66*, 264–278.

Mackey, M. (2005) Northern lights and northern readers: Background knowledge, affect linking, and literary understanding. In M. Lenz with C. Scott (eds), *His Dark Materials*

*Illuminated: Critical Essays on Philip Pullman's Trilogy*. Detroit: Wayne State University Press. pp. 57–67.

Mackey, M. (2010) Reading from the feet up: The local work of literacy. *Children's Literature in Education, 41*(4), 323–339.

Mackey, M. (2016) *One Child Reading: My Auto-Bibliography*. Edmonton: University of Alberta Press.

Maine, F. (2015) *Dialogic Readers: Children Talking and Thinking Together About Visual Texts*. London: Routledge.

Mangan, L. (2018) *BookWorm: A Memoir of Childhood Reading*. London: Square Peg.

Mangen, A. (2016) What hands may tell us about reading and writing. *Educational Theory, 66*(4), 457–477.

Mangen, A. and Kuiken, D. (2014) Lost in an iPad: Narrative engagement on paper and tablet. *Scientific Study of Literature, 4*(2), 150–177.

Mangen, A. and van der Weel, A. (2016) The evolution of reading in the age of digitisation: An integrative framework for reading research. *Literacy, 50*(3), 116–124.

Manresa, M. (2018) Adolescent reading habits: The effect of school activities on reading practices. In E. Arizpe and G. Cliff-Hodges (eds), *Young People Reading: Empirical Research Across International Contexts*. London: Routledge. pp. 123–136.

Mar, R.A. (2011) The neural bases of social cognition and story comprehension. *Annual Review of Psychology, 62*, 103–134.

Marks, H.M. (2000) Student engagement in instructional activity: Patterns in the elementary, middle and high school years. *American Educational Research Journal, 37*(1), 153–184.

Marsh, J. (2014) Purposes for literacy in children's use of the online virtual world Club Penguin. *Journal of Research in Reading, 37*(2), 179–195.

Massumi, B. (2002) *Parables for the Virtual: Movement, Affect, Sensation*. Durham, NC: Duke University Press.

Maybin, J. (2013) What counts as reading? PIRLS, EastEnders and the man on the flying trapeze. *Literacy, 47*(2), 59–66.

Maybin, J. (2017) *Brian Street, 1943–2017*. Obituary included in the Royal Anthropological Institute. Available at: https://therai.org.uk/archives-and-manuscripts/obituaries/brian-street-1943-2017 (accessed 19 December 2019).

McCarthey, S.J. and Moje, E.B. (2002) Identity matters. *Reading Research Quarterly, 37*(2), 228–238.

McDougall, J. (2009) A crisis of professional identity: How primary teachers are coming to terms with changing views of literacy. *Teaching and Teacher Education, 24*, 1–9.

McGeown, S.P, Norgate, R. and Warhurst, A. (2012a) Exploring intrinsic and extrinsic reading motivation among very good and very poor readers. *Educational Research, 54*(3), 309–322.

McGeown, S., Goodwin, H., Henderson, N. and Wright, P. (2012b) Gender differences in reading motivation: Does sex or gender identity provide a better account? *Journal of Research in Reading*, 35(3), 328–336.

McGeown, S.P., Duncan, L.G., Griffiths, Y.M. and Stothard, S.E. (2015) Exploring the relationship between adolescent's reading skills, reading motivation and reading habits. *Reading and Writing*, 28(4), 545–569.

McGrane, J., Stiff, J., Baird, J., Lenkeit, J. and Hopfenbeck-Oxford, T. (2017) *Progress in International Reading Literacy Study (PIRLS): National Report for England*. London: Department for Education.

McPhee, D. and Sanden, S. (2016) Motivated to engage: Learning from the literacy stories of pre-service teachers. *Reading Horizons*, 55(1), 3–5.

Mead, G.H. (1934) *Mind, Self, and Society: From the Standpoint of a Social Behaviorist* (Works of George Herbert Mead, Vol. 1). Chicago: Chicago University Press.

Medwell, J., Wray, D., Poulson, L. and Fox, R. (1998) *Effective Teachers of Literacy*. Final Report to Teacher Training Agency, School of Education, Exeter University.

Meek, M. (1988) *How Texts Teach What Readers Learn*. Stroud: Thimble Press.

Meek, M. (2002) *What More Needs Saying About Imagination?* Address at the 19th International Reading Association World Congress on Reading, Edinburgh, Scotland.

Meek, M. (2011) *On Being Literate*, 3rd edn. London: Random House (RHCP Digital).

Mercer, N. (1995) *The Guided Construction of Knowledge: Talk Amongst Teachers and Learners*. Clevedon, UK: Multilingual Matters Ltd.

Mercer, N. (2000) *Words and Minds: How we Use Language to Think Together*. London: Routledge.

Mercer, N. and Littleton, K. (2007) *Dialogue and the Development of Children's Thinking: A Sociocultural Approach*. Abingdon: Routledge.

Mercer, N., Wegerif, R. and Dawes, L. (1999) Children's talk and the development of reasoning in the classroom. *British Educational Research Journal*, 25(1), 95–111.

Merga, M.K. (2016) 'I don't know if she likes reading': Are teachers perceived to be keen readers, and how is this determined? *English in Education*, 50(3), 255–269.

Methe, S.A. and Hintze, J.M. (2003) Evaluating teacher modelling as a strategy to increase student reading behavior. *School Psychology Review*, 32(4), 617–624.

Miller, D. (2009) *The Book Whisperer: Awakening the Inner Reader in every Child*. San Francisco: Jossey Bass.

Miyamoto, A., Pfost, M. and Artelt, C. (2018) Reading motivation and reading competence: A comparison between native and immigrant students in Germany. *Journal of Research in Reading*, 41(1), 176–196.

Moje, E.B. and Dillon, D. (2006) Adolescent identities as demanded by science classroom discourse communities. In D.E. Alvermann, K.A. Hinchman, D.W. Moore, S.F.

Phelps and D.R. Waff (eds), *Reconceptualizing the Literacies in Adolescents' Lives*, 2nd edn. Mahwah, NJ: Lawrence Erlbaum. pp. 85–106.

Moje, E., Luke, A., Davies, B. and Street, B. (2009) Literacy and identity: Examining the metaphors in history and contemporary research. *Reading Research Quarterly*, 44(4), 415–437.

Mol, S.E. and Bus, A.G. (2011) To read or not to read: A meta-analysis of print exposure from infancy to early adulthood. *Psychological Bulletin*, 137, 267–296.

Moll, L., Amanti, C., Neff, D. and González, N. (1992) Funds of knowledge for teaching: Using a qualitative approach to connect homes and classrooms. *Theory into Practice*, 31, 132–141.

Morris, J.A., Miller, B.W., Anderson, R.C., Nguyen-Jahiel, K.T., Lin, T.J., Scott, T. and Ma, S. (2018) Instructional discourse and argumentative writing. *International Journal of Educational Research*, 90, 234–247.

Moses, L. and Kelly, L. (2018) 'We're a little loud. That's because we like to read!': Developing positive views of reading in a diverse, urban first grade. *Journal of Early Childhood Literacy*, 18(3), 307–337.

Moss, G. (2000) Raising boys' attainment in reading: Some principles for intervention. *Reading*, 34(3), 101–106.

Moss, G. (2007) *Literacy and Gender: Researching Texts, Contexts and Readers*. London and New York: Routledge.

Moss, G. (2011) Policy and the search for explanations for the gender gap in literacy attainment. *Literacy*, 45(3), 111–118.

Moss, G. and McDonald, J.W. (2004) The borrowers: Library records as unobtrusive measures of children's reading preferences. *Journal of Research in Reading*, 27, 401–412.

Mottram, M. and Hall, C. (2009) 'Diversions and diversity: Does the personalisation agenda offer real opportunities for taking children's home literacies seriously?, *English in Education*, 43(2), 98–112.

Mullis, I.V.S., Martin, M.O., Foy, P. and Drucker, K.T. (2012) *Progress in International Reading Literacy Study in Primary Schools, 2011*. Chestnut Hill, MA: TIMSS & PIRLS International Study Center, Boston College.

Munzer, T., Miller, A., Weeks, H., Kaciroti, N. and Radesky, J. (2019) Differences in parent–toddler interactions with electronic versus print books. *Pediatrics*, 143(4). Available at: https://doi.org/10.1542/peds.2018-2012 (accessed 18 December 2019).

Nathanson, S., Pruslow, J. and Levitt, R. (2008) The reading habits and literacy attitudes of inservice and prospective teachers: Results of a questionnaire survey. *Journal of Teacher Education*, 59(4), 313–321.

Nell, V. (1988) The psychology of reading for pleasure: Needs and gratifications. *Reading Research Quarterly*, 23, 6–50.

Nelson, K. and Fivush, R. (2004) The emergence of autobiographical memory: A social cultural developmental theory. *Psychological Review, 111,* 486–511.

Nicholas, M. and Paatsch, L. (2018) Mothers' views on shared reading with their two-year olds using printed and electronic texts: Purpose, confidence and practice. *Journal of Early Childhood Literacy.* Available at: https://doi.org/10.1177%2F1468798418792614 (accessed 29 December 2019).

Nikolajeva, M. (2002) *The Rhetoric of Character in Children's Literature.* Lanham, MD: Scarecrow Press.

Nikolajeva, M. (2005) *Aesthetic Approaches to Children's Literature: An Introduction.* Lanham, MD: Scarecrow Press.

Nikolajeva, M. (2013) Picturebooks and emotional literacy. *The Reading Teacher, 67*(4), 249–254.

Nikolajeva, M. (2014) Memory of the present: Empathy and identity in young adult fiction. *Narrative Works, 4*(2), 86–107.

Nisbet, J. (2008) What is educational research? Changing perspectives. In D. Matheson (ed.), *An Introduction to the Study of Education,* 3rd edn. London: Routledge. pp. 319–333.

Nystrand, M., Wu, L., Gamorgan, A., Zeiser, S. and Long, D. (2003) Questions in time: Investigating the structure and dynamics of unfolding classroom discourse. *Discourse Processes, 35*(2), 135–198.

Oakhill, J., Cain, K. and Elbro, C. (2015) *Understanding and Teaching Reading Comprehension: A Handbook.* London: Routledge.

Oatley, K. (1999) Why fiction may be twice as true as fact: Fiction as cognitive and emotional simulation. *Review of General Psychology, 3,* 101–117.

Oatley, K. (2009) An emotion's emergence, unfolding, and potential for empathy: A study of resentment by the 'psychologist of Avon'. *Emotion Review, 1*(1), 24–30.

Oatley, K. (2016) Fiction: Simulation of social worlds. *Trends in Cognitive Sciences, 20*(8), 618–628.

O'Donnell, B. and Hallam, S. (2014) *Read for my School: Digital Versus Paper Books.* Paper presented at London Book Fair Conference.

OECD (2010) *PISA 2009 Results: Learning to Learn – Student Engagement, Strategies and Practices (Volume III).* Paris: OECD Publishing. Available at: http://dx.doi.org/10.1787/9789264083943-en (accessed 16 December 2019).

OECD (2016) *PISA 2018 Draft Analytical Frameworks.* Available at: www.oecd.org/pisa/data/PISA-2018-draft-frameworks.pdf (accessed 18 December 2019).

OECD (2017a) *The Pursuit of Gender Inequality: An Uphill Battle.* Paris: OECD Publishing.

OECD (2017b) *Education at a Glance 2017: OECD Indicators.* Paris: OECD Publishing.

OECD (2018) *Reading Performance (PISA) (Indicator).* Available at: https://doi.org/10.1787/79913c69-en (accessed 29 December 2019).

Open University (2019) *Reading for Pleasure.* Available at: https://researchrichpedagogies.org/research/reading-for-pleasure (accessed 28 September 2019).

Orkin, M., Pott, M., Wolf, M., May, S. and Brand, E. (2018) Beyond gold stars: Improving the skills and engagement of struggling readers through intrinsic motivation. *Reading & Writing Quarterly, 34*(3), 203–217.

Paley, V.G. (1990) *The Boy Who Would Be a Helicopter: The Uses of Storytelling in the Classroom.* Cambridge, MA: Harvard University Press.

Papadakis, S. and Kalogiannakis, M. (2017) Mobile educational applications for children: What educators and parents need to know. *International Journal of Mobile Learning and Organisation, 11*(3), 256–277.

Papadakis, S., Kalogiannakis, M. and Zaranis, N. (2017) Designing and creating an educational app rubric for preschool teachers. *Education and Information Technologies, 22*(6), 3147–3165.

Park, H. (2008) Home literacy environments and children's reading performance: A comparative study of 25 countries. *Educational Research and Evaluation, 14*(6), 489–505.

Parry, B. and Taylor, L. (2018) Readers in the round: Children's holistic engagements with texts. *Literacy, 52*(2), 103–110.

Pea, R.D. (1993) Practices of distributed intelligence and designs for education. In G. Salomon (ed.), *Distributed Cognitions: Psychological and Educational Considerations.* New York: Cambridge University Press. pp. 47–87.

Pérez, B. and McCarthy, T.L. (eds) (2004) *Sociocultural Contexts of Language and Literacy.* Mahwah, NJ: Lawrence Erlbaum Associates.

Picton, I. and Clark, C. (2015) *The Impact of Ebooks on the Reading Motivation and Reading Skills of Children and Young People: A Study of Schools Using RM Books*, Final Report. London: National Literacy Trust.

Pihl, J. (2012) Can library use enhance intercultural education? *Issues in Educational Research, 22*(1), 79–90.

Pino-Pasternak, D., Whitebread, D. and Neale, D. (2018) The role of regulatory, social, and dialogic dynamics on young children's productive collaboration in group problem solving. *New Directions for Child and Adolescent Development, 162,* 41–66.

Prensky, M. (2001) Digital natives, digital immigrants, Part 1. *On the Horizon, 9*(5), 1–6.

Price, L. (2019) *What We Talk About When We Talk About Books: The History and Future of Reading.* New York: Basic Books.

Priddis, L.E. and Howieson, N.D. (2010) Narrative as a window to the inner mental world of young children: Attachment representations, affect and memory. *Journal of Early Childhood Research, 8*(2), 161–174.

Proust, M. (2013) *Swann's Way: In Search of Lost Time* (Vol. 1). Princeton: Yale University Press.

Ragin, C.C. and Amoroso, L.M. (2011) *Constructing Social Research: The Unity and Diversity of Method.* New York: Pine Forge Press.

Repaskey, L., Schumm, J. and Johnson, J. (2017) First and fourth grade boys' and girls' preferences for and perceptions about narrative and expository text. *Reading Psychology*, 38(8), 808–847.

Rey, F.L.G. (2009) Historical relevance of Vygotsky's work: Its significance for a new approach to the problem of subjectivity in psychology. *Outlines. Critical Practice Studies*, 11(1), 59–73.

Rosenbaum, P.R. (2010) *Design of Observational Studies* (Vol. 10). New York: Springer.

Rosenblatt, L.M. (1978/1994) *The Reader, the Text, the Poem: The Transactional Theory of Literary Work*. Carbondale, IL: South Illinois University Press.

Rosenblatt, L.M. (1986) The aesthetic transaction. *Journal of Aesthetic Education*, 20(4), 122–128.

Rosenblatt, L.M. (1994) *The Reader, the Text, the Poem: The Transactional Theory of the Literary Work*. Carbondale, IL: South Illinois University Press.

Rosenblatt, L.M. (1995) *Literature as Exploration*. New York: Modern Languages Association of America.

Rosenblatt, L.M. (2005) *Making Meaning with Texts: Selected Essays*. New York: Heinemann Educational Books.

Roskos, K., Burstein, K. and You, B.-K. (2012) A typology for observing children's engagement with ebooks at preschool. *Journal of Interactive Online Learning*, 11(2), 47–66.

Rosnay, M. and Hughes, C. (2006) Conversation and theory of mind: Do children talk their way to socio-cognitive understanding? *British Journal of Developmental Psychology*, 24(1), 7–37.

Ross, C.S., McKechnie, L. and Rothbauer, P.M. (2006) *Reading Matters: What Research Reveals About Reading, Libraries and Community*. Westport: Libraries Unlimited.

Rothbauer, P.M. (2004) 'People aren't afraid anymore but it's hard to find books': Reading practices that inform personal and social identities of self-identified lesbian and queer young women. *Canadian Journal of Information and Library Science*, 27, 4.

Rouxel, A. (2005) *Lectures Cursives: Quel Accompagnement?* Paris: Delagrave.

Rowe, D.W. and Neitzel, C. (2010) Interest and agency in 2- and 3-year olds' participation in emergent writing. *Reading Research Quarterly*, 45(2), 169–195.

Rowsell, J. and Wohlwend, K. (2016) Free play or tight spaces? Mapping participatory literacies in apps. *The Reading Teacher*, 70(2), 197–205.

Rundell, K. (2019) *Why You Should Read Children' Books, Even Though You Are So Old and Wise*. London: Bloomsbury.

Rutherford, L., Merga, M. and Singleton, A. (2018) Influences on Australian adolescents' recreational reading. *Australian Journal of Language and Literacy*, 41(1), 44–56.

Ryan, M.L. (2006) *Avatars of Story*. Minnesota: University of Minnesota Press.

Salomon, G. (1998) Novel constructivist learning environments and novel technologies: Some issues to be concerned with. *Learning and Instruction*, 8, 3–12.

Sari, B., Takacs, Z.K. and Bus, A.G. (2017) What are we downloading for our children? Best-selling children's apps in four European countries. *Journal of Early Childhood Literacy*, 19(4).

Sarroub, L.K. and Pernicek, T. (2016) Boys, books and boredom: A case study of three high school boys and their encounters with literacy. *Reading and Writing Quarterly*, 32(1), 27–55.

Saxe, R.R., Whitfield-Gabrieli, S., Scholz, J. and Pelphrey, K.A. (2009) Brain regions for perceiving and reasoning about other people in school-aged children. *Child Development*, 80(4), 1197–1209.

Schaffner, E., Schiefele, U. and Ulferts, H. (2013) Reading amount as a mediator of the effects of intrinsic and extrinsic reading motivation on reading comprehension. *Reading Research Quarterly*, 48(4), 369–385.

Schaffner, E., Philipp, M. and Schiefele, U. (2016) Reciprocal effects between intrinsic reading motivation and reading competence? A cross-lagged panel model for academic track and nonacademic track students. *Journal of Research in Reading*, 9(1), 19–36.

Schank, R.C. and Abelson, R.P. (1977) *Scripts, Plans, Goals, and Understanding: An Inquiry into Human Knowledge Structures*. London: Psychology Press.

Scherer, L. (2016) *Children, Literacy and Ethnicity: Reading Identities in the Primary School*. Basingstoke: Palgrave Macmillan.

Schiefele, U., Schaffner, E., Moller, J. and Wigfield, A. (2012) Dimensions of reading motivation and their relation to reading behavior and competence. *Reading Research Quarterly*, 47(4), 427–463.

Schugar, H. and Dreher, M. (2017) US fourth graders' informational text comprehension: Indicators from NAEP. *International Electronic Journal of Elementary Education*, 9(3), 523–552.

Schwartz, B. (2004) *The Paradox of Choice: Why More is Less*. New York: Ecco.

Seilman, U. and Larsen, S.F. (1989) Personal resonance to literature: A study of remindings while reading. *Poetics*, 18(1–2), 165–177.

Selwyn, N. (2016) *Education and Technology: Key Issues and Debates*. London: Bloomsbury Publishing.

Sénéchal, M., Hill, S. and Malette, M. (2018) Individual differences in grade 4 children's written compositions: The role of online planning and revising, oral storytelling, and reading for pleasure. *Cognitive Development*, 45, 92–104.

Silverman, D. (2006) *Interpreting Qualitative Data: Methods for Analysing Talk, Text and Interaction*. London: SAGE.

Skeeters, K., Campbell, B., Dubitsky, A., Faron, E., Gieselmann, K., George, D., Goldschmidt, B. and Wagner, E. (2016) The top five reasons we love giving students choice in reading English. *Leadership Quarterly*, 38(3), 6–7.

Skowron, E.A. and Schmitt, T.A. (2003) Assessing interpersonal fusion: Reliability and validity of a new DSI fusion with others subscale. *Journal of Marital and Family Therapy*, 29, 209–222.

Smagorinsky, P. (2011) Vygotsky's stage theory: The psychology of art and the actor under the direction of perezhivanie. *Mind, Culture, and Activity, 18*(4), 319–341.

Smith, J.K., Smith, L.F., Gilmore, A. and Jameson, M. (2012) Students' self-perception of reading ability, enjoyment of reading and reading achievement. *Learning and Individual Differences, 22*(2), 202–206.

Sparrow, B., Liu, J. and Wegner, D.M. (2011) Google effects on memory: Cognitive consequences of having information at our fingertips. *Science, 333*(6043), 776–778.

Spring, E. (2018) 'I think I was born with a suitcase': Blackfoot adolescent readers' responses top Sherman's Alexie's The Absolutely True Diary of a part-time Indian. In A. Arizpe and G. Cliff-Hodges (eds), *Young People Reading: Empirical Research Across International Contexts*. London: Routledge. pp. 106–120.

Spufford, F. (2002) *The Child that Books Built*. London: Faber and Faber.

Stanovich, K.E. (1986) Matthew effects in reading: Some consequences of individual differences in the acquisition of literacy. *Reading Research Quarterly, 21*, 360–407.

Steenberg, M. (2017) Literary reading as a social technology. In P. Rothbauer, K.I. Skjerdingstad, L. McKechnie and K. Oterholm (eds), *Plotting the Reading Experience: Theory/Practice/ Politics*. Ontario: Wilfrid Laurier University Press. pp. 183–197.

Stephens, M. and Coleman, M. (2007) *Comparing PIRLS and PISA with NAEP in Reading, Mathematics, and Science*, Working Paper, US Department of Education. Washington, DC: National Center for Education Statistics. Available at: http://nces.ed.gov/Surveys/PISA/pdf/comppaper12082004.pdf (accessed 3 January 2020).

Street, B.V. (1984) *Literacy in Theory and Practice* (Vol. 9). Cambridge: Cambridge University Press.

Street, B.V. (2008) New literacies, new times: Developments in literacy studies. In B.V. Street and N. Hornberger (eds), *Encyclopedia of Language and Education*, Volume 2: Literacy. New York: Springer. pp. 3–14.

Strouse, G.A. and Ganea, P.A. (2017a) Parent–toddler behavior and language differ when reading electronic and print picture books. *Frontiers in Psychology, 8*, 677.

Strouse, G. and Ganea, P. (2017b) A print book preference: Caregivers report higher child enjoyment and more adult–child interactions when reading print than electronic books. *International Journal of Child Computer Interaction, 12*, 8–15. Available at: https://doi.org/10.1016/j.ijcci.2017.02.001 (accessed 18 December 2019).

Sulentic-Dowell, M., Beal, G.D. and Capraro, R.M. (2006) How do literacy experiences affect the teaching propensities of elementary pre-service teachers? *Reading Psychology, 27*, 235–255.

Sullivan, A. and Brown, M. (2015) Reading for pleasure and progress in vocabulary and mathematics. *British Educational Research Journal, 41*(6), 971–991.

Sumara, D.J. (1998) Fictionalising acts: Reading and the making of identity. *Theory into Practice, 37*(3), 203–210.

Suter, W.N. (2011) *Introduction to Educational Research: A Critical Thinking Approach.* London: SAGE.

Swann, J. (2012) Creative interpretations: A discursive approach to literary reading. In R. Jones (ed.), *Discourse and Creativity*. London: Pearson Education.

Taboada, A., Tonks, S.M., Wigfield, A. and Guthrie, J.T. (2009) Effects of motivational and cognitive variables on reading comprehension. *Reading and Writing: An Interdisciplinary Journal, 22,* 85–106.

Takacs, Z.K., Swart, E.K. and Bus, A.G. (2014) Can the computer replace the adult for storybook reading? A meta-analysis on the effects of multimedia stories as compared to sharing print stories with an adult. *Frontiers in Psychology, 5,* 1366.

Takacs, Z.K., Swart, E.K. and Bus, A.G. (2015) Benefits and pitfalls of multimedia and interactive features in technology-enhanced storybooks: A meta-analysis. *Review of Educational Research, 85*(4), 698–739.

Taylor, C.A. (2016) Edu-crafting a cacophonous ecology: Posthumanist research practices for education. In C.A. Taylor and C. Hughes (eds), *Posthuman Research Practices in Education*. London: Springer. pp. 5–24.

Terranova, T. (2007) Futurepublic: On information warfare, bio-racism and hegemony as Noopolitics. *Theory, Culture and Society, 24*(3), 125–145.

Thomson, P. (2002) *Schooling the Rustbelt Kids: Making the Difference in Changing Times.* England: Trentham Books.

Trelease, J. (2013) *The Read Aloud Handbook*, 7th edn. New York: Penguin.

Troseth, G.L., Strouse, G.A., Flores, I., Stuckelman, Z.D. and Johnson, C.R. (2019) An enhanced eBook facilitates parent–child talk during shared reading by families of low socioeconomic status. *Early Childhood Research Quarterly*. doi: 10.1016/j.ecresq.2019.02.009.

Turner, M. (1996) *The Literary Mind: The Origins of Thought and Language*. Oxford: Oxford University Press.

Turner, T., Spruijt-Metz, D., Wen, C.F. and Hingle, M.D. (2015) Prevention and treatment of pediatric obesity using mobile and wireless technologies: A systematic review. *Pediatric Obesity, 10*(6), 403–409.

Uccelli, P., Dobbs, C.L. and Scott, J. (2013) Mastering academic language: Organization and stance in the persuasive writing of high school students. *Written Communication, 30*(1), 36–62.

Vaismoradi, M., Turunen, H. and Bondas, T. (2013) Content analysis and thematic analysis: Implications for conducting a qualitative descriptive study. *Nursing & Health Sciences, 15*(3), 398–405.

Vaknin-Nusbaum, N., Nevo, E., Brande, S. and Gambrell, L. (2018) Developmental aspects of reading motivation and reading achievement among second grade low achievers and typical readers. *Journal of Research in Reading, 41*(3), 438–454.

van Kleeck, A., Stahl, S.A. and Bauer, E.B. (eds) (2003) *On Reading Books to Children: Parents and Teachers*. London: Routledge.

van Manen, M. (1990) *Researching Lived Experience: Human Science for an Action Sensitive Pedagogy*. Albany, NY: State University of New York Press.

Veresov, N. and Fleer, M. (2016) Perezhivanie as a theoretical concept for researching young children's development. *Mind, Culture, and Activity, 23*(4), 325–335.

Vygotsky, L.S. (1964) Thought and language. *Annals of Dyslexia, 14*(1), 97–98.

Vygotsky, L. (1978) *Mind in Society: The Development of Higher Psychological Processes*. Cambridge, MA: Harvard University Press.

Vygotsky, L.S. (1980) *Mind in Society: The Development of Higher Psychological Processes*, 2nd edn. Cambridge, MA: Harvard University Press.

Vygotsky, L.S. (1986) *Thought and Language*. Cambridge, MA: MIT Press.

Vygotsky, L.S. (1987) *The Collected Works of L.S. Vygotsky: Volume 1 – Thinking and Speech* (trans. N. Minick). New York: Plenum Press.

Waller, A. (2019) *Rereading Childhood Books: A Poetics: Perspectives on Children's Literature*. London: Bloomsbury.

Wang, J.H.Y. and Guthrie, J.T. (2004) Modeling the effects of intrinsic motivation, extrinsic motivation, amount of reading, and past reading achievement on text comprehension between US and Chinese students. *Reading Research Quarterly, 39*(2), 162–186.

Wang, Q. and Fivush, R. (2005) Mother–child conversations of emotionally salient events. *Social Development, 14*, 473–495.

Wasik, B.A. and Bond, M.A. (2001) Beyond the pages of a book: Interactive book reading and language development in preschool classrooms. *Journal of Educational Psychology, 93*(2), 243.

Weiser, C. (2018) Evidence and its integration into teacher knowledge: Foucaultian perspectives to link research knowledge and teaching. *Journal of Education for Teaching, 44*(5), 637–650.

Wells, G. (1999) *Dialogic Inquiry: Towards a Sociocultural Practice and Theory of Education*. Cambridge: Cambridge University Press.

Westbrook, J., Sutherland, J., Oakhill, J. and Sullivan, S. (2018) 'Just reading': The impact of a faster pace of reading narratives on the comprehension of poorer adolescent readers in English classrooms. *Literacy, 53*(2), 60–68.

Wetherell, M. and Maybin, J. (1996) The distributed self: A social constructionist perspective. In R. Stevens (ed.), *Understanding the Self*. London: Sage. pp. 219–279.

Wilhelm, J. (2016) Recognizing the power of pleasure: What engaged adolescent readers get from their free-choice reading, and how teachers can leverage this for all. *Australian Journal of Language and Literacy, 39*(1), 30–41.

Williams, R. (1976) *Keywords: A Vocabulary of Culture and Society*. London: Fontana.

Williams, R. (1982) *The Sociology of Culture*. New York: Schocken.

Williams, T.J. (2009) *Save Our Children: The Struggle Between Black Parents and Schools*. New York: African American Images.

Williamson, B. (2016) Digital education governance: Data visualization, predictive analytics, and 'real-time' policy instruments. *Journal of Education Policy*, *31*(2), 123–141.

Williamson, B. (2017) Decoding ClassDojo: Psycho-policy, social-emotional learning and persuasive educational technologies. *Learning, Media and Technology*, *42*(4), 440–453.

Wilson, J. (2001) *Sleepovers*. London: Young Corgi.

Wolf, M. (2018a) *Reader, Come Home: The Reading Brain in a Digital World*. New York: HarperCollins.

Wolf, M. (2018b) Skim reading is the new normal. The effect on society is profound. *The Guardian*, 25 August. Available at: www.theguardian.com/commentisfree/2018/aug/25/skim-reading-new-normal-maryanne-wolf (accessed 18 December 2019).

Wood, D., Bruner, J.S. and Ross, G. (1976) The role of tutoring in problem solving. *Journal of Child Psychology and Psychiatry*, *17*(2), 89–100.

Worton, M. and Still, J. (1991) Introduction. In M. Worton and J. Still (eds), *Intertextuality: Theories and Practices*. Manchester: Manchester University Press. pp. 1–45.

Wu, Y.H. (2010) The magical matter of books: Amazon. com and The Tales of Beedle the Bard. *Children's Literature Association Quarterly*, *35*(2), 190–207.

Yokota, J. and Teale, W.H. (2014) Picture books and the digital world: Educators making informed choices. *The Reading Teacher*, *67*(8), 577–585.

Zhao, S. and Unsworth, L. (2016) Touch design and narrative interpretation: A social semiotic approach to picture book apps. In N. Kucirkova and G. Falloon (eds), *Apps, Technology and Younger Learners*. London: Routledge. pp. 109–121.

# INDEX